★ OUR COUNTRY'S ★
PRESIDENTS

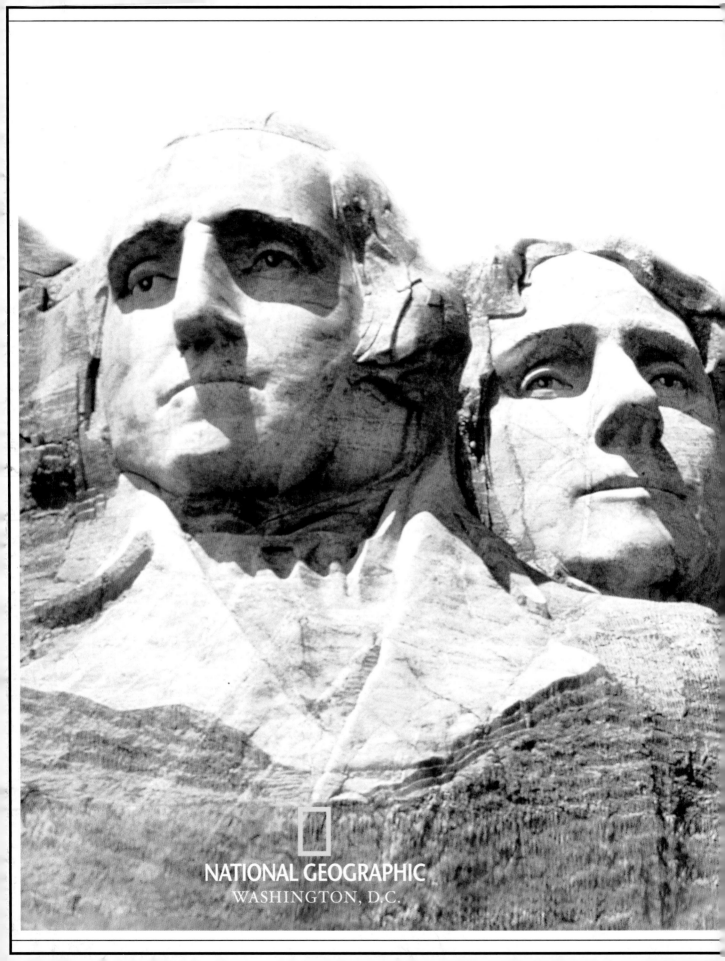

NATIONAL GEOGRAPHIC

WASHINGTON, D.C.

OUR COUNTRY'S
PRESIDENTS

ALL YOU NEED TO KNOW ABOUT THE PRESIDENTS, FROM GEORGE WASHINGTON TO BARACK OBAMA

Ann Bausum

WITH A FOREWORD BY
PRESIDENT BARACK OBAMA

TABLE OF CONTENTS

Barack Obama

THE HISTORY of the American Presidency is an extraordinary collection of individual stories of triumph, hard work, and sacrifice. Since our nation's founding, 42 Presidents before me have held this office, and no path to it has been the same. Some have served as generals, some as farmers, some as war heroes, and some as educators. What is so exceptional about the American Presidency is that any American can seek it.

As a student, I was impressed by the story of another man from my home state of Illinois who served as our nation's leader some 150 years ago – Abraham Lincoln. He came from a humble background and had little formal education, and yet rose to become one of our nation's most important Presidents. As you will learn in this book, President Lincoln helped save our union, free a people, and called on all Americans to rise above their differences and come together around a common purpose. His life is an example that all of us can strive to follow.

Many of our Presidents faced extraordinary challenges, and overcame great odds to make our nation stronger and more prosperous. This collection tells their stories – from George Washington, Franklin Roosevelt, and Dwight Eisenhower to John Kennedy, Ronald Reagan, and Bill Clinton. These Presidents led our nation through wars, guided our country in times of crisis, and offered a helping hand to lift up our people.

Our nation's history is one of struggle and progress, heartache and hope. But the overriding lesson of our past is that people who love their country can change it. That is the lesson that inspired me to enter public service, and it is the lesson I hope you take away from the pages that follow.

Barack Obama

44TH PRESIDENT OF THE UNITED STATES

About the Presidency

An Introduction

ON FEBRUARY 4, 1789, a few dozen men held simultaneous meetings in the various United States. By unanimous vote they selected George Washington to be the nation's first President. These electors hoped Washington would head an unbroken chain of capable national leaders. At that point, though, no one knew for certain whether the American experiment in democracy would last. Only time would tell.

Eleven years later the nation's second President, John Adams, moved into the still unfinished home that is known today as the White House. "May none but Honest and Wise Men ever rule under this Roof," he wrote. Those who followed him to the Presidency have tried to honor his hopes, and so will the men and women who become President in the future.

Each President takes a short oath of office:

"I do solemnly swear that I will faithfully execute the Office of the President of the United States, and will to the best of my ability, preserve, protect and defend the Constitution of the United States."

Each person meets a simple list of qualifications in order to seek the Presidency: he or she must be born as a U.S. citizen, be at least 35 years old, and have lived in the country for at least 14 years. Each candidate represents the best hopes of fellow countrymen for meeting the nation's needs.

Places change over time. The 1790 census counted not even four million people in the United States, including more than half a million slaves. Women, African Americans, and Native Americans could not vote. Broader rights came later on. Over the years, transportation advanced from horse power to steam

George Washington (center) placed his hand on a Bible to take the first presidential oath of office on Thursday, April 30, 1789, in New York City, one of the nation's early capitals. His Vice President, John Adams, stands to his left. Both men wore clothes made of American-made fabric, not European cloth, to celebrate their confidence in the independence of their new nation. Today January 20 serves as Inauguration Day. Before 1937, March 4 was favored. Since the passage of a 1951 Constitutional amendment, Presidents are limited to two elected terms as Chief Executive.

power to jet power. Inventors, scientists, and explorers changed the landscape with factories, technologies, and discoveries. The United States grew from a tentative experiment in democracy into a world superpower.

U.S. Presidents helped shape this evolution. Some, such as Abraham Lincoln, led the nation through critical periods of national and world history. Others, such as Thomas Jefferson, transformed the country's geography and outlook with their visions for change. Many left a personal stamp on the outcome of the nation. Most served as good stewards; they tried to do their best work. All marked their place in the history of the nation.

U.S. Presidents are a favorite topic of study for young and old alike. Presidents attract attention for different reasons, whether it's for bold policies, as with Franklin D. Roosevelt, for their power to inspire, as with John F. Kennedy, or simply for their adventuresomeness, as with Teddy Roosevelt. Readers are curious about how Presidents coped with the challenges of their eras and how they lived their personal lives.

Presidents come with funny stories (like the one who got stuck in his bathtub), unexpected facts (some were slaveholders), and overlooked insights (how they helped establish national traditions). They give us words that inspire ("Ask not what your country can do for you—ask what you can do for your country.") and words that reassure ("The only thing we have to fear is fear itself.").

We give Presidents nicknames—from Uncle Jumbo to Tricky Dick, from Honest Abe to Old Rough-and-Ready. We remember them for their extremes, their milestones, and their originality. Who was the only unmarried President? Who won the closest election? How many Presidents died on the Fourth of July? How many died in office? Who was our youngest President? Who was the oldest? Which Presidents are regarded as our best leaders? Who might be seen as among the worst?

Our Country's Presidents answers these questions and hundreds more. It introduces the Presidents as individuals, with full disclosure of good traits as well as flaws. By viewing the Presidents in full dimension, it is possible to breathe life into the darkened portraits that survive them. Readers may measure their own dreams, accomplishments, and challenges against those of their national leaders, perhaps gaining personal knowledge along the way.

The Presidents' stories, both personal and professional, are part of the nation's story. By understanding them, they become part of the reader's extended family history. Welcome to the stories of our country's Presidents.

How to Use This Book

You may choose to read *Our Country's Presidents* from cover to cover, just browse through the photos, or investigate one topic of interest. Knowing a bit more about how the book is organized should help you use it with greater success.

TIME LINES

This book presents the U.S. Presidents in chronological order grouped by six historical periods. A brief essay explains the common themes shared by the Presidents within these groupings. An illustrated time line accompanies the essay. It introduces readers to important events of the period, from wars to inventions, from explorations to protests.

PROFILES

Individual essays present key elements of the history of each President, including family background, childhood, education, prepresidential careers, election highlights, important events during the Presidency, and activities pursued in retirement years. The opening paragraph of each essay summarizes major points about the significance of each leader and his administration. Multiple illustrations provide a visual dimension to the story. Profiles range in length from two to six pages depending on the significance of the individual. Longer essays feature notable quotes by

the Presidents that have been highlighted with large-format type.

PRESIDENTIAL PORTRAITS

Each presidential profile is introduced by a full-page reproduction of the leader's official portrait. These paintings are unveiled after the President leaves office and are displayed throughout the White House. The portraits of the most recent Presidents hang in places of honor near the main entrance to the White House.

FACT BOXES

A fact box appears on the opening spread of each profile. It features the President's signature as well as quick reference facts in categories ranging from the person's nickname to his chief election opponent, from important dates to the number of states in the Union at the start of each Presidency. Each box includes a list of selected landmarks that help readers make geographic connections with the lives of the Presidents.

THEMATIC SPREADS

More than a dozen two-page spreads are placed strategically throughout the book to explain particular themes that relate to the Presidency. By reading these topical essays, you will be able to make connections between

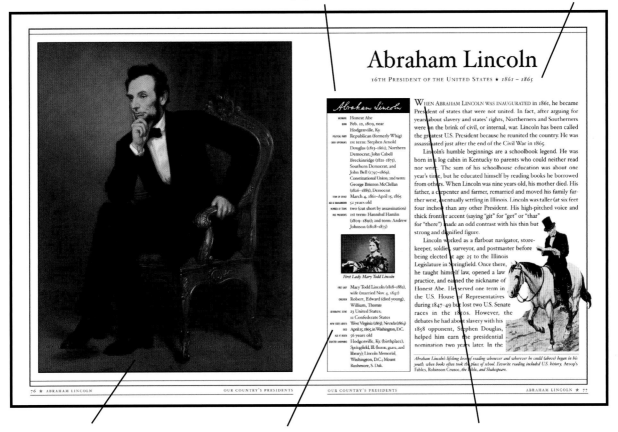

SIGNATURE

TERM OF OFFICE DATES

Abraham Lincoln

16TH PRESIDENT OF THE UNITED STATES ★ 1861 – 1865

WHEN ABRAHAM LINCOLN WAS INAUGURATED in 1861, he became President of states that were not united. In fact, after arguing for years about slavery and states' rights, Northerners and Southerners were on the brink of civil, or internal, war. Lincoln has been called the greatest U.S. President because he reunited the country. He was assassinated just after the end of the Civil War in 1865.

Lincoln's humble beginnings are a schoolbook legend. He was born in a log cabin in Kentucky to parents who could neither read nor write. The sum of his schoolhouse education was about one year's time, but he educated himself by reading books he borrowed from others. When Lincoln was nine years old, his mother died. His father, a carpenter and farmer, remarried and moved his family farther west, eventually settling in Illinois. Lincoln was taller (at six feet four inches) than any other President. His high-pitched voice and thick frontier accent (saying "git" for "get" or "thar" for "there") made an odd contrast with his thin but strong and dignified figure.

Lincoln worked as a flatboat navigator, storekeeper, soldier, surveyor, and postmaster before being elected at age 25 to the Illinois Legislature in Springfield. Once there, he taught himself law, opened a law practice, and earned the nickname of Honest Abe. He served one term in the U.S. House of Representatives during 1847–49 but lost two U.S. Senate races in the 1850s. However, the debates he had about slavery with his 1858 opponent, Stephen Douglas, helped him earn the presidential nomination two years later. In the

Abraham Lincoln's lifelong love of reading whenever and wherever he could (above) began in his youth, when books often took the place of school. Favorite reading included U.S. history, Aesop's Fables, Robinson Crusoe, the Bible, and Shakespeare.

OFFICIAL PRESIDENTIAL PORTRAIT

FACT BOX

INTRODUCTORY SUMMARY PARAGRAPH

Presidents. Your understanding of U.S. history and the function of the federal government will grow, too. Some essays cover topics of human interest, such as background about the wives and children of the Presidents. Others explain how the government functions, including the workings of the electoral college and the three branches of government. Additional thematic spreads help readers understand the election process, from the start of campaigns to the exciting conclusion of Election Day.

REFERENCE AIDS

A summary of U.S. election history introduces the reference material in the final pages of *Our Country's Presidents*. This chart shows the results of every election, including victors and major challengers. A resource guide follows with ideas for how to find out more about the Presidents. Information on sources used for the book's text and photos as well as a comprehensive index conclude the book.

THE PRESIDENCY AND HOW IT GREW

★ *1789 – 1837* ★

1789

Delegates wrote a new set of laws for governing the United States at the Constitutional Convention of 1787. By 1789 the Constitution was ratified, and the nation's first President was in place.

1795

The Constitution put the federal government in charge of issuing money. The $10 "eagle" coin was minted from 1795 to 1933. The capped figure of "Liberty" faced the coin.

1803

Thomas Jefferson offered to buy the Mississippi port of New Orleans. France sold it and the rest of its North American lands to the United States as the Louisiana Purchase.

1804–1806

A handful of men and Sacagawea, a Native American woman, helped Meriwether Lewis and William Clark explore the land between the Mississippi River and the Pacific Ocean.

The authors of the U.S. Constitution only sketched a loose outline of the Presidency when they defined the federal government in 1787. They expected the first Presidents to work out the details of the job in cooperation with Congress and the Supreme Court. As a result, the first officeholders helped shape the way Presidents make decisions, fight wars, work with Congress, add territory to the country, entertain, and so on. The Presidency became a position that could be revised and improved as needed by future Presidents.

1810

John Marshall served as the nation's Chief Justice longer than anyone else. His 1810 Supreme Court ruling in Fletcher v. Peck *was the first to declare a state law unconstitutional.*

1814

Francis Scott Key wrote a poetic description of the British bombardment of Baltimore's Fort McHenry near the end of the War of 1812. It became the U.S. national anthem.

circa 1820

Eli Whitney's cotton gin made it possible for cotton to be grown and processed on a large scale. Slaves labored on sizable plantations to raise more of the crop.

1836

Susanna Dickinson and her baby were among the few survivors of the Battle of the Alamo. Texans battled Mexico for two more months before gaining independence.

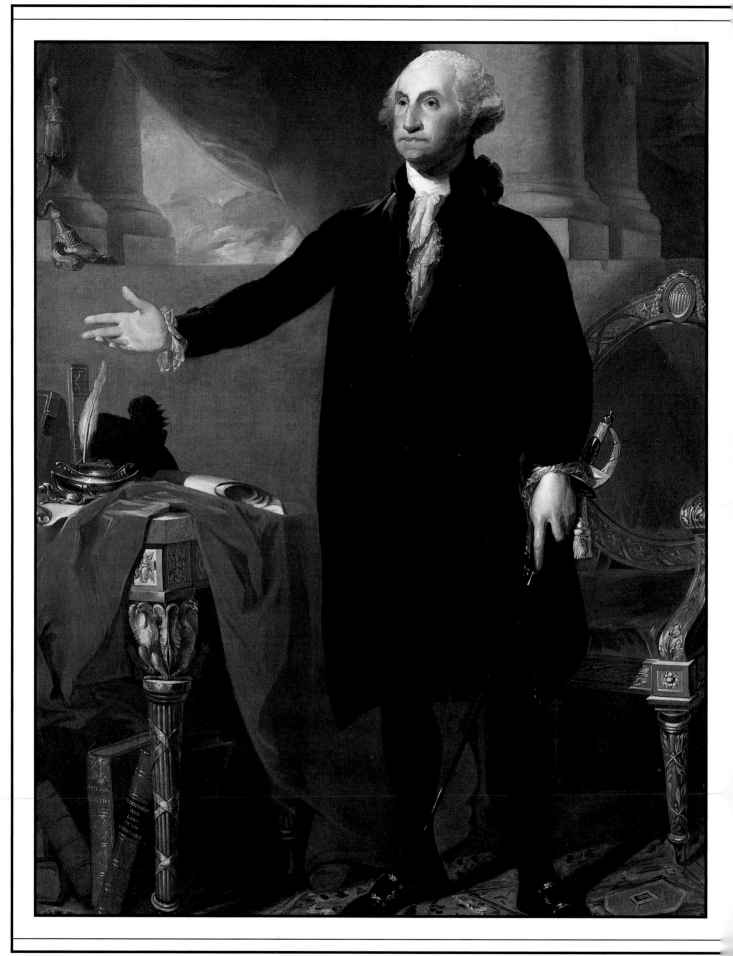

George Washington

NICKNAME	Father of His Country
BORN	Feb. 22, 1732, at Pope's Creek, Westmoreland County, Va.
POLITICAL PARTY	Federalist
CHIEF OPPONENTS	none (elected unanimously)
TERM OF OFFICE	April 30, 1789–March 3, 1797
AGE AT INAUGURATION	57 years old
NUMBER OF TERMS	two
VICE PRESIDENT	John Adams (1735–1826)
FIRST LADY	Martha Dandridge Custis Washington (1731–1802), wife (married Jan. 6, 1759)
CHILDREN	none; 2 stepchildren from his wife's first marriage
GEOGRAPHIC SCENE	11 states and 2 former colonies still debating ratification of the Constitution
NEW STATES ADDED	Vermont (1791), Kentucky (1792), Tennessee (1796)
DIED	Dec. 14, 1799, at Mount Vernon, Va.
AGE AT DEATH	67 years old
SELECTED LANDMARKS	Pope's Creek, Va. (birthplace); Valley Forge National Historical Park, Valley Forge, Pa.; Mount Vernon, Va. (homestead and grave); Washington Monument, Washington, D.C.; Mount Rushmore National Memorial, Keystone, S. Dak.

George's legendary cherry tree confession

GEORGE WASHINGTON HELPED TRANSFORM 13 British colonies into a new nation through a lifetime of public service as both a military leader and a statesman. As the first President of the United States, he set precedents, or patterns of behavior, for future Presidents to follow. After his death, he was praised for being "first in war, first in peace, and first in the hearts of his countrymen."

Little is known about the early life of the man who grew up to be called the "Father of His Country." Stories about his virtues—such as his honest confession of chopping down his father's cherry tree—were actually invented by an admiring "biographer" soon after Washington's death. The son of a Virginia landowner and planter, Washington grew up in colonial Virginia. His father died when George was 11, and his older brother, Lawrence, helped raise him. Washington was educated in basic subjects including reading, writing, and mathematics, but he did not attend college.

His skill with mathematics led to early work as a surveyor, or measurer and mapper of land. While still a teenager, Washington surveyed the unsettled wilderness of Virginia's Blue Ridge Mountains. He ventured farther

George Washington survived an icy crossing of the Allegheny River (above) as a British scout in 1753. Later, he made a trustworthy President because citizens knew Washington, being childless, could not place a family heir in power to succeed him. He truly was the "Father of His Country."

General George Washington served as commander-in-chief of the Continental Army throughout the Revolutionary War. He led a daring attack across the ice-filled Delaware River in 1776 (below), struggled to keep up morale among troops wintering over at Valley Forge, Pennsylvania, in 1777–1778 (left), and planned battle strategy for the defeat of the British at Yorktown, Virginia, in 1781 (above). Weapons, ammunition, food, shelter, clothing, and even shoes were often in short supply.

west during his 20s—this time as a soldier. Washington fought in the French and Indian War, Great Britain's territorial dispute with France over the lands of the Ohio River Valley. His reputation spread after he published first-hand accounts of his experiences.

Virginians elected Washington to their colonial legislature, the House of Burgesses, when he was 26. Soon after, Washington married Martha Dandridge Custis, a wealthy widow with two young children. They settled at Mount Vernon, a family home Washington had inherited.

As a colonial legislator, Washington spoke out against unfair aspects of British rule. Later he was one of Virginia's representatives at the First and Second Continental Congresses. These meetings led to the organization of a Continental Army, opposed to the British. Washington, who attended the meetings in his military uniform, was chosen to head the Army. He was 43 years old. His selection added an influential Southerner to a Revolutionary War movement that was led mostly by Northerners.

> "Liberty, when it begins to take root, is a plant of rapid growth."
>
> George Washington, letter to James Madison, March 2, 1788

New York residents gave George Washington a hero's welcome (right) when he entered the city in 1783 after the end of the Revolutionary War. Four years later he presided over the Constitutional Convention (below) in Philadelphia. Delegates drafted a plan for a new national government with hopes that Washington would serve as the country's first President.

Washington held the Continental Army together for six years of fighting against British forces. His troops suffered significant defeats, but they won important victories in the fight for independence, too. Aided by the French, Washington finally forced the British to surrender most of their troops on October 19, 1781, at Yorktown, Virginia. He retired from the Army after the 1783 peace treaty and returned to private life.

Six years passed between the signing of a peace treaty with Great Britain and the election of Washington as President. During that time the former colonies operated under the Articles of Confederation, a document that reserved most power for the states. Each state printed its own money, for example. There was no national Chief Executive. States sent representatives to a federal Congress, but this legislature did not even have the authority to collect taxes. Neither the states nor the federal government was able to repay the millions of dollars that had been spent on the Revolutionary War. The states were so poorly linked

George Washington helped lay the cornerstone of the U.S. Capitol (left) during his first year as President. He is shown (right, at far right) with key Cabinet advisers (from left to right): Thomas Jefferson (State), Henry Knox (War), Alexander Hamilton (Treasury), and Edmund Randolph (Attorney General).

that their fate as a nation seemed in jeopardy.

In 1787 state representatives gathered in Philadelphia to try to resolve these problems. George Washington, one of Virginia's delegates at this Constitutional Convention, was selected to preside. By the time the convention ended four months later, the delegates had written the Constitution of the United States. This document outlined the basic design for a strong federal government, with two chambers of legislators, a federal court system, and a President. It continues to serve as the foundation for the United States government today.

Nine state governments were required to ratify, or approve, the document before the new federal government

could form. By the next summer more than enough states had ratified the Constitution for it to take effect. Following the Constitution's directions, states chose representatives to serve as electors for the President. These members of the first electoral college cast two votes apiece. All of them gave one vote—for a total of 69—to George Washington, thus making him President. John Adams received the greatest number of remaining votes and became Vice President. Washington was reelected unanimously four years later, with Adams again voted in as Vice President. No other

Former President George Washington welcomed a stream of visitors, including his Revolutionary War ally the Marquis de Lafayette of France, to Mount Vernon. His wife, Martha, is seated at the far right with her family members. Washington's image has been preserved over the years on everything from postage stamps (above) to geographic landmarks. He is the only President to have a state named for him.

President was ever unanimously elected.

In 1789 Washington traveled to New York City, then the nation's capital, for his inauguration. The next year the capital moved temporarily to Philadelphia. Washington brought slaves from his plantation to help staff the President's home. Although Washington helped plan a permanent national capital, his Presidency ended before the federal government moved to the city later named in his honor.

President Washington set many precedents for future Chief Executives to follow. A few, like bowing in greeting, quickly went out of fashion. (Thomas Jefferson introduced the custom of shaking hands.) Many other precedents, such as seeking regular advice from department secretaries in Cabinet meetings, remain essential today. Washington established how the U.S. negotiates treaties, if presidential vetoes could encourage the reworking of legislation (yes), whether the Chief Justice had to be the oldest member of the Supreme Court (no), if the President could decide who would join the Cabinet (yes), and even how many terms he thought a President should serve. He established speechmaking traditions, too, from his Inaugural Addresses to State of the Union messages to a farewell address upon leaving office.

Washington appointed the first federal judges, signed laws that established basic government services like banking and currency, and sought to keep the nation out of wars with Native American and European nations. During his Presidency, political parties began to form despite Washington's objections. He became identified with the Federalist Party.

After retiring from the Presidency, George Washington returned to his family estate, Mount Vernon, Virginia. An expert horseman, he loved to review his property on horseback. Washington had perfected his skills in the saddle during his youth. As a teenager, Washington had wanted to join the British navy. His mother, widowed when George was 11, refused to grant his wish.

Martha Washington, who had joined her husband at winter battle camps during the Revolutionary War, left Mount Vernon again to be with him during his Presidency. "Lady Washington," as she was called, helped set presidential social customs.

Washington established one more tradition—attending the Inauguration of his successor—before he and his wife retired to Mount Vernon in 1797. He was not left at peace for long. In 1798 he agreed to take charge of the Army once more, this time to defend the country in case war developed with France. (It did not, and he was able to complete his service from home.)

In December 1799 Washington became ill after spending hours riding around his property in poor weather. What started as a simple sore throat developed into what was probably a strep infection. Doctors tried the usual cures of the day, including draining nearly a third of the blood from his body, but his condition did not improve. His throat became so swollen that he could not swallow or breathe. He died within two days of falling ill. Washington, one of the largest slaveholders in the country, arranged in his will for his own slaves to be freed by the time of his wife's death.

"Many things which appear of little importance in themselves and at the beginning may have great and durable consequences."

George Washington, letter to John Adams, May 10, 1789

John Adams

2ND PRESIDENT OF THE UNITED STATES ★ 1797 – 1801

John Adams

NICKNAME	Father of American Independence
BORN	Oct. 30, 1735, in Braintree (now Quincy), Mass.
POLITICAL PARTY	Federalist
CHIEF OPPONENT	Thomas Jefferson, (1743–1826) Democratic-Republican
TERM OF OFFICE	March 4, 1797–March 3, 1801
AGE AT INAUGURATION	61 years old
NUMBER OF TERMS	one
VICE PRESIDENT	Thomas Jefferson (1743–1826)
FIRST LADY	Abigail Smith Adams (1744–1818), wife (married Oct. 25, 1764)
CHILDREN	Abigail, John Quincy, Charles, Thomas, plus a daughter died young
GEOGRAPHIC SCENE	16 states
NEW STATES ADDED	none
DIED	July 4, 1826, in Quincy, Mass.
AGE AT DEATH	90 years old
SELECTED LANDMARKS	Adams National Historical Site, Quincy, Mass. (birthplace and family home); United First Parish Church, Quincy, Mass. (grave)

JOHN ADAMS DEVOTED HIS ADULT LIFE to the twin causes of creating the United States and securing its long-term survival. Adams—as the President who succeeded, or followed, George Washington—showed that the nation's most important office could survive a change of leadership. He helped his new country avoid war with France during his single term of office.

The man who became known as the "Father of American Independence" was born a British subject in the colony of Massachusetts. The son of an educated farmer and leather craftsman, Adams grew up enjoying toy boats, marbles, kites, hunting, books, and learning. He graduated from Harvard University in 1755 and took up the study of law.

Adams practiced law in Boston for 12 years and served briefly in the Massachusetts Legislature before becoming a delegate to the First and Second Continental Congresses. At these meetings in Philadelphia he encouraged the colonists to seek independence from Great Britain. It was Adams who suggested that George

This pair of farmhouses served as the birthplaces for two U.S. Presidents: John Adams and his son, John Quincy Adams.

John Adams, the nation's second President, went to school in a setting like the one pictured in this illustration. Adams cherished his status as a U.S. citizen, a right he earned thanks to the American Revolution. "I have not one drop of blood in my veins, but what is American," Adams said two years before becoming President.

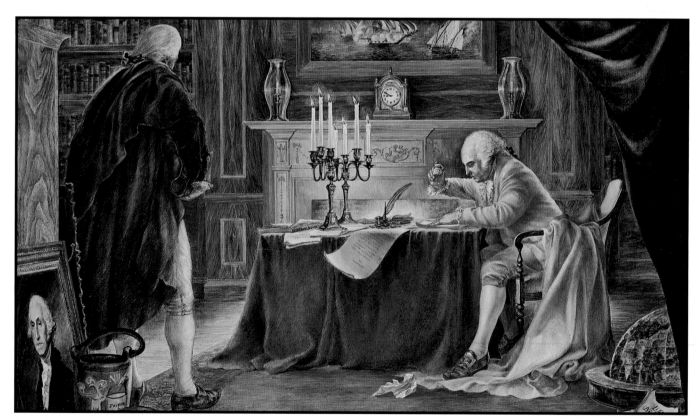

Abigail Adams and her husband wrote hundreds of letters to each other during their marriage because John Adams was frequently away on government business. In 1776, when he was a delegate to the Continental Congress in Philadelphia, she reminded him to "remember the ladies. Be more generous and favorable to them than your ancestors." She went on to suggest that women should "not hold ourselves bound by any laws in which we have no voice or representation." It would be the 20th century before politicians honored her wishes.

Washington command the new Continental Army, and Adams coordinated the crafting of the Declaration of Independence.

Adams was overseas during much of the Revolutionary War. He represented his new country to governments in Europe. During his stay in the Netherlands he arranged for important loans to help fund the Revolutionary War effort. Later he helped negotiate the peace treaty that ended the war with Great Britain.

After the war, Adams served as the first U.S. Ambassador, or representative, to Great Britain. He returned to the United States in 1788 just as a federal government was being organized with the new U.S. Constitution. He was elected to serve as Vice President to George Washington. Adams held the post for both of Washington's terms, but he found the job dull. He observed: "My country has in its wisdom contrived for me the most insignificant office that ever the invention of man contrived or his imagination conceived." His efforts while Vice President to establish flattering terms of address for the President (such as "His Highness") only earned him nasty nicknames like "His Rotundity" (Adams was very overweight) and "Bonny Johnny Adams."

Whereas Washington had become President by

John Adams at work in the new White House. Adams at times felt overshadowed by other significant figures of the day. He joked: "The history of our Revolution will be one continued lie from one end to the other. The essence of the whole will be that Dr. Franklin's electrical rod smote the earth and out sprang General Washington. That Franklin electrified him with his rod and thenceforward these two conducted all the policies, negotiations, legislatures, and war."

John Adams is called the "Father of the American Navy" for establishing a permanent U.S. naval fleet. Among the ships constructed during his Presidency was the Philadelphia *(left). The U.S.* Constellation *captured* L'Insurgente *of France in 1799 (right) when the two nations were on the brink of war.*

a unanimous vote of the electoral college, Adams had no such luck. The Constitution originally called for all candidates to be considered for President. It directed that the runner-up, or second-place finisher, become Vice President. This plan failed to anticipate the development of political parties. (A constitutional amendment in 1804 established separate votes for each office.) In 1796 Adams (a Federalist) became President with only a three-vote lead over Thomas Jefferson, a member of the rival Democratic-Republican Party. Tensions developed between Adams and Jefferson during their shared administration. Adams was defeated by Jefferson during his bid for a second presidential term.

Adams devoted much of his Presidency to avoiding war with France. Relations with this former Revolutionary War ally had become tense over the United States war settlement with Great Britain. Adams helped the U.S. establish an uneasy balance of relations with both of these European superpowers. He appointed hundreds of new federal judges, too,

including the influential Chief Justice John Marshall. However, many of his final choices, the so-called midnight judges, were named too late in his term to take their seats.

In 1801 Adams retired to his home in Massachusetts. Throughout his life he had a close, respectful relationship with his wife, Abigail. The pair shared one of the longest marriages of any presidential couple–54 years.

After their Presidencies were over, John Adams and Thomas Jefferson restored the friendship of their Revolutionary War days through lively letter writing. The two men were the only signers of the Declaration of Independence to become President. Curiously, they both died on the same day—the 50th anniversary of the Declaration of Independence. That day, Adams observed: "It is the glorious Fourth of July. God bless it." His final words were: "Thomas Jefferson still survives." He did not know his friend had died only a short while earlier. Adams, who had been ill, stopped breathing later that day.

"I am but an ordinary man.
The times alone have destined me to fame."

John Adams, diary entry, April 26, 1779

The White House

★ The Building and Its History ★

SINCE 1800 every U.S. President has lived in the national landmark known today as the White House. George Washington was the only President who never slept there, but he left his mark on the structure by choosing its location and approving its design. The place has been endlessly modified, expanded, and rebuilt ever since John Adams moved into the incomplete house near the end of his term of office.

Thomas Jefferson, the home's second resident, directed many early improvements to the structure and its grounds. Subsequent Presidents have added basic conveniences such as running water, toilets, and electricity; others have modernized it with telephones, elevators, and a movie theater. The West Wing evolved from a temporary office building added by Theodore Roosevelt. Franklin D. Roosevelt added the present Oval Office that has become the President's center of business. Harry Truman had the original White House structure shored up and rebuilt after one inspector proclaimed that the building "was standing up purely from habit." More recently, workers painstakingly removed all of the building's exterior paint, some 40 layers thick, then repainted it its trademark white. Today the President's home includes 132 rooms on four main floors (plus two basement levels).

Over the years the occupants of the White House have sat for portraits, collected priceless furnishings, and obtained notable works of art. Many of these items remain in use today, making the White House a living museum. Although the White House closed its doors to individual visitors for security reasons in 2001, groups may arrange for free self-guided tours of public areas. An off-site visitors center provides general information for everyone.

An artist from the 20th century imagined the scene (above, lower) of George Washington viewing the construction with architect James Hoban of what was first called simply the President's House. The modern White House (top, and see cutaway and key) serves as office and residence to the President and family. Its surrounding 18 acres are enjoyed by modern first families for croquet, tennis, horseshoes, golf, swimming, basketball, and jogging. The White House is shared with the nation through events like the annual Easter Egg Roll, when more than 20,000 children use spoons to roll colored eggs down the sloping lawn. During the War of 1812, invading British forces (right) destroyed all but the outer walls of the White House. Before setting it ablaze, they ate the dinner left behind by its fleeing residents. Later on, workers put a fresh coat of white paint on the building to hide scorch marks left by the fire.

FIRST FLOOR

F7

* F6

* F5

* F3

F4

G6

GROUND FLOOR

* F8

* F9

* F1

* F2

G5

G4

G3

G1

Thomas Jefferson

3RD PRESIDENT OF THE UNITED STATES ★ *1801 – 1809*

NICKNAME	Father of the Declaration of Independence
BORN	April 13, 1743, at Shadwell, Goochland (now Albemarle) County, Va.
POLITICAL PARTY	Democratic-Republican
CHIEF OPPONENTS	1st term: President John Adams, Federalist (1735–1826) and Aaron Burr, Democratic-Republican (1756–1836); 2nd term: Charles Cotesworth Pinckney, Federalist (1746–1825)
TERM OF OFFICE	March 4, 1801–March 3, 1809
AGE AT INAUGURATION	57 years old
NUMBER OF TERMS	two
VICE PRESIDENTS	1st term: Aaron Burr (1756–1836); 2nd term: George Clinton (1739–1812)
FIRST LADIES	Dolley Dandridge Payne Todd Madison (1768–1849), friend, and Martha "Patsy" Jefferson Randolph (1772–1836), daughter
WIFE	Martha Wayles Skelton Jefferson (1748–1782), married Jan. 1, 1772
CHILDREN	Martha, Mary, plus three daughters and a son died young
GEOGRAPHIC SCENE	16 states
NEW STATES ADDED	Ohio (1803)
DIED	July 4, 1826, at Monticello, Charlottesville, Va.
AGE AT DEATH	83 years old
SELECTED LANDMARKS	Monticello, Charlottesville, Va. (homestead and grave); Poplar Forest, Bedford County, Va. (homestead retreat); Jefferson Memorial, Washington, D.C.; Mount Rushmore National Memorial, Keystone, S. Dak.

BEFORE HIS DEATH, Thomas Jefferson listed the accomplishments he wanted carved on his gravestone. Serving as the nation's third President did not make his list. Nonetheless, Jefferson remains one of the most important Presidents in U.S. history. The Louisiana Purchase he made during his first term of office extended the country beyond the Mississippi River toward the Pacific.

Jefferson had the skills for many careers. However, because he came of age during the American Revolution, he devoted himself most notably to service as a statesman. Jefferson was born in 1743 near the western frontier of colonial Virginia. His father, a landowner, surveyor, and government official, died when his son was 14. From the age of nine, Jefferson studied some distance from home and boarded with his tutor. Later he enrolled at the College of William and Mary in Williamsburg, Virginia. His education was broad and comprehensive, including science,

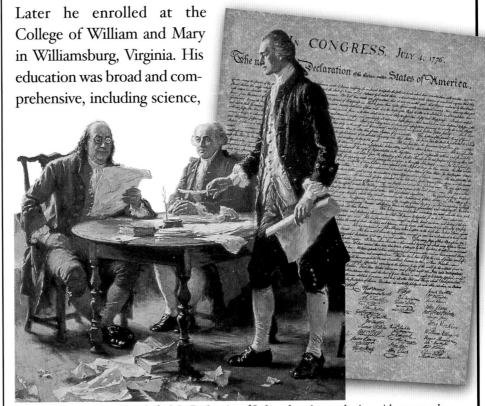

Thomas Jefferson (standing) drafted the Declaration of Independence in consultation with, among others, Benjamin Franklin (seated on left) and John Adams. Adams suggested that Jefferson compose the document. "You can write ten times better than I can," said Adams, plus "I am obnoxious, suspected, and unpopular."

In 1804 Aaron Burr, who was Thomas Jefferson's Vice President, killed Alexander Hamilton, a political rival, in a duel (left). During the Tripolitan War of 1801–1805, the U.S. fought with the Barbary pirates and their allies in North Africa (right) to stop lawlessness on the seas. French troops turned over New Orleans and the territory of Louisiana to U.S. forces on December 20, 1803. During the ceremony (below) the Stars and Stripes of the U.S. replaced the tricolor French flag at the Mississippi river port. Eventually all or parts of 15 states would be carved from Thomas Jefferson's Louisiana Purchase.

mathematics, philosophy, law, English language and literature, Latin, Greek, French, and even dancing.

After college Jefferson became an attorney. By age 26 he was a member of Virginia's House of Burgesses. Jefferson spoke out there against British policies during the final years of colonial government. On June 7, 1776, Jefferson and other delegates at the Second Continental Congress in Philadelphia were asked to consider whether "these United Colonies are, and of right ought to be, free and independent States."

Soon after, Jefferson,

Benjamin Franklin, John Adams, and two others were appointed to draft a declaration, or statement, in favor of independence. Jefferson spent about two weeks putting their ideas on paper. On July 2 the delegates agreed to declare their independence. Two days later, after a few revisions, members approved Jefferson's official declaration. This document is treasured for its persuasive calls for freedom and equality. It is the first achievement Jefferson listed on his gravestone.

During the Revolutionary War, Jefferson tried to put his democratic dreams into action. He wrote the "Statute for Religious Freedom" while serving in the Virginia Legislature. This document called for the separation of church and state, a concept that says it is improper for religious groups and the government to interact. Later this idea was adopted as one of the

"We hold these truths to be self-evident, that all men are created equal, that they are endowed by their Creator with certain unalienable Rights, that among these are Life, Liberty and the pursuit of Happiness."

Thomas Jefferson, Declaration of Independence, July 4, 1776

basic principles of the national government. Jefferson listed this achievement on his gravestone, too.

Over the next 20 years Jefferson served as governor of Virginia, a representative to the Continental Congress, U.S. minister to France, secretary of state for George Washington, and Vice President for John Adams. These last two posts left Jefferson frustrated. Some government leaders, known as Federalists, favored a strong federal, or national, government ruled by the country's most prosperous and well-educated citizens. They patterned their beliefs and social customs after those of wealthy Britons. Jefferson opposed these stands. His supporters were called the Anti-Federalists, Democratic-Republicans, National Republicans, or eventually, the Democrats. Jefferson expressed his dislike of Federalism by resigning from Washington's administration. He chose not to powder his hair, too, and he encouraged states to disobey federal laws that they disliked.

When the electoral college voted in 1800, Jefferson and Aaron Burr tied for the Presidency. It took the House of Representatives 36 ballots and two months to decide that Jefferson should be the

winner. The Constitution was amended by the time of the next presidential elections, so that separate votes were held for President and Vice President. Jefferson was then easily reelected.

As President, Jefferson reversed what he saw as the most offensive Federalist programs. He restored full freedom of speech to the press, reduced restrictions on immigration, increased land sales in the West, ended U.S. taxes, decreased the national debt, closed the national bank, and canceled the last-minute "midnight judges" appointments that Adams had made as he left office. During his second term Congress, with his approval, ended the practice of importing slaves into the United States from other countries.

Jefferson invented new codes of presidential behavior, too. He dressed casually around guests,

Thomas Jefferson is called a "Renaissance Man" because of his broad range of talents. He excelled as a farmer, an architect, an inventor, a lawyer, a writer, a musician, and an educator, as well as a statesman. Among his inventions were swivel chairs and the polygraph (right), a machine that duplicated an original document as it was being composed. He designed and founded the University of Virginia in Charlottesville (below) during his retirement years. Jefferson's personal library of 6,500 books became the foundation for a new Library of Congress after the Library's original collections were destroyed during the War of 1812.

Thomas Jefferson inspects the effectiveness of a plow he invented for use at his estate, Monticello. He depended on slaves to provide the labor there, both in the fields and in his house. Thomas Jefferson is the only person to serve two full terms as President after serving as Vice President. The Jefferson Memorial (below) was constructed in his honor 200 years after his birth.

even answered the White House door himself sometimes, and invited ordinary citizens to visit the President's home on New Year's Day and Independence Day. His administration, and the two like-minded ones that followed it, led to the end of the Federalist Party.

Jefferson's most noted presidential triumph was the Louisiana Purchase of 1803. When Jefferson tried to buy the port of New Orleans, the French offered to sell all of their western lands, not just the port. They were too busy preparing to fight the British to defend this distant territory. The price was 60 million francs, or about $15 million. The United States nearly doubled in size by gaining more than 800,000 square miles of territory west of the Mississippi River. Many Federalists failed to see the value of buying "a howling wilderness." Jefferson, however, was thrilled.

Even before the Louisiana Purchase, Jefferson had been planning an exploration of the West. He asked Meriwether Lewis, his personal secretary, to lead the trip. News of the Louisiana Purchase reached the U.S. on Independence Day in 1803, just as Lewis was about to set off from the East. Lewis joined forces with William Clark and a small corps of explorers in St. Louis, Missouri. The next spring they set off up the Missouri River in search of a water passageway to the Pacific. Instead they found the Rocky Mountains. They finally reached the Pacific Ocean by way of the Columbia River in December 1805. The Lewis and Clark expedition returned by a similar route to St. Louis the following fall. Their 8,000-mile trip helped open the Louisiana Purchase for settlement.

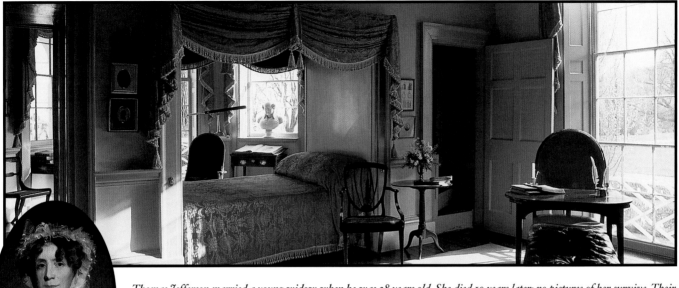

Thomas Jefferson married a young widow when he was 28 years old. She died 10 years later; no pictures of her survive. Their elder daughter, Martha (left), served sometimes as her father's First Lady. Jefferson spent five decades perfecting his beloved mountaintop home, Monticello. In Italian, Monticello (pronounced Mont-ti-chello) means "little mountain." Jefferson added clever details to his house (above) such as hiding beds, dumbwaiters, octagonal rooms, skylights, revolving storage space, a clock that kept track of the days of the week, and pairs of doors that opened when only one of them was pushed. As a naturalist, Jefferson enjoyed seeing a magpie and prairie dog (below) that were collected during the Lewis and Clark expedition.

Jefferson retired to Monticello at the end of his second term. For the remaining 17 years of his life he made improvements to his beloved home, surrounded himself with grandchildren, entertained distinguished guests, and juggled the mounting debts that came with his lavish lifestyle. He accomplished the third and final credit for his gravestone during these years: Jefferson is called the Father of the University of Virginia for designing and organizing this institution. Jefferson, like his old Revolutionary War friend John Adams, died 50 years to the day after the approval of the Declaration of Independence.

Jefferson left a complicated legacy. His estate was so in debt that Monticello had to be sold.

Modern genetic tests seem to confirm old rumors that Jefferson had a long-term relationship with one of his slaves, Sally Hemings, after his wife's death and that he fathered children with her. Jefferson freed only five slaves when he died (including some who were probably his children). The rest of his 200 slaves were sold to pay his bills.

From today's perspective it is hard to reconcile Jefferson's use of slavery with his passion for freedom. In truth, Jefferson's lavish lifestyle forced him to depend on slave labor. Jefferson, troubled by the institution of slavery, wrote: "I tremble for my country when I reflect that God is just." Jefferson knew it would be left for future generations to end slavery and that the process would most likely be painful.

> ## "I shall not die without a hope that light and liberty are on a steady advance."
>
> Thomas Jefferson, letter to John Adams, September 12, 1821

James Madison

4TH PRESIDENT OF THE UNITED STATES ★ 1809 – 1817

NICKNAME	Father of the Constitution
BORN	March 16, 1751, at Belle Grove, Port Conway, Va.
POLITICAL PARTY	Democratic-Republican
CHIEF OPPONENTS	1st term: Charles Cotesworth Pinckney, Federalist (1746–1825); 2nd term: DeWitt Clinton, Federalist (1769–1828)
TERM OF OFFICE	March 4, 1809–March 3, 1817
AGE AT INAUGURATION	57 years old
NUMBER OF TERMS	two
VICE PRESIDENTS	1st term: George Clinton (1739–1812); 2nd term: Elbridge Gerry (1744–1814)
FIRST LADY	Dolley Dandridge Payne Todd Madison (1768–1849), wife (married Sept. 15, 1794)
CHILDREN	none
GEOGRAPHIC SCENE	17 states
NEW STATES ADDED	Louisiana (1812), Indiana (1816)
DIED	June 28, 1836, at Montpelier, Orange County, Va.
AGE AT DEATH	85 years old
SELECTED LANDMARKS	Montpelier, Orange County, Va. (homestead and grave); The Octagon, Washington, D.C. (temporary executive home after destruction of the White House)

Dolley Madison

JAMES MADISON IS REMEMBERED MOST for the hand he had in creating the basic rules for governing the United States—the Constitution and its Bill of Rights. Madison made sure that his new country had a strong and democratic government. Later, as President, he struggled to lead the United States safely through its first war since the American Revolution: the War of 1812.

Madison devoted his adult life to the creation of the United States. Born a British subject in the colony of Virginia, he completed his education at the college that became Princeton University. Madison was the smallest man in the history of the Presidency. He stood 5 feet 4 inches tall and weighed only 100 pounds.

After serving in the Virginia legislature and with the Continental Congress, Madison was sent to the Constitutional Convention of 1787. He and other delegates spent 86 days inventing the structure of the U.S. government, including its Congress, Presidency, and federal court system. His detailed notes remain a valuable record of the entire event. As one of the authors of *The Federalist Papers,* Madison helped influence states to ratify, or accept, the new Constitution. These 85 essays supported the idea of a strong federal, or national, government. As a Representative in the first U.S. Congress, Madison helped secure passage of the Bill of Rights. This companion document to the Constitution sets down the basic privileges of the nation's citizens and states. Because Madison played such a central role

James Madison had studied hundreds of books on history and government by the time delegates gathered at the Constitutional Convention of 1787 to organize a new government (above). Madison joked that he earned the scar on his nose in "defense of his country." Actually it resulted from the frostbite he suffered during a long ride home after a 1788 debate with James Monroe during a U.S. Congressional campaign.

Wars raged on many fronts during the Presidency of James Madison. U.S. soldiers were guided by future President William Henry Harrison in their repulse of an attack by Native Americans at the Tippecanoe River, Indiana Territory, in 1811 (left). Forced recruitment of its sailors by the British navy (right) helped draw the U.S. into the War of 1812 with Great Britain. This conflict featured many battles at sea (below).

in these events, he became known as the "Father of the Constitution." Madison thought otherwise. The Constitution was not "the off-spring of a single brain," he insisted, but "the work of many heads and many hands." Madison and George Washington are the only men who signed the Constitution and later became Presidents.

Madison served four terms in Congress, then worked in Virginia's state government before his friend Thomas Jefferson asked him to join his new presidential administration as secretary of state. At the end of his two terms, Jefferson favored Madison as his successor. Madison easily defeated his opponent, Charles Pinckney, in the electoral college voting. Pinckney, noting the popularity of Madison's wife, Dolley, observed that he "might have had a better chance had I faced Mr. Madison alone."

When Madison became President, the United States was being drawn into conflict with the British over their war with France. Americans were frustrated because the British were halting U.S. cargo ships bound for France and seizing U.S. sailors and goods. If modern forms of communication had existed in Madison's time, war might have been avoided. Not knowing that the British were ending these seizures, the U.S. declared war against Great Britain.

During the War of 1812 (which lasted until 1814), American forces were beaten regularly on land and at sea. The greatest humiliation occurred late in the war when the British entered Washington and set fire to the White House and the U.S. Capitol building. The final contest, the Battle of New Orleans, was fought after a peace treaty had been signed in Europe but

Scenes from the War of 1812: U.S. and British sailors compete for control of the Great Lakes in 1813 (above, left); Dolley Madison supervises the packing of White House valuables (above, right) as the British march on the nation's capital in 1814. Francis Scott Key (right) captures the drama of a British naval attack at Baltimore in 1814 by writing the poem that became the U.S. national anthem.

before that news could reach North America. Madison was praised after the war for having allowed others to criticize his wartime policies without fear of trial or imprisonment. He insisted it was important for the United States to be able to fight a war without limiting the constitutional rights of its citizens, including the right of free speech.

First Lady Dolley Madison gained lasting fame during the war. She rescued government documents and a famous portrait in the White House of George Washington, just hours before the British raided the capital. She was famous, too, for her role as a hostess. She gave lively parties, made pleasant conversation, and dressed lavishly, often topping her head with a turban, jewels, or feathers.

After eight years in the White House, Dolley and her husband, "Jemmey," returned to Montpelier, his family homestead. From there James Madison helped Jefferson create the University of Virginia, spoke out against slavery, argued against secession (the idea that a state could quit being part of the United States), and organized his notes from the Constitutional Convention. He outlived all of the other Founding Fathers, the men who had influenced the American Revolution and written the U.S. Constitution. Madison died in 1836, six days shy of the nation's 60th Independence Day celebration.

"If men were angels,
no government would be necessary."

James Madison, *The Federalist Papers*, #51, 1788

The Powers of the President

★ *The Executive Branch in Government* ★

THE STRUCTURE of the United States government was established by the Constitution in 1787. That document and its 27 amendments explain the basic organization of the nation. The three branches, or divisions, of government are the legislative, executive, and judicial forms of federal power. The legislative branch is represented by the U.S. Congress, which consists of the House of Representatives and the Senate. The judicial branch contains the federal court system, including its Supreme Court. The executive branch includes the President and the departments of the government. Originally there were three departments—State, War, and Treasury. Today (*see chart*) there are 15 departments.

The Constitution lists the central powers of the President: serve as Commander in Chief of the armed forces; make treaties with other nations; grant pardons; inform Congress on the state of the union; and appoint ambassadors, officials, and judges. Over time the government has evolved so the branches operate within a system of checks and balances. For example, most of the President's actions require the approval of Congress. Likewise, the laws passed in Congress must be signed by the President before they can take effect. This system prevents one area of government from becoming so powerful as to overly influence the business of the nation.

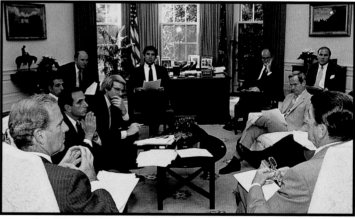

The powers of the President at work: Setting policy with cabinet officers from the earliest Presidency (left) to modern times with Ronald Reagan (right); directing the opinions of the judicial system by appointing new judges (top); asking Congress to declare war (far right, next page); and addressing Congress. John Adams (left, next page) was the last President to address Congress in person until Woodrow Wilson (right, next page). Other Presidents sent written messages instead.

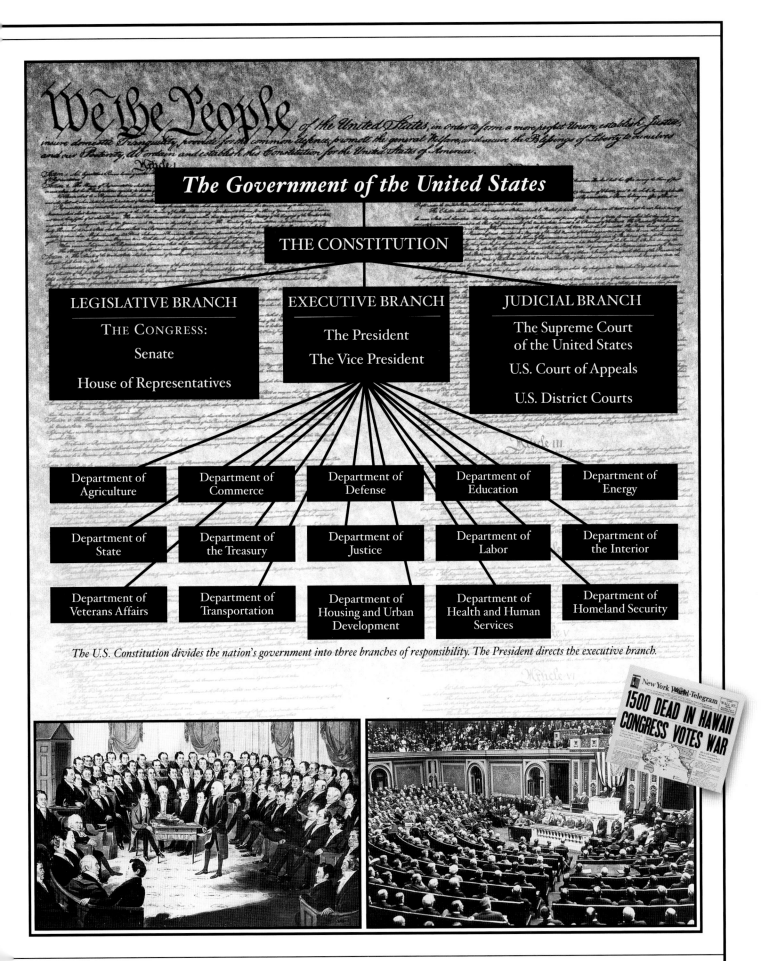

The Government of the United States

THE CONSTITUTION

LEGISLATIVE BRANCH

THE CONGRESS:

Senate

House of Representatives

EXECUTIVE BRANCH

The President

The Vice President

JUDICIAL BRANCH

The Supreme Court
of the United States

U.S. Court of Appeals

U.S. District Courts

Department of
Agriculture

Department of
Commerce

Department of
Defense

Department of
Education

Department of
Energy

Department of
State

Department of
the Treasury

Department of
Justice

Department of
Labor

Department of
the Interior

Department of
Veterans Affairs

Department of
Transportation

Department of
Housing and Urban
Development

Department of
Health and Human
Services

Department of
Homeland Security

The U.S. Constitution divides the nation's government into three branches of responsibility. The President directs the executive branch.

New York World-Telegram

1500 DEAD IN HAWAII CONGRESS VOTES WAR

James Monroe

5TH PRESIDENT OF THE UNITED STATES ★ 1817 – 1825

NICKNAME	Era of Good Feelings President
BORN	April 28, 1758, in Westmoreland County, Va.
POLITICAL PARTY	Democratic-Republican
CHIEF OPPONENTS	1st term: Rufus King, Federalist (1755–1827); 2nd term: none
TERM OF OFFICE	March 4, 1817–March 3, 1825
AGE AT INAUGURATION	58 years old
NUMBER OF TERMS	two
VICE PRESIDENT	Daniel D. Tompkins (1774–1825)
FIRST LADY	Elizabeth Kortright Monroe (1768–1830), wife (married Feb. 16, 1786)
CHILDREN	Eliza, Maria, plus a son died young
GEOGRAPHIC SCENE	19 states
NEW STATES ADDED	Mississippi (1817), Illinois (1818), Alabama (1819), Maine (1820), Missouri (1821)
DIED	July 4, 1831, in New York, N.Y.
AGE AT DEATH	73 years old
SELECTED LANDMARKS	Ash Lawn-Highland, Charlottesville, Va. (homestead); James Monroe Museum and Memorial Library, Fredericksburg, Va.; Hollywood Cemetery, Richmond, Va.

James Monroe retired to Oak Hill in 1825.

JAMES MONROE WAS THE LAST U.S. PRESIDENT who had been an adult during the Revolutionary War. He presided over a country in the midst of widespread change. New thinking was developing about the role of political parties, the issue of slavery, and the fate of European colonies in the Americas.

Monroe grew up during an earlier period of change. He was born in Virginia as tensions increased between the American colonists and their motherland, Great Britain. Although he entered the College of William and Mary, he interrupted his education to join in early revolutionary activities. At age 17 he raided the local armory with other students; the next year he dropped out of school to join the Continental Army. Monroe served under the command of General George Washington, rising in rank to major. He crossed the Delaware River with Washington's troops, was severely wounded during a heroic capture of British cannons in the Battle of Trenton, and wintered at Valley Forge.

Near the end of the war Monroe studied law in Thomas Jefferson's law practice and later opened his own. He also began his lifelong career of public service. Before being elected President, Monroe served in the Virginia Assembly, the Continental Congress, the U.S. Senate, and as governor of Virginia. He held foreign affairs

James Monroe was a tall President, just over six feet in height. He chose to be inaugurated outdoors (above) in 1817. Monroe added to his popularity as President by taking two extensive "goodwill tours" during his administration. In 1817 he traveled north and west as far as Maine and Michigan. Two years later he headed south to Georgia, went as far west as the Missouri Territory, and traveled back to Washington through Kentucky.

The White House (above, center) and adjacent federal office buildings as they appeared in 1820. The building of canals and locks expanded the opportunities for travel and commerce (below) during James Monroe's Presidency.

posts under three of the first four Presidents. He was Washington's minister to France, Jefferson's minister to Great Britain, and secretary of state and secretary of war for James Madison. In 1803 President Jefferson sent him to France to help negotiate the Louisiana Purchase.

Both Jefferson and outgoing President Madison favored Monroe's election as President in 1816. Some Democratic-Republicans spoke of their desire to pass over Monroe, a Virginian, and end the "Virginia Dynasty" of Presidents. (Three of the first four Presidents had come from Virginia. Eventually 7 of the first 12 would be Virginians.) Monroe's abilities were more important than concerns about his birthplace, though, and he was elected by a wide margin. Four years later he ran without opposition and earned all but one electoral vote. Legend says he lost this single vote because an elector wanted to preserve George Washington's record of unanimous election. Facts suggest, however, that the elector simply did not support Monroe and put forth another candidate (John Quincy Adams) instead. During his Presidency a newspaper credited

TREATY
OF
AMITY, COMMERCE,
AND
NAVIGATION,
BETWEEN
His Britannic Majesty
AND
The United States of America,
CONDITIONALLY RATIFIED
By the Senate of the United States,
At Philadelphia, June 24, 1795.
TO WHICH IS ANNEXED,
A Copious Appendix.

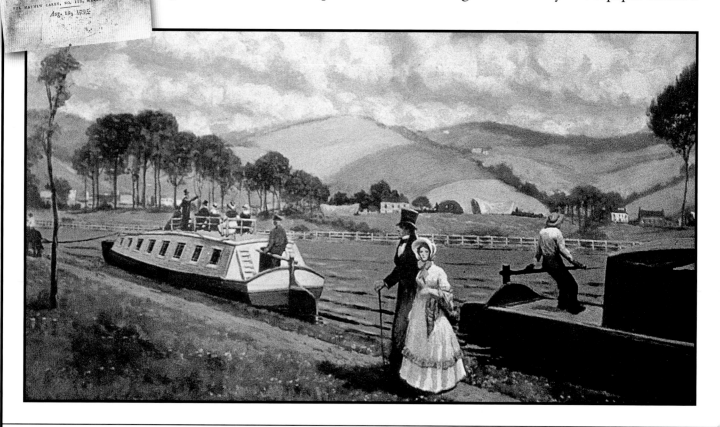

> "The American continents…are henceforth not to be considered as subjects for future colonization by any European powers."
>
> James Monroe,
> The Monroe Doctrine, December 2, 1823

As President, James Monroe (right, by globe) framed a new vision for the role of the U.S. government in the Western Hemisphere. During earlier diplomatic years, his wife, Elizabeth (below), influenced French radicals to free the condemned wife of the Marquis de Lafayette.

Monroe with bringing the nation an "era of good feelings." The phrase stuck and came to be associated with him like a nickname.

The United States underwent significant geographic changes during Monroe's leadership. Five new states joined the nation. Only one administration would add more. (Six states joined the nation during Benjamin Harrison's single term in office.) In addition, Monroe purchased Florida from Spain and resolved key border concerns with Canada. Most important, he stated a vital U.S. position about the Western Hemisphere: The American continents were off-limits for further colonizing by European nations. This policy came to be known as the Monroe Doctrine. It set the stage for the expansion of the United States westward to the Pacific Ocean during the next two decades.

The greatest controversy of Monroe's administration was whether Missouri should enter the Union as a state that permitted slavery. Politicians organized along regional lines—North against South—over this issue. In the end the Missouri Compromise admitted Missouri as a "slave state" with Maine entering as a "free state." Since each "side" in the debate gained one state, balance between opposing viewpoints was maintained. Legislators agreed to prohibit further expansion of slavery north and west of Missouri's southern border. This position would be reconsidered by future administrations during an increasingly tense debate over slavery.

In 1825 Monroe and his wife, Elizabeth, retired to their northern Virginia home, which was designed by Jefferson. When Elizabeth died in 1830, James moved to New York City. He lived there with his younger daughter, Maria, and her family. Within the year Monroe died, too. He was the last U.S. President to die on the Fourth of July. His death followed those of Presidents Jefferson and Adams by exactly five years.

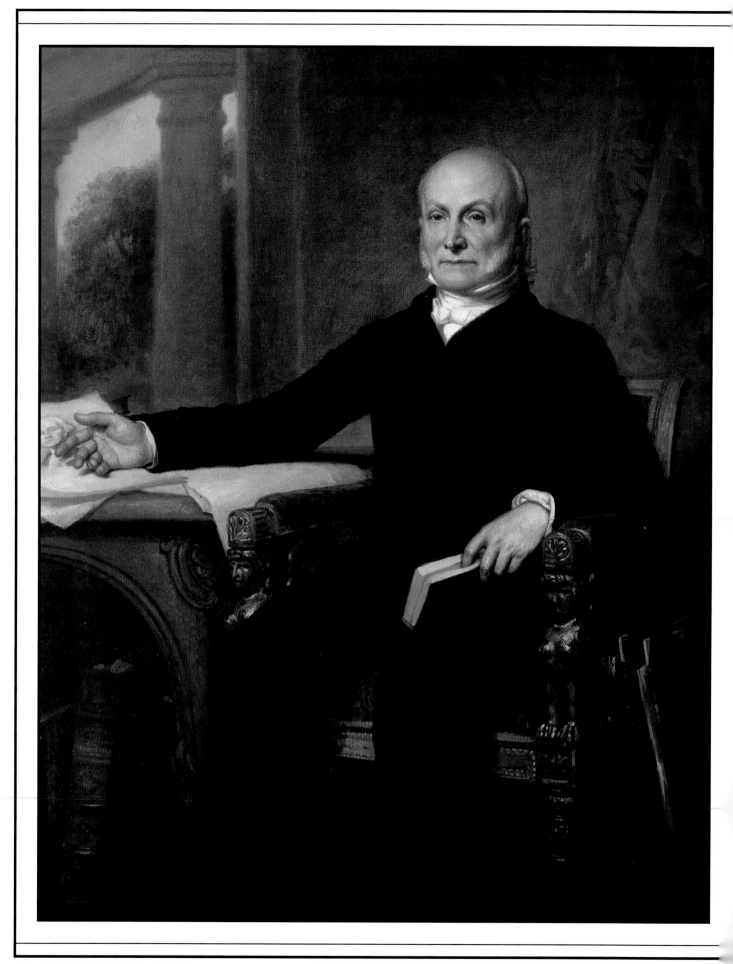

John Quincy Adams

6TH PRESIDENT OF THE UNITED STATES ★ *1825 – 1829*

NICKNAME	Old Man Eloquent
BORN	July 11, 1767, in Braintree (now Quincy), Mass.
POLITICAL PARTY	Democratic-Republican
CHIEF OPPONENT	Andrew Jackson, Democratic-Republican (1767–1845)
TERM OF OFFICE	March 4, 1825–March 3, 1829
AGE AT INAUGURATION	57 years old
NUMBER OF TERMS	one
VICE PRESIDENT	John Caldwell Calhoun (1782–1850)
FIRST LADY	Louisa Catherine Johnson Adams (1775–1852), wife (married July 26, 1797)
CHILDREN	George, John, Charles, plus a daughter died young
GEOGRAPHIC SCENE	24 states
NEW STATES ADDED	none
DIED	Feb. 23, 1848, at the U.S. Capitol, Washington, D.C.

The collapse of Congressman Adams

AGE AT DEATH	80 years old
SELECTED LANDMARKS	Adams National Historical Site, Quincy, Mass. (birthplace and family home); United First Parish Church, Quincy, Mass. (grave)

JOHN QUINCY ADAMS, like his father, earned more lasting fame for his accomplishments beyond the White House than for his Presidency. His single term of office took place following important overseas service and preceded a celebrated career in Congress. Adams was the only son of a Chief Executive to seek and gain the Presidency until George W. Bush did so in the 2000 election.

Adams grew up in Massachusetts during the American Revolution. He witnessed the Battle of Bunker Hill at age eight. He traveled abroad while his father was a diplomat and later earned a degree from Harvard University. After studying law, he served his country with each of the nation's first Presidents. He was a U.S. ambassador for George Washington and his father, a senator under Thomas Jefferson, an ambassador for James Madison, and secretary of state to James Monroe.

The 1824 electoral votes failed to give majority support to one candidate. After an ugly debate, the House of Representatives named Adams the victor. As Chief Executive, Adams ignored political strategy, stuck to his principles, and found himself generally miserable. It seemed that no one supported him. Jealous political rivals accused him of corruption. Congress refused to fund his plan for a national transportation system of roads and canals. Newspapers slandered him. Adams felt it was undignified to personally campaign for reelection and lost at the polls in 1828.

Adams is the only President to serve later in the House of Representatives. He won election to the chamber in 1830 at age 63. Adams earned the nickname "Old Man Eloquent" for his passionate arguments. He fought for eight years to overturn the 1836 "gag rule" that prohibited discussion of slavery. His speeches were fiery, both about the restrictions and, once lifted, about slavery itself. On February 21, 1848, Adams had a stroke at his desk on the House floor. Realizing he was deathly ill, Adams asked to be tended to in a nearby office so he could die in his beloved Capitol building. He did so two days later.

John Quincy Adams enlivened his gloomy White House years by playing billiards, writing in his diaries, and exercising. Often he swam nude in the Potomac River. Once someone stole his clothes, and he had to ask a passing boy to fetch new ones for him from the White House.

White House Traditions

★ *Easter Eggs, State Dinners, and Presidential Portraits* ★

JOHN AND ABIGAIL ADAMS established one of the oldest and longest-lasting White House traditions soon after their arrival at the incomplete mansion in the fall of 1800. The following New Year's Day they invited members of the public to visit their home at an open house. All were welcomed. Those first guests would have exchanged bows with the presidential couple, but from Thomas Jefferson's Presidency on, handshakes came into fashion.

As the popularity of the New Year's Day open house grew, so did the length of the lines of visitors waiting to enter. Abraham Lincoln found himself shaking hands for three hours on New Year's Day in 1863. President Hoover ended the tradition of greeting the public on New Year's Day in 1932.

A newer tradition that continues to this day is the annual Easter Egg Roll on the south lawn of the White House. This activity migrated to the President's yard in 1878 after it was banned from the lawn of the U.S. Capitol as too damaging to the turf. The custom has continued with some interruptions, such as during wartime, ever since and has gained in popularity in recent decades. The tradition of decorating a Christmas tree at the White House dates back almost as far as the Easter Egg Roll; it began in 1889 during Benjamin Harrison's administration.

The Easter Egg Roll gets underway as children race to the finish line on the South Lawn of the White House. In 1933, Eleanor Roosevelt greeted visitors and listeners to the Egg Roll for the first time over the radio. She introduced games at the event, but the most famous event of the modern Easter Egg Roll, the egg-rolling race, began in 1974.

When the Presidents, premiers, and rulers of other countries visit the U.S., they are guests of honor with the nation's first family at what is called a State Dinner. Tradition calls for the presidential couple to escort the visiting dignitaries to dinner by way of what is known as the grand staircase of the White House. The U. S. Marine Band performs, and the presidential party pauses for news photographers when they and other dishes used at official events. Periodically a presidential couple will order new dishes for the White House. Considerable thought is given to the design and manufacturing of the china. In early administrations such tableware had to be imported from Europe; now preference is given to goods made in the United States.

Over the years it has become a tradition for portraits to be painted of the

Candles lit the first decorated Christmas tree in the White House. Frances Cleveland switched to electric lights in 1895. By the 1920s the First Family had added an electrified tree to the White House lawn (above), too. Queen Elizabeth II addressed President George W. Bush and guests during a State Dinner at the White House (left). First Lady Mamie Eisenhower admired her official portrait (right) prior to its hanging in the White House.

reach the adjoining entrance hall. If dancing is planned, custom dictates that the presidential couple exchange dances with their guests of honor. They usually offer gifts to one another, too, and deliver ceremonial toasts to the health of the leaders and their nations.

Guests lucky enough to be invited to stay at the White House often sleep in what is known as the Lincoln Bedroom. Lincoln never actually slept there, but furnishings from his administration help decorate the room.

First Lady Caroline Harrison helped establish the tradition of preserving and displaying china

President and spouse as their stay in the White House comes to a close. The portraits remain behind, taking their places alongside those of past Presidents and First Ladies.

Tradition calls for the portraits of the most recent Presidents to be hung in a place of honor on the main floor of the White House. The portrait of the departing President takes the place on the wall held by the painting of his predecessor, and that portrait moves to a spot of honor nearby—a reminder that Presidents are an integral part of the traditions and history of the White House.

Andrew Jackson

7TH PRESIDENT OF THE UNITED STATES ★ *1829 – 1837*

Andrew Jackson

NICKNAME	Old Hickory
BORN	March 15, 1767, in the Waxhaw border region of North and South Carolina
POLITICAL PARTY	Democrat
CHIEF OPPONENTS	1st term: President John Quincy Adams, National Republican (1767–1848); 2nd term: Henry Clay, National Republican (1777–1852)
TERM OF OFFICE	March 4, 1829–March 3, 1837
AGE AT INAUGURATION	61 years old
NUMBER OF TERMS	two

The Inauguration of Andrew Jackson, 1829

VICE PRESIDENTS	1st term: John Caldwell Calhoun (1782–1850); 2nd term: Martin Van Buren (1782–1862)
FIRST LADY	Emily Donelson (1807–1836), niece
WIFE	Rachel Donelson Robards Jackson (1767–1828), married Aug. 1791 and Jan. 17, 1794
CHILDREN	Andrew (adopted)
GEOGRAPHIC SCENE	24 states
NEW STATES ADDED	Arkansas (1836), Michigan (1837)
DIED	June 8, 1845, in Nashville, Tenn.
AGE AT DEATH	78 years old
SELECTED LANDMARKS	The Hermitage, Nashville, Tenn. (homestead and grave)

THE ELECTION OF ANDREW JACKSON put in the White House for the first time a man who seemed to represent the background and ambitions of "ordinary" Americans. His leadership style differed from that of his predecessors, too. Jackson set new patterns for presidential power that continue to be used today.

Jackson grew up earning his "man-of-the-people" reputation. He was the son of Scotch-Irish immigrants, born to a family on the move following the sudden death of his father just a few days earlier. His exact birthplace remains uncertain. He is considered the first of the log cabin Presidents. In 1776 he was able, at age nine, to read aloud the text of the new Declaration of Independence to nonreading neighbors. Although he never learned proper grammar and spelling, he was well-spoken.

Jackson's education was interrupted by the American Revolution. At 13 he served as a messenger for American troops and was captured by the British. Jackson is the only President who was a prisoner of war, and the last one who served in the Revolutionary War.

A British officer attacked Andrew Jackson (above) after he refused to polish the captor's boots during the Revolutionary War. Jackson's face bore a lifelong scar from his wound.

Andrew Jackson's reputation as a war hero made him a popular candidate for President (above). He had led troops against Indians (right) and the British during the War of 1812. Jackson's wife, Rachel, became ill when she learned that their marital history was a campaign issue. The couple had been married twice; the second ceremony occurred after they learned that their first wedding had taken place before she was properly divorced from an earlier husband. Rachel died of a heart attack before her husband became President.

Jackson tried several professions after the war before he took up the study of law and became an attorney. He settled in Tennessee. Jackson practiced law there and established a cotton plantation, worked by slaves, named the Hermitage. Later he served briefly in both the House and Senate of the U.S. Congress.

More than a decade later—during the War of 1812—Jackson earned the national reputation that carried him to the White House. He served as an officer for volunteers from Tennessee and became a U.S. general. General Jackson became famous for his leadership during the Battle of New Orleans, the last conflict in the War of 1812. Jackson's sol-

diers thought their leader was as tough as an old hickory tree. The nickname "Old Hickory" stuck with Jackson for life.

During the 1828 presidential election the opposition party sought to discredit Jackson. It issued a thick booklet about his "youthful indiscretions," or mistakes, including accounts of his numerous fights and duels. (Jackson lived the last four decades of his life with a bullet lodged near his heart from one of his duels.) Jackson's supporters dished out their own round of slander, and Jackson defeated his rival, President John Quincy Adams. Citizens stormed the White House during Jackson's Inaugural Reception. They

General Jackson (above) went on to become the first President to have his life threatened by an assassin. The unlucky assailant (who was later ruled insane) fired two guns at the President from close range in the U.S. Capitol rotunda, but neither one fired properly. Jackson was so angry that he beat the gunman with his cane.

> "The great can protect themselves, but the poor and humble, require the arm and shield of the law."
>
> Andrew Jackson, 1821

General Andrew Jackson became the "hero of New Orleans" after his forces killed or wounded 2,000 British soldiers who were attacking the city at the end of the War of 1812. U.S. casualties were only 71. Jackson's fame helped earn him the Presidency 14 years later.

were eager to see the "People's President." Muddy boots climbed on silk chairs, fists flew, china crashed, and ladies fainted in the crush of visitors. Jackson escaped out a back door to the safety of a hotel. Finally, staff members placed tubs of punch on the White House lawn to lure the crowd outside, then locked the doors.

Jackson marked his two terms of office by assuming greater powers of leadership than any prior President. Critics nicknamed him "King Andrew the First." Future Presidents would thank him for setting standards that fortified their own administrations. Jackson insisted the President could hire and fire his own Cabinet members by replacing ones who refused to follow his orders. He upheld the authority of the U.S. government over state governments by insisting it was treasonous for

South Carolina to ignore federal import tax law. He encouraged the practice of awarding federal jobs to political supporters. He defied the Supreme Court by ignoring its support of Cherokee Indians. Jackson insisted that Native Americans living east of the Mississippi should be relocated to new land in the West.

Although his bold actions shocked many politicians, they were generally popular with citizens. Jackson was the last two-term President until Abraham Lincoln. After his second term he retired to the Hermitage, where he continued to influence politics. He took particular pleasure in the presidential elections of two of his protégés—his own Vice President, Martin Van Buren, and, later on, James K. Polk, a fellow Tennessean. "Old Hickory" died shortly after Polk became President.

Andrew Jackson, who grew up in a simple log cabin (left), was called "a barbarian who...hardly could spell his own name" by political rival John Quincy Adams. Jackson's final home, the Hermitage (right), reflected the advances he had made during his lifetime. In 1833 Jackson responded playfully to his introduction, delivered in Latin, at a Harvard University ceremony in his honor. He joked: "All the Latin I know is E pluribus unum." (This motto on the U.S. seal means "out of many, one.") The crowd applauded with delight.

FROM SEA TO SHINING SEA

★ *1837 – 1861* ★

1845

Frederick Douglass increased public concern over the treatment of slaves when he published his autobiography. He worked with abolitionists to end slavery.

circa 1846

By 1846 large parties of settlers were traveling the Oregon Trail from Missouri to the western United States. They rested at Independence Rock before crossing the Rocky Mountains.

1846–1848

The Mexican War began with battles at disputed Texas border spots such as Palo Alto. By the end of the war, U.S. boundaries stretched to California.

1849

The discovery of gold in California triggered a massive gold rush to the territory. Prospectors flocked to the region in search of the valuable metal.

Presidents faced a delicate balancing act before the Civil War. Efforts to expand U.S. land holdings always seemed to spark renewed debate over whether to expand slavery as well. Presidents had greater success at adding land than at resolving what to do about slavery. Native Americans suffered when they were pushed from their homelands by new waves of settlers. None of the Presidents from this era served more than one term in office. Rather, they left by choice, lost reelection bids, or died in office.

1850s

The number of miles of railroad track in use throughout the United States tripled during the 1850s. A spreading web of routes moved people and freight across vast distances.

1854

Commodore Matthew C. Perry, backed up by a strong show of military might, established trading rights between the United States and Japan during his visit there.

1860

By 1860 more than one-third of all Southerners—some 3.5 million people—were slaves. Disagreement over the expansion of slavery erupted into the Civil War a year later.

1860–1861

Pony Express riders could deliver mail between Missouri and California in ten days or less. Rides ceased after telegraph wires spanned the continent in October 1861.

Martin Van Buren

8TH PRESIDENT OF THE UNITED STATES ★ *1837 – 1841*

NICKNAME	Little Magician
BORN	Dec. 5, 1782, in Kinderhook, N.Y.
POLITICAL PARTY	Democrat
CHIEF OPPONENT	William Henry Harrison, Whig (1773–1841)
TERM OF OFFICE	March 4, 1837–March 3, 1841
AGE AT INAUGURATION	54 years old
NUMBER OF TERMS	one
VICE PRESIDENT	Richard M. Johnson (1780–1850)
FIRST LADY	Angelica Singleton Van Buren (1816–1878), daughter-in-law
WIFE	Hannah Hoes Van Buren (1783–1819), married Feb. 21, 1807
CHILDREN	Abraham, John, Martin, Smith
GEOGRAPHIC SCENE	26 states
NEW STATES ADDED	none
DIED	July 24, 1862, in Kinderhook, N.Y.
AGE AT DEATH	79 years old
SELECTED LANDMARKS	Lindenwald, Kinderhook, N.Y. N.Y. (homestead); Kinderhook Cemetery, Kinderhook, N.Y.

The "Little Magician" seeks reelection.

MARTIN VAN BUREN EARNED THE RESPECT and support of the Democratic Party by inventing new ways to expand political influence. The financial panic that began soon after he entered the White House in 1837 clouded his bright prospects as President. This popular Vice President of Andrew Jackson failed to win election to a second term.

Van Buren was an unlikely President to lose a reelection bid. He had spent his adult life creating the political system that earned him his first term in office. A native of New York, he was the first President born as a citizen of the United States. (Earlier Presidents, although born as British subjects, were considered U.S. citizens by their association with the new nation.) Van Buren, the descendant of Dutch immigrants, completed his formal schooling before his 14th birthday. He then took up the study of law. By age 21 he was a practicing attorney.

A successful political career followed. Between 1812 and 1829 Van Buren—originally a Democratic-Republican—served as a member of the New York State Senate, then as a U.S. senator, and briefly as governor of his home state. Along the way he revolutionized party politics.

Martin Van Buren's birthplace (above) was in Kinderhook, New York. Van Buren earned many nicknames because of his political cleverness and success. He was called the "Little Magician," "Enchanter," "Wizard," and "Red Fox of Kinderhook." In 1840 Democrats in New York City formed the "O.K. Club," after "Old Kinderhook," another Van Buren nickname. Soon "OK" came to mean "all right."

A HARD ROAD TO HOE!

"The less government interferes with private pursuits the better for the general prosperity."

Martin Van Buren, 1837

Martin Van Buren's Presidency was troubled by obstacles (left), such as how to manage the federal money supply and how to overcome the popular frontier-style image, complete with hard cider, of his 1840 political opponent, William Henry Harrison. When Martin Van Buren became President, the nation's population had almost quadrupled to over 15 million people since the start of George Washington's administration nearly 50 years earlier.

Van Buren wanted to defeat those who held office as a result of their personal wealth and influence. He worked with others who shared this view to stir up popular support over issues such as the costly construction of canals. He and his supporters identified themselves by displaying the tail of a buck deer on their hats. The "Bucktail" Democrats gained broad influence by unseating their aristocratic rivals.

Once in power, the Bucktails rewarded their supporters with thousands of state jobs, thus assuring continued loyalty to the party. This practice came to be known as the "spoils system" because it distributed the riches, or spoils, of office among party members. It was these supporters who helped Van Buren get elected to the U.S. Senate. Later, Andrew Jackson gained his place in the White House thanks, in part, to the practice of Van Buren-style politics. Jackson rewarded Van Buren for his support by naming him secretary of state. When Jackson ran for reelection, he chose Van

Buren as his Vice President. He supported Van Buren's own bid for the Presidency four years later.

Van Buren gained Jackson's post in the election of 1836, but he did not enjoy the same popularity as his predecessor. Nor did his administration enjoy the same prosperity. Soon after his Inauguration, the national economy collapsed in what became known as the Panic of 1837. Banks failed, businesses closed, and tens of thousands of workers lost their jobs. In some cities, angry residents rioted and stole food. It was the worst financial crisis the nation had ever experienced, and it lasted for five years. Van Buren handled the problem poorly. He continued Jackson's financial policies without realizing they were making matters worse, not better.

Van Buren had better luck managing other threats to the nation. Using diplomacy, he quieted tensions with Mexico over the newly independent republic of Texas. His antistatehood position on Texas helped reduce North-South concerns over

During Martin Van Buren's Presidency, federal troops drove some 15,000 Cherokees out of their homes in or near Georgia to the Indian Territory in present-day Oklahoma. Close to a third of these Native Americans died because of the harsh conditions along what became known as the Trail of Tears.

the possible expansion of slavery there. He avoided war with Great Britain in two disputes, one over the Maine-Canada border and the other regarding American support of rebels from Ontario, Canada.

Van Buren continued the Indian Removal Act policies of the Jackson administration. As a result, the United States waged a vicious war against Seminole Indians in Florida, forcing survivors to move West. These battles and other Indian removal efforts cost the federal government some $50 million. This flow of money unexpectedly helped improve the economy, although not early enough before the election to earn Van Buren a second term in office. The "Little Magician" found himself out of tricks when faced for the second time with a challenge by William Henry Harrison. Van Buren was defeated by someone whose own party had grown stronger using the same tactics Van Buren had promoted earlier with the Democrats.

Van Buren returned to his hometown in upstate New York. He lived at Lindenwald, an estate he had purchased there some years earlier. Van Buren made two more unsuccessful runs for the White House, most notably in 1848 with the short-lived Free Soil Party. He supported President Abraham Lincoln's pro-Union policies during the Civil War but died before the end of the conflict.

Martin Van Buren (far left) became a widower in 1819 after the death of his wife, Hannah (right), at age 35. He never remarried.

William Henry Harrison

9TH PRESIDENT OF THE UNITED STATES ★ *1841*

NICKNAME	Tippecanoe
BORN	Feb. 9, 1773, in Charles City County, Va.
POLITICAL PARTY	Whig
CHIEF OPPONENT	President Martin Van Buren, Democrat (1782–1862)
TERM OF OFFICE	March 4, 1841–April 4, 1841
AGE AT INAUGURATION	68 years old
NUMBER OF TERMS	one (cut short by death)
VICE PRESIDENT	John Tyler (1790–1862)
FIRST LADY	Jane Irwin Harrison (dates unknown), daughter-in-law
WIFE	Anna Tuthill Symmes Harrison (1775–1864), married Nov. 25, 1795
CHILDREN	Elizabeth, John, Lucy, William, John, Benjamin, Mary, Carter, Anna, plus a son died young
GEOGRAPHIC SCENE	26 states
NEW STATES ADDED	none
DIED	April 4, 1841, in the White House, Washington, D.C.
AGE AT DEATH	68 years old
SELECTED LANDMARKS	Berkeley Plantation, Charles City County, Va. (birthplace); Grouseland, Vincennes, Ind. (family home); Harrison Tomb State Memorial, North Bend, Ohio

WILLIAM HENRY HARRISON had a Presidency of extremes. At 68 he was the oldest man at that point in time to become President. He gave the longest Inaugural Address ever—one hour and 40 minutes, and he was the first President to die in office. But Harrison is remembered most for having the shortest term of office: one month.

Harrison was also the last President born before the start of the American Revolution. Harrison's father signed the Declaration of Independence when William Henry was three years old. Harrison attended Hampden-Sydney College in Virginia before studying medicine and becoming a soldier. He battled Indians at the Tippecanoe River (hence his nickname) and fought in the War of 1812. He was the governor of Indiana Territory, an Ohio state senator, the ambassador to Colombia, and a U.S. representative and senator before seeking the Presidency. Harrison represented the Whigs, a new party that evolved from the Federalists. He and his 1840 presidential running mate were billed as the ticket of "Tippecanoe and Tyler Too." They won.

Harrison delivered his lengthy Inaugural Address outdoors in brisk weather, yet he refused to wear a hat or coat. He caught cold soon after, perhaps because of this mistake. Several weeks later, still recovering from his cold, he was soaked in a sudden downpour. His illness worsened, and he developed pneumonia. "I am ill, very ill," he concluded. Harrison died five days later, exactly one month after taking office. His death triggered the first promotion of a Vice President to the Presidency without benefit of an election. Years later Harrison's grandson, Benjamin Harrison, became the nation's 23rd President.

Harrison defeated Tecumseh in 1813.

The Whig Party urged voters to "keep the ball rolling on to Washington" by supporting its candidate.

John Tyler

10TH PRESIDENT OF THE UNITED STATES ★ 1841 – 1845

The first telegraph message was sent in 1844.

JOHN TYLER WAS THE FIRST VICE PRESIDENT to complete a different Chief Executive's term. He took firm command of the office immediately after the death of William Henry Harrison. This confident action set the standard for future midterm successions.

A Virginian like his predecessor, Tyler was a graduate of the College of William and Mary in Williamsburg. Before being named to the 1840 presidential ticket, he had served Virginia in the state legislature, as governor, and in the U.S. House and Senate.

Tyler was dubbed "His Accidency" after Harrison's unexpected death. The Constitution was vague about how a Vice President should take over as President. Tyler insisted that he was a true President, not an acting one. He took the oath of office, moved into the White House, and prepared to serve out Harrison's term. He even delivered a brief Inaugural Address (and did not catch cold).

As President, Tyler favored greater power for state governments and less for the federal government. His policies added to North-South tensions and helped lead the country to civil war later on. Tyler supported settlement of the West, helped resolve a dispute with Great Britain over Canada's boundaries with Maine, and led efforts to bring the Republic of Texas (then an independent country) into the Union.

Tyler was kicked out of the Whig Party after he vetoed its pro-banking legislation. Without the backing of a party, he had no easy way to seek reelection. He and his family retired to Virginia. When civil war seemed likely, Tyler, who was a slaveholder, encouraged his state to leave the Union. He was elected to serve in the Confederate Congress, but he died before he could take office.

John Tyler fathered more offspring than any other President: 15 children by two wives. He and his future wife, Julia, escaped harm in 1844 when a cannon misfired during their visit to the warship Princeton *(above). After Julia hosted a popular White House ball at the end of her husband's Presidency, Tyler, who had been kicked out of his political party, joked: "They cannot say now that I am a President without a party."*

The Vice Presidents

★ Leaders Just a Heartbeat Away ★

FORTY-SEVEN MEN have served as Vice President of the United States since 1789. Fourteen have eventually become President, starting with John Adams, the first Vice President. The others, although important political figures in their day, have tended to fade from popular memory.

The Vice Presidency was created at the same time as the Presidency with the writing of the U.S. Constitution in 1787. The office received only brief definition. It took two Constitutional amendments to clarify how Vice Presidents should be chosen and what role they should play when a President becomes ill or dies in office.

The earliest Vice Presidents earned their posts by being the runners-up in the voting for President by the Electoral College. By the late 1820s, after the expansion of popular elections, political parties began identifying their own candidates for the two offices. Today such selection is directed by each presidential nominee. Then and now vice presidential nominees often balance and broaden the appeal of an election ticket by representing, for example, a different geographic region or age.

Early Vice Presidents were not seen as Presidents-in-waiting the way they are today. In fact, lawmakers disagreed over whether the Vice President even had this responsibility. It was not until the death of President William Henry Harrison in 1841 that this uncertainty was resolved. John Tyler, Harrison's Vice President, insisted that he deserved all the rights and responsibilities of President. His

Aaron Burr was among the most notorious Vice Presidents, particularly after he shot Alexander Hamilton in an 1804 duel (far left). Hamilton later died, leaving Burr open to murder charges while serving in Thomas Jefferson's administration. Modern Vice Presidents juggle a growing set of duties, whether ceremonial (left, Hubert Humphrey with Martin Luther King, Jr., during Lyndon B. Johnson's administration), advisory (right, Al Gore with President Bill Clinton), or directive (far right, Dick Cheney during the 43rd Presidency). They support favored legislation, too. Their official residence (top) lies a short drive from the White House.

decisive example set the pattern for future presidential successions.

The Constitution spells out one main responsibility for the Vice President: to preside over the U.S. Senate. In that role the Vice President is expected to cast deciding votes whenever the tally of senators' ballots results in a tie. Vice President John Adams was called upon to fulfill this duty on 29 occasions, more than any other Vice President.

With such a limited job description, early Vice Presidents often spent little time in the nation's capital, especially when the Senate was out of session. Many returned to their home states and took up old responsibilities. It was not until the 1970s that the Vice President even earned an official residence. The home is a 33-room house on the grounds of the U.S. Naval Observatory, a short drive from the White House. Walter Mondale, second in command to Jimmy Carter, became the first Vice President to inhabit this space.

Over the years Vice Presidents have shared similar backgrounds with Presidents, starting with a common average age, about 55 years old. New York State, a popular home for Presidents, gave more Vice Presidents to the country than any other state. Eight were born there, and 11 lived there prior to taking office. Like Presidents, many Vice Presidents served first as governors (15 of them did) or members of Congress (in 34 cases) before running for national office. Many had presidential ambitions of their own but settled for the post of Vice President, perhaps with the hope that the

Only two Vice Presidents, John C. Calhoun and Spiro T. Agnew, have resigned from office. Calhoun left Andrew Jackson's administration to become a U.S. senator. Agnew was forced from office (above) during Richard Nixon's Presidency for failing to properly pay his income taxes. Ten months later scandal forced Nixon to resign.

job would serve as a stepping stone to the Presidency later on.

About half of the Vice Presidents served at least one four-year term in office; only eight have completed two terms as Vice President. Others either succeeded to the Presidency by death (on eight occasions), or because of resignation (once), died in office themselves (in seven instances), resigned from their duties (twice), or filled unexpired terms of other Vice Presidents (once). Former Vice Presidents have variously retired from political life, won seats in Congress, or, in the case of five men, gone on to be elected President. One, Al Gore, even earned a Nobel Peace Prize.

Until the U.S. Constitution was amended in 1967, vacancies in the office of Vice President remained unfilled until the next presidential election. Now the 25th Amendment asks the President to nominate someone to serve as Vice President, subject to approval by a majority of the members of Congress. Richard Nixon was the first President to use this provision. All together there have been 19 occasions totaling nearly 38 years when the nation has had no one serving as Vice President.

The role a Vice President plays in an administration is set by each individual President. During the 20th century, Vice Presidents gained greater influence and were given increasingly important duties. Today's Vice Presidents juggle a growing range of responsibilities. At the same time they live each day knowing they are but a heartbeat away from becoming President of the United States.

James K. Polk

IITH PRESIDENT OF THE UNITED STATES ★ 1845 – 1849

NICKNAME	Young Hickory
BORN	Nov. 2, 1795, near Pineville, Mecklenburg County, N.C.
POLITICAL PARTY	Democrat
CHIEF OPPONENT	Henry Clay, Whig (1777–1852)
TERM OF OFFICE	March 4, 1845–March 3, 1849
AGE AT INAUGURATION	49 years old
NUMBER OF TERMS	one
VICE PRESIDENT	George Mifflin Dallas (1792–1864)
FIRST LADY	Sarah Childress Polk (1803–1891), wife (married Jan. 1, 1824)
CHILDREN	none
GEOGRAPHIC SCENE	27 states
NEW STATES ADDED	Texas (1845), Iowa (1846), Wisconsin (1848)
DIED	June 15, 1849, at Nashville, Tenn.
AGE AT DEATH	53 years old
SELECTED LANDMARKS	Pineville, N.C. (reconstructed birthplace); State Capitol Grounds, Nashville, Tenn. (grave)

Polk camps with his father on a surveying trip.

USING A COMBINATION OF WAR AND ROUGH DIPLOMACY, James Knox Polk increased the nation's size by two-thirds. By the end of his single term, he had secured the land that would form almost all of the 48 contiguous United States. However, disagreements over the expansion of slavery into the new territories left the nation more divided than ever.

Polk came to Washington with the nickname "Young Hickory" because of his ties to Andrew Jackson, the famed "Old Hickory" President. Like Jackson, Polk was born in the Carolinas and settled in Tennessee. He was the son of a prosperous landowner, planter, and slaveholder. Polk's formal education began at age 17. He earned a degree with honors from the University of North Carolina, studied law, became an attorney, and sought a career in politics.

After a few years in the Tennessee Legislature, Polk gained election to the U.S. House of Representatives. He served there for 14 years and

James K. Polk grew up in the backwoods of North Carolina and Tennessee. Polk pushed the U.S. boundaries to the Pacific Ocean. The first U.S. postage stamps, the U.S. Naval Academy, and the Smithsonian Institution all began during his administration.

Posters compare the candidates for President in 1844 (left). James K. Polk was a "dark horse," or unexpected choice, for his political party. When word of his nomination reached Washington, D.C., by the new Morse telegraph, some doubted that the machine was working correctly. A political cartoon (right) questions whether trouble caused by President Polk's policies will collapse on him like a house of cards. An artist illustrated his policy of Manifest Destiny by showing the symbolic figure of Columbia (below) leading settlers westward.

was eventually elected Speaker, or leader, of the House. He earned Andrew Jackson's friendship in those years by supporting the President's policies. Later Polk served as governor of Tennessee.

Despite this record of public service, the nomination of Polk for President in 1844 came as a surprise. Most Democrats had expected the party to renominate former President Martin Van Buren, with Polk as a possible vice presidential candidate. Van Buren, however, had lost favor because of his antislavery stand against Texas statehood. Polk, a slaveholder, supported bringing Texas into the Union as a slave state and became the compromise nominee. He narrowly defeated the noted statesman Henry Clay at the polls.

Polk came into office determined, as were many citizens then, to expand his country's borders to the Pacific Ocean.

"The people of this continent alone have the right to decide their own destiny."

James K. Polk, Message to Congress, December 2, 1845

This belief—that the U.S. had the right to take over lands to the West—was called Manifest Destiny. This unquestionable confidence was used to justify the nation's expansion regardless of harm done to those who were displaced.

Polk started with the Oregon Territory. Previously this Northwestern region, which included parts of present-day Oregon, Idaho, Washington State, and Canada's British Columbia, had been settled by British and Americans alike. U.S. pioneers traveled to it by way of the Oregon Trail. Polk bluffed that he expected the British to give up all land south of latitude 54° 40', the southern border of Russia's Alaskan Territory. Otherwise he would fight to take it. Hence the popular slogan: "Fifty-four forty, or fight." In the end Polk was delighted to settle on the 49th parallel, which still forms most of the U.S.-Canada border.

Next Polk concentrated on the southern U.S. border. Texans had won their independence from Mexico in 1836. Polk angered Mexico by granting Texas statehood soon after he became President. Then a boundary dispute erupted over the new state's southern border. Mexico insisted the Nueces River, the boundary of Texas as a Mexican state, was still its southern border. The U.S. claimed territory all the way to the Rio Grande—about half of the country of Mexico.

On Polk's instructions, U.S. soldiers provoked the Mexicans to attack by crossing into the disputed region in early 1846. From then on, U.S. forces never lost a battle in a war that ultimately took them all the way to Mexico City. When the Mexican War ended in the fall of 1847, the United States had gained not only the border it wanted for Texas but considerable other new land as well. Eventually, some or all of the states of Arizona, California, Colorado, Nevada, New Mexico, Utah, and Wyoming would take shape in the extra territory. Mexico was paid $15 million for its loss of land. Ulysses S. Grant, the future Civil War general and U.S. President, was among those who fought in the war. He described it as "one of the most unjust ever waged by a stronger against a weaker nation."

In all, Polk added 1.2 million square miles of territory to the United States. It came with a heavy price. Northerners opposed to slavery and Southerners who supported it debated furiously over whether slavery had a place in the vast new lands. The two sides seemed ready to come to blows over the issue, and they finally did when the Civil War erupted some dozen years later.

Polk left the White House after one term, fulfilling an election promise not to run again. He enjoyed the shortest retirement of any President—three months—in part because he had literally exhausted himself on the job. Polk became ill, possibly with cholera, and died. His wife, Sarah, lived in their Tennessee home 42 years longer, remaining neutral during the Civil War.

James K. Polk and his wife, Sarah (right), had no children. They retired to "Polk Place" (left) after his Presidency. Sarah was well educated, and she devoted her energies to her husband's career. She traveled with him, helped with his speeches, reviewed newspapers for him, and served as the White House hostess. Because of her religious beliefs, she disapproved of alcohol, gambling, and dancing. When she entered the room for her husband's Inaugural Ball, the dancing ended. The Polks started the White House traditions of an annual Thanksgiving dinner and the playing of "Hail to the Chief" for the President's arrival.

Zachary Taylor

12TH PRESIDENT OF THE UNITED STATES ★ 1849 – 1850

NICKNAME	Old Rough-and-Ready
BORN	Nov. 24, 1784, in Orange County, Va.
POLITICAL PARTY	Whig
CHIEF OPPONENT	Lewis Cass, Democrat (1782–1866)
TERM OF OFFICE	March 4, 1849–July 9, 1850
AGE AT INAUGURATION	64 years old
NUMBER OF TERMS	one (cut short by death)
VICE PRESIDENT	Millard Fillmore (1800–1874)
FIRST LADIES	Margaret Mackall Smith Taylor (1788–1852), wife (married June 21, 1810); Mary Elizabeth Taylor Bliss (1824–1909), daughter
CHILDREN	Ann, Sarah, Mary, Richard, plus two daughters died young
GEOGRAPHIC SCENE	30 states
NEW STATES ADDED	none
DIED	July 9, 1850, in the White House, Washington, D.C.
AGE AT DEATH	65 years old
SELECTED LANDMARKS	Zachary Taylor National Cemetery, Louisville, Ky.

General Zachary Taylor often wore old farm clothes into battle. He made a straw hat part of his standard battle dress.

ZACHARY TAYLOR WAS A SOLDIER BY TRAINING, not a politician, but he discovered unexpected similarities between those two professions after becoming President. Politicians in the nation's capital could become as combative as soldiers, he learned, particularly when the matter of slavery was discussed. He threatened to use military force to settle the debate over slavery; then he died in office before he could.

Taylor was the first President who had never held another elected office. In fact, he had never even voted in a presidential election because he felt his loyalty as a soldier for the U.S. government required him to stay neutral politically. Born in Virginia, Taylor was raised on a plantation in Kentucky and was one of the last slave owners to become President. He never attended college. Instead he entered into a 40-year career as an officer in the U.S. Army. His relaxed style of military dress, reputation for bravery, and consistent victories earned him the nickname "Old Rough-and-Ready."

Being a military hero helped Taylor win the election, but his Army career was poor training for the national debate on slavery. When he suggested that new states should decide for themselves whether to be slave or free, all sides protested. Northerners wanted Taylor to restrict slavery, not expand it. Southerners feared new antislavery states would diminish their own pro-slavery influence in Congress. When Southerners threatened to secede from, or leave, the Union, Taylor offered to lead the U.S. Army against them. We must "preserve the Union at all hazards," he said.

Then Taylor died. An Independence Day snack of iced buttermilk and cherries was probably contaminated with bacteria. He developed cholera and succumbed to his illness five days later.

Zachary Taylor's legs were so short that he needed help mounting a horse. He liked to ride sidesaddle. Eventually both Taylor and his 1848 running mate (above) served as President of the nation.

Millard Fillmore

13TH PRESIDENT OF THE UNITED STATES ★ *1850 – 1853*

NICKNAME	Last of the Whigs
BORN	Jan. 7, 1800, in Cayuga County, N.Y.
POLITICAL PARTY	Whig
CHIEF OPPONENT	none; succeeded Taylor
TERM OF OFFICE	July 10, 1850–March 3, 1853
AGE AT INAUGURATION	50 years old

Millard Fillmore failed to be elected in 1856.

NUMBER OF TERMS	one (partial)
VICE PRESIDENT	none
FIRST LADIES	Abigail Powers Fillmore (1798–1853), wife (married Feb. 5 1826); Mary Abigail Fillmore (1832–1854), daughter
SECOND WIFE	Caroline Carmichael McIntosh Fillmore (1813–1881), married Feb. 10, 1858
CHILDREN	Millard, Mary
GEOGRAPHIC SCENE	30 states
NEW STATES ADDED	California (1850)
DIED	March 8, 1874, in Buffalo, N.Y.
AGE AT DEATH	74 years old
SELECTED LANDMARKS	Fillmore Glen State Park, Moravia, N.Y. (reconstructed birthplace); The Millard Fillmore House, East Aurora, N.Y.; Forest Lawn Cemetery, Buffalo, N.Y.

MILLARD FILLMORE OFFERED COMPROMISE, in contrast to the threatening style of his predecessor, as a way to end the ongoing tense debate over slavery. Despite being born a Northerner, Fillmore seemed to sympathize with Southern concerns. In the end, the compromises he signed only delayed civil war between North and South.

Born in a log cabin in upstate New York, Fillmore fulfilled the American dream of rising from simple beginnings to national importance. He was poorly educated. He is said to have seen his first map of the United States upon entering school at age 19. (Later he married his schoolteacher.) He never attended college, but he trained himself to be a lawyer. He won election to government posts in New York State and the U.S. House of Representatives before agreeing to run as Vice President for Zachary Taylor's ticket in 1848.

When Fillmore became President after Taylor died in office, he chose to compromise with lawmakers over quarrelsome debates about slavery. Their five agreements became known as the Compromise of 1850. These deals admitted California as a free state, settled border disputes between Texas and New Mexico, gave territory status to New Mexico, closed the slave markets in the nation's capital, and allowed federal law officers to return runaway slaves to their owners. Each side gained something, and war seemed less likely.

Fillmore showed little interest in the next election, so the Whigs selected a different candidate and lost in 1852. The party then fell into confusion and disappeared, earning Fillmore the nickname "Last of the Whigs." Fillmore retired to Buffalo, New York. In 1856 he ran for President with the new Know-Nothing Party, but he came in third. He died in 1874.

Millard Fillmore was tall, handsome, and well mannered, in striking contrast with the rough-and-ready image of his predecessor. He and his wife, Abigail, established the first permanent library at the White House. Abigail traveled in an elegant carriage (above). Sadly, she caught cold and died after attending the Inauguration of her husband's successor.

Pathways to the Presidency

★ *Campaign Strategies and Party Politics* ★

THE PRESIDENTIAL CAMPAIGNS of modern times are vastly different from those waged by earlier candidates for President. In fact, the concept of campaigning for the Presidency did not even gain favor until well into the 19th century. Prior to that time supporters spoke on behalf of candidates. Sitting Presidents, in particular, preferred not to mix the politics of campaigning with their work as chief executive.

Today's candidates begin their official presidential campaigns more than a year before Election Day and raise hundreds of millions of dollars in order to support their bids for votes. During the opening months of an election year, members of the various political parties compete against one another in a series of statewide contests called primaries and caucuses. Votes earned at the state level determine how many delegates will support each candidate during summer nominating conventions.

The party conventions bring thousands of delegates and leaders together to make official their nomination for President based on these statewide spring elections. Each presidential

Presidential hopefuls have followed many pathways to the Presidency, from traveling by train on a whistle-stop campaign (top, Warren G. Harding in 1920) to appearing on television (center, the first televised presidential debates, held in 1960 between Richard Nixon and John F. Kennedy). Opportunities to vote increased during the 1960s when reforms ended an era that sought to exclude African Americans from participating in Southern elections (left, marking ballots in Alabama). Controversies still occur, though, as they did in 2000 with the counting of votes in Florida (right).

Presidential hopeful Barack Obama spoke to the largest political convention crowd ever when he accepted the Democratic Party nomination for President in 2008. More than 80,000 people gathered at Denver's Invesco Field at Mile High for an occasion that featured political speeches, performances by pop stars, and celebration. Confetti and fireworks took the place of the traditional balloon drop of most convention finales.

candidate has the responsibility of selecting a Vice Presidential running mate, and that person's nomination is made official at the conventions, too. Other convention business includes determining the party's platform, a statement that summarizes what the party and candidates will support if elected.

The fall campaign season pits candidates from the major parties against one another in a series of debates and political action. Political campaigns compete for support for their candidates through advertising blitzes and weeks of cross-country appearances where the candidates deliver stump speeches, similar material repeated over and over for new audiences. Campaigns employ each innovation in communications technology—from radio to television to the Internet to cell phones—to influence voters.

Election Day occurs in November on the first Tuesday after the first Monday in the month. U.S. citizens 18 or older, regardless of race, gender, or beliefs, may register to vote. Voter turnout, the number of people who actually vote on Election Day, can be a critical factor in a candidate's success or defeat. Although a surprising number of people choose not to vote even when they are eligible to do so, many others value this action as one of their most cherished responsibilities as citizens. The final outcome of the election is determined by tallies within each state that identify the electoral college support of each candidate.

Usually the results of elections are known within hours after the closing of polls. Winning candidates celebrate with victory speeches, while the losers concede, or admit defeat, in concession speeches. Occasionally election results are unclear or become controversial, and some time may be required in order to determine who will emerge victorious.

A President's level of support during an election is seen as a measure of national confidence in that person. Someone who wins by a wide margin is said to hold a mandate, or the sign of widespread national support. Presidents elected with a mandate bring considerable political influence to their work.

Franklin Pierce

14TH PRESIDENT OF THE UNITED STATES ★ 1853 – 1857

NICKNAME	Handsome Frank
BORN	Nov. 23, 1804, in Hillsborough (now Hillsboro), N.H.
POLITICAL PARTY	Democrat
CHIEF OPPONENT	Winfield Scott, Whig (1786–1866)
TERM OF OFFICE	March 4, 1853–March 3, 1857
AGE AT INAUGURATION	48 years old
NUMBER OF TERMS	one
VICE PRESIDENT	William Rufus De Vane King (1786–1853)
FIRST LADY	Jane Means Appleton Pierce (1806–1863), wife (married Nov. 10, 1834)
CHILDREN	Frank, Benjamin, plus a son died young
GEOGRAPHIC SCENE	31 states
NEW STATES ADDED	none
DIED	Oct. 8, 1869, in Concord, N.H.
AGE AT DEATH	64 years old
SELECTED LANDMARKS	Hillsboro, N.H. (boyhood home); Concord, N.H. (adult home); Old North Cemetery, Concord, N.H.

Benjamin Pierce (above, with mother) died in a train crash shortly before his father's Inauguration.

WHEN FRANKLIN PIERCE BECAME PRESIDENT, the national debate about slavery had quieted. Pierce, a man with an undistinguished record in public office, carelessly renewed the controversy by supporting the option of slavery in Kansas. This stand re-opened the slavery issue and helped push the country closer to civil war.

In large part Pierce was nominated for President because he had not made many political enemies or taken a firm stand about slavery. His party decided it would be easier to elect "Handsome Frank" than other, more controversial Democrats. Pierce had been born in a log cabin in New Hampshire. A graduate of Maine's Bowdoin College, he took up law and served in the New Hampshire Legislature. Later he spent 10 years in Washington, D.C., as a representative and a senator. While there Pierce earned more notice for his heavy drinking than for his lawmaking. Democrats campaigned for his Presidency with the slogan: "We Polked you in 1844; we shall Pierce you in 1852."

As President, Pierce infuriated Northerners by supporting the Kansas-Nebraska Act of 1854. This measure ended the Missouri Compromise of 1820 by permitting slavery to spread north of Missouri's southern border. Using a policy called popular sovereignty, the act suggested that residents of new states should determine for themselves whether to permit slavery within their borders. Casualties climbed to about 200 in "Bleeding Kansas" after both pro-slavery and antislavery settlers rushed to the territory and began fighting.

The Democratic Party was so embarrassed by the scene that it did not renominate Pierce for a second term. Pierce retired to New Hampshire in disgrace. His death in 1869 went largely unrecognized.

Franklin Pierce seemed to find trouble wherever he turned during the stormy pre–Civil War years of his Presidency. Debates over slavery turned particularly ugly in "Bleeding Kansas" (above). Improving the White House, with hot and cold running water and a hot-water-based heating system, proved more manageable than policymaking.

James Buchanan

NICKNAME	Ten-Cent Jimmy
BORN	April 23, 1791, in Cove Gap, Pa.
POLITICAL PARTY	Democrat
CHIEF OPPONENT	John C. Frémont, Republican (1813–1890)
TERM OF OFFICE	March 4, 1857–March 3, 1861
AGE AT INAUGURATION	65 years old
NUMBER OF TERMS	one
VICE PRESIDENT	John Cabell Breckinridge (1821–1875)
FIRST LADY	Harriet Lane (1830–1903), niece
WIFE	never married
CHILDREN	none
GEOGRAPHIC SCENE	31 states
NEW STATES ADDED	Minnesota (1858), Oregon (1859), Kansas (1861)
DIED	June 1, 1868, in Lancaster, Pa.
AGE AT DEATH	77 years old
SELECTED LANDMARKS	Mercersburg Academy, Mercersburg, Pa. (relocated boyhood home); Wheatland, Lancaster, Pa. (homestead); Woodward Hill Cemetery, Lancaster, Pa.

SOUTH CAROLINA'S "ULTIMATUM"

"Don't fire 'til I get out of office," exclaims James Buchanan in this political cartoon. The departing President told his successor, Abraham Lincoln: "If you are as happy, my dear sir, on entering this house as I am on leaving it and returning home, you are the happiest man on earth."

JAMES BUCHANAN, in an effort to hold the Union together, offered concession after concession to the South, regardless of the anger his actions provoked in the North. When Southern states began to secede anyway, he protested but claimed to have no constitutional authority to force them to come back.

Buchanan's unhappy single term in the White House followed a distinguished, 40-year career of public service in the United States and abroad. Buchanan was born in a log cabin in Pennsylvania. The son of an Irish immigrant, he graduated from Dickinson College, studied law, and entered public service. He served briefly in the state legislature, then spent a decade each in the U.S. House and Senate. In addition, he was minister to Russia under Andrew Jackson, James K. Polk's secretary of state, and minister to Great Britain for Franklin Pierce. This final post helped earn him the presidential nomination. By being abroad he had avoided the latest slavery debates.

Shortly after Buchanan's Inauguration, the Supreme Court issued its *Dred Scott* ruling. The slave Dred Scott had argued he should be free if his master moved with him to a free state. The Court disagreed, saying slaves were property, not citizens, and remained slaves anywhere. Although Buchanan disliked slavery (he even bought slaves in order to free them), he hated breaking laws even more. (His nickname recalled his insistence on precise bookkeeping, for example.) Buchanan stood by the ruling, infuriating Northerners. He could not resolve the financial Panic of 1857 or the secession of Southern states from the Union. Having stated he would serve only one term, Buchanan was delighted to leave office. Buchanan, the only President who never married, retired to Pennsylvania to write his memoirs. He died in 1868.

Dred Scott

James Buchanan had one good eye for each type of vision—close up and distant. In order to see well he cocked his head to one side or the other depending on which eye he needed to use.

A NEW BIRTH OF FREEDOM

★ *1861 – 1897* ★

1863

Union forces defeated Confederate troops at the Battle of Gettysburg after the Southern Army crossed over onto Northern soil. The four-year-long Civil War ended in 1865.

1865–1870

Many Northerners who moved South after the Civil War carried their belongings in suitcases made from carpets. These "carpetbaggers" tried to influence the Reconstruction of the South.

1871

Fires burned across Chicago for more than 24 hours beginning on October 8. The city rebuilt itself into a vibrant midwestern business center, complete with early skyscrapers.

1879

Thomas Edison invented the electric lightbulb. Other inventions by Edison included the phonograph, microphone, and motion pictures. He developed the scientific research laboratory, too.

Years of disagreement between Northerners and Southerners over slavery and related issues finally led to Civil War between the two regions. After the four-year war ended in 1865, a series of Presidents struggled with Reconstruction, the process of reuniting and rebuilding the splintered nation. Post–Civil War Presidents more often found themselves watching history unfold than shaping it. The growth of industry in the East and the expansion of western settlement drove the United States toward its modern form.

1886

The Statue of Liberty became a beacon of welcome to immigrants after its dedication. Within a decade, more than 350,000 newcomers were arriving annually. The figure had more than doubled by 1906.

1889

When the federal government opened up central Oklahoma for settlement in April, some 50,000 "sodbusters" rushed to stake their claims in the new territory on one day.

1890

Susan B. Anthony spent half a century trying without success to earn women the right to vote. In 1890 she became president of the National American Woman Suffrage Association.

1893

The Duryea brothers built the first successful gasoline-powered car in the United States. Within a dozen years more than 1.5 million cars were being produced in the country.

Abraham Lincoln

16TH PRESIDENT OF THE UNITED STATES ★ *1861 – 1865*

Abraham Lincoln

NICKNAME	Honest Abe
BORN	Feb. 12, 1809, near Hodgenville, Ky.
POLITICAL PARTY	Republican (formerly Whig)
CHIEF OPPONENTS	1st term: Stephen Arnold Douglas (1813–1861), Northern Democrat; John Cabell Breckinridge (1821–1875), Southern Democrat; and John Bell (1797–1869), Constitutional Union; 2nd term: George Brinton McClellan (1826–1885), Democrat
TERM OF OFFICE	March 4, 1861–April 15, 1865
AGE AT INAUGURATION	52 years old
NUMBER OF TERMS	two (cut short by assassination)
VICE PRESIDENTS	1st term: Hannibal Hamlin (1809–1891); 2nd term: Andrew Johnson (1808–1875)

First Lady Mary Todd Lincoln

FIRST LADY	Mary Todd Lincoln (1818–1882), wife (married Nov. 4, 1842)
CHILDREN	Robert, Edward (died young), William, Thomas
GEOGRAPHIC SCENE	23 United States; 11 Confederate States
NEW STATES ADDED	West Virginia (1863), Nevada (1864)
DIED	April 15, 1865, in Washington, D.C.
AGE AT DEATH	56 years old
SELECTED LANDMARKS	Hodgenville, Ky. (birthplace); Springfield, Ill. (home, grave, and library); Lincoln Memorial, President's Cottage, Washington, D.C.; Mount Rushmore, S. Dak.

WHEN ABRAHAM LINCOLN WAS INAUGURATED in 1861, he became President of states that were not united. In fact, after arguing for years about slavery and states' rights, Northerners and Southerners were on the brink of civil, or internal, war. Lincoln has been called the greatest U.S. President because he reunited the country. He was assassinated just after the end of the Civil War in 1865.

Lincoln's humble beginnings are a schoolbook legend. He was born in a log cabin in Kentucky to parents who could neither read nor write. The sum of his schoolhouse education was about one year's time, but he educated himself by reading books he borrowed from others. When Lincoln was nine years old, his mother died. His father, a carpenter and farmer, remarried and moved his family farther west, eventually settling in Illinois. Lincoln was taller (at six feet four inches) than any other President. His high-pitched voice and thick frontier accent (saying "git" for "get" or "thar" for "there") made an odd contrast with his thin but strong and dignified figure.

Lincoln worked as a flatboat navigator, storekeeper, soldier, surveyor, and postmaster before being elected at age 25 to the Illinois Legislature in Springfield. Once there, he taught himself law, opened a law practice, and earned the nickname of Honest Abe. He served one term in the U.S. House of Representatives during 1847–49 but lost two U.S. Senate races in the 1850s. However, the debates he had about slavery with his 1858 opponent, Stephen Douglas, helped him earn the presidential nomination two years later. In the

Abraham Lincoln's lifelong love of reading whenever and wherever he could (above) began in his youth, when books often took the place of school. Favorite reading included U.S. history, Aesop's Fables, Robinson Crusoe, *the* Bible, *and works by Shakespeare.*

four-way presidential race of 1860, Lincoln was the top vote-getter.

Lincoln was elected on a platform that considered it treason for Southern states to secede, or withdraw, from the nation. It agreed to continue slavery in the South but outlawed its spread elsewhere. Southern leaders threatened to secede rather than accept this Republican plan. After Lincoln's victory, but before his Inauguration, these states began to act on their threat to leave the Union. The Civil War officially began on April 12, 1861, at Fort Sumter, South Carolina, when forces from the new Confederate States of America attacked this U.S. fort.

Lincoln grew strong by splitting logs into thousands of rails for fences. At 21, he "paid" 400 rails per yard for pants fabric.

Lincoln had promised in his Inaugural oath to "preserve, protect, and defend" the Union. Now he began to act, competing with Confederate leaders for the allegiance of states not yet committed to either side. With Congress out of session until July, Lincoln broke laws when they stood in his way of protecting the Constitution. "Often limb must be amputated to save a life," he reasoned. Lincoln expanded the size of the Army and Navy, jailed people who might encourage secession of border states, stopped trade with the Confederacy, and spent government funds without the approval of lawmakers. His efforts strengthened the Northern cause; later they were approved by Congress and the courts. In the end, 11 states joined the Confederacy and 23 remained in the Union, including the crucial border states of Missouri, Kentucky, and Maryland.

The outcome of the Civil War remained unclear during the early years of fighting. While the North held the upper hand on the seas, the South generally beat Union forces on land. It was not until the Battle of Gettysburg, in July 1863, that Southern dominance of the battlefield ended. Through speeches such as his Gettysburg Address, Lincoln encouraged Northerners to keep fighting whatever the costs. In this famous three-minute dedication of the battlefield cemetery, he urged citizens to assure "that these dead shall not have died in vain—that this nation, under God, shall have a new birth of freedom—and that government of the people, by the people, for the people, shall not perish from the earth." Earlier that same year Lincoln called for the end of slavery in his Emancipation Proclamation.

Consistent military victories, including the capture of Atlanta, Georgia, in September 1864, helped Lincoln win reelection. His selection of Southern-born Andrew Johnson as his new running mate balanced his ticket. Only Union states participated in the election. By the following March, Union victory in the war was certain; the only question was when. Lincoln's second Inaugural Address made it clear that the Northern states would keep fighting "until every drop of blood drawn with the lash, shall be paid by another drawn with the sword."

Lincoln joked that he mostly battled mosquitoes during the Black Hawk War of 1832. The war pushed Native Americans farther west.

Lincoln and his running mate, Hannibal Hamlin, won the 1860 election even though many Southern states left them off their ballots.

Yet Lincoln urged citizens to end the war free from bitterness, "with malice toward none; with charity for all." Victory came on April 9, 1865, at Appomattox Court House, Virginia, when Confederate General Robert E. Lee surrendered to Union General Ulysses S. Grant. More than 600,000 soldiers had died during the four-year conflict.

Seeing the Union successfully through the Civil War was Lincoln's greatest presidential responsibility, but it was not his only accomplishment. Together with Congress, he inaugurated a national banking system, established the Department of Agriculture, standardized paper currency, supported the development of a transcontinental railroad, enacted the Homestead Act, which opened up vast holdings of federal land to settlers, and crafted the 13th Amendment, which ended slavery.

> "A house divided against itself cannot stand."
>
> Abraham Lincoln,
> June 1858

Lincoln's personal life in the White House revolved around his wife, Mary, and two young sons, William and Thomas, known as Willie and Tad. (Son Robert was already away at

Northerners and Southerners differed for years over whether the federal government had the right to control the practice of slavery. Disagreement about matters such as returning runaway slaves to their owners (above) caused Southern states to secede from the Union and led to the Civil War.

Citizens saw the toll war took on their President (left) and their countrymen thanks to early photographs made during the nation's four-year Civil War.

school.) Lincoln often romped with his sons and their friends. A teenage guest recalled how she once entered a room to find the President flattened on the floor with four boys holding down his limbs. "Come quick and sit on his stomach," invited Tad. Lincoln forgave the boys their wildness. "It's a diversion," he told a visitor, "and we need diversion at the White House." Lincoln told jokes, tall tales, anecdotes, and stories to relieve wartime tensions.

In 1862 humor lost its place for a while when

Left to right: Mary, Willie, Robert, Tad, and Abraham Lincoln. By 1871 only Mary and Robert remained alive.

Willie became the only child to die in the White House. He was a victim of typhoid fever. Mary, already saddened by criticism of her performance as First Lady, grieved deeply and long. First falsely accused of being sympathetic to the Confederacy (she had relatives in the South), then scolded for her lavish spending, she was now chided by the public for neglecting her official duties. The subsequent deaths of her husband and Tad left her so grief-stricken that some people considered her insane.

Lincoln spent much of the final weeks of his life away from the White House. He met with military commanders, such as Ulysses S. Grant (who would become the 18th President), and discussed surrender terms. Lincoln's plans for Reconstruction, or the reunion, of the United States were flexible and generous. However, he would barely live to enjoy the end of the war, much less shape its peace. He became the first President to be assassinated when he was shot on April 14, 1865.

Lincoln had received thousands of death threats since 1860. The day he was shot, he confided to his daytime bodyguard that he

> "That on the 1st day of January, A.D. 1863, all persons held as slaves...shall be then, thence-forward, and forever free."

Abraham Lincoln,
from the Emancipation Proclamation,
January 1, 1863

had dreamed for the three previous nights of being assassinated. His nightmare became a reality that evening when he went out to see a play. His nighttime bodyguard left Lincoln's box seat unguarded so he could watch the performance too. John Wilkes Booth, an actor familiar with the theater, was thus able to enter the President's box unnoticed. Booth hoped to revive the Confederate cause by killing the President. He shot Lincoln in the back of the head, then jumped to the stage floor, breaking his leg in the process. He escaped the theater nonetheless and remained on the loose for nearly two weeks. Eventually he was shot and killed while being captured.

The wounded and unconscious President was carried to a boardinghouse across the street. His long body had to be placed diagonally across the standard-size bed in order to recline properly. He died the following morning, said to be wearing an expression of happiness and repose on his face. His body lay in state at the U.S. Capitol and at other sites in the North before traveling home for burial in Illinois.

From the Lincoln-Douglas Debates of 1858 to the Emancipation Proclamation and Gettysburg Address of 1863 (top), Lincoln promoted freedom and unity. He was silenced by gunshot in 1865 (bottom, left). The President's death at the end of the Civil War (bottom, right) unsettled the fragile nation.

Andrew Johnson

17TH PRESIDENT OF THE UNITED STATES ★ *1865 – 1869*

NICKNAME	The Veto President
BORN	Dec. 29, 1808, in Raleigh, N.C.
POLITICAL PARTY	Democrat
CHIEF OPPONENT	none; succeeded Lincoln
TERM OF OFFICE	April 15, 1865–March 3, 1869
AGE AT INAUGURATION	56 years old
NUMBER OF TERMS	one (partial)
VICE PRESIDENT	none
FIRST LADIES	Eliza McCardle Johnson (1810–1876), wife (married May 17, 1827); Martha Johnson Patterson (1828–1891), daughter
CHILDREN	Martha, Charles, Mary, Robert, and Andrew, Jr.
GEOGRAPHIC SCENE	36 states
NEW STATES ADDED	Nebraska (1867)
DIED	July 31, 1875, in Carter's Station, Tenn.
AGE AT DEATH	66 years old
SELECTED LANDMARKS	Mordecai Historic Park, Raleigh, N.C. (relocated birthplace); Andrew Johnson National Historic Site, Greenville, Tenn. (includes two residences and grave)

Andrew Johnson opened a tailor's shop (above) when he was 17. He continued to make his own clothes even after becoming a legislator. During his Presidency the U.S. purchased the Alaskan Territory from Russia. In 1875 the retired President returned to the U.S. Senate. No other President has gone on to become a senator. At his request he was buried wrapped in a U.S. flag with his head resting on his copy of the Constitution.

THE CRISIS OF WAR BETWEEN THE STATES was followed by a crisis within the U.S. Presidency. It began with the assassination of Abraham Lincoln and continued through the Presidency of his successor, Andrew Johnson. The climax came with Johnson's impeachment and near removal from office by Congress.

Johnson grew up with more poverty and hardship than any other President. His parents were illiterate laborers; his father died when Andrew was three. He never attended a day of school. Nonetheless, by age 20 Johnson had been elected to be an alderman, or city legislator. Later he became a mayor, then a Tennessee state senator, U.S. representative, Tennessee governor, and U.S. senator. Johnson was the only Southern legislator who stayed on to work in the U.S. Senate during the Civil War. Southerners branded him a traitor, but Lincoln rewarded him by making him the military governor of Tennessee.

Although Johnson was a Democrat, Republicans put him on Lincoln's 1864 presidential ticket as a representative from the South. Thus, the party allegiance of the Presidency changed with Lincoln's death. Johnson was the last slave owner to become President. He argued with politicians about how to "reconstruct" the United States after the Civil War. He routinely vetoed, or rejected, Congress's ideas and became known as "The Veto President."

His leadership style angered legislators so much that, in 1868, the House of Representatives impeached him, or charged that he should be removed from office. House members identified 11 articles, or reasons, for removal. Nine of them dealt with the President's controversial firing of his secretary of war, an ally of Congress. The Senate considered the House charges but fell one vote short of convicting Johnson, so he completed his term of office.

Andrew Johnson—the first President ever impeached—received a summons (above) for his Senate trial.

U. S. Political Parties

★ *The Two-Party System* ★

THE FOUNDING FATHERS hoped that representatives of the new United States government would work together in harmony without dividing into opposing groups called parties. Yet, soon after George Washington became President, political parties began to form. Leaders partnered with others who shared their geographic background, foreign policy beliefs, or other ideas for governing the country.

Today, as then, the party with the largest number of elected members in the U.S. House of Representatives and the U.S. Senate holds a majority of influence over those chambers. Its members outnumber those of the minority, or opposing, parties. Occasionally the same party will control both chambers of Congress and the Presidency. With that much political power, it can significantly influence the nature of government. Usually each party will control only one or two of these three areas. In that case, political parties will have to compromise and cooperate with one another in order to enact new laws and policies.

During George Washington's Presidency, lawmakers divided into two groups, depending on whether or not they believed that a strong federal government should oversee weaker state governments. Ever since, although names and opinions may change, two political parties have dominated the U.S. government. Today's leaders are primarily members of the Democratic and Republican parties. Each group can trace its origins well back into the 19th century.

The Democratic Party evolved from the early groups who opposed a strong federal government. Leaders such as Thomas Jefferson shaped these lawmakers into a collection of politicians known variously as the Democratic-Republicans, the National Republicans, or, eventually, the Democrats.

The modern Republican Party was formed during the 1850s to combat the spread of slavery. Its first successful presidential candidate was Abraham Lincoln. Sometimes it is referred to as the Grand Old Party (GOP).

The Democratic and Republican Parties have shared fairly equally in the control of the White House. There have been several occasions, however, when one party has had a long period of domination. From Lincoln's election in 1860 through the election of 1908, for example, all but two

A campaign banner (center) promotes the 1920 ticket of the Democratic Party. (It lost.) A 19th-century political cartoonist popularized the use of animals to symbolize the Republican and Democratic Parties. He drew an elephant to represent the colossal size of Republican Party support in 1874. He chose a donkey for the Democrats, knowing that Andrew Jackson had adopted that symbol after being called a jackass during the feisty campaign of 1828.

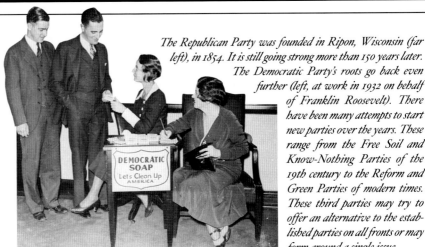

The Republican Party was founded in Ripon, Wisconsin (far left), in 1854. It is still going strong more than 150 years later. The Democratic Party's roots go back even further (left, at work in 1932 on behalf of Franklin Roosevelt). There have been many attempts to start new parties over the years. These range from the Free Soil and Know-Nothing Parties of the 19th century to the Reform and Green Parties of modern times. These third parties may try to offer an alternative to the established parties on all fronts or may form around a single issue.

Presidents were Republicans. The Democratic Party earned its longest streak of control—20 years—from 1933 to 1953. Its predecessor, the Democratic-Republican Party, had an even longer streak—28 years, from 1801–1829.

Two other political parties had members become Chief Executives, too. Washington and his successor, John Adams, were associated with the Federalist Party. The Whig Party evolved from these early Federalists. Four of its members became President. Two Whigs won outright election: William Henry Harrison and Zachary Taylor. Both of them died in office. Their Whig Vice Presidents, John Tyler and Millard Fillmore, replaced them.

Often the presidential ballot will include candidates from third parties, those groups that exist beyond the two major parties. Occasionally a candidate will run for office as an "independent," that is, without the support of a political party. No independent or third-party candidates have ever made it to the White House. Even so, these candidates may influence an election by dividing the support of voters or by directing attention to a particular issue or cause. In recent decades, third party and independent candidates have frequently siphoned support away from Republican and Democratic candidates in ways that helped secure a victory for the opposing major party. In 2000, for example, the Green Party attracted just enough support to play a role in placing the Republican Party's candidate in office.

Andrew Jackson (left) was the first President to campaign under the banner of the same Democratic Party that exists today. Former Republican President Theodore Roosevelt (right) tried to return to the White House as the nominee of the Progressive, or Bull Moose, Party. He finished second in the 1912 election, ahead of the sitting Republican President William Howard Taft. In no other presidential election has a third party surpassed one of the two major parties.

Ulysses S. Grant

18TH PRESIDENT OF THE UNITED STATES ★ *1869 – 1877*

NICKNAME	Unconditional Surrender Grant
BORN	April 27, 1822, in Point Pleasant, Ohio
POLITICAL PARTY	Republican
CHIEF OPPONENTS	1st term: Horatio Seymour, Democrat (1810–1886); 2nd term: Horace Greeley, Democrat (1811–1872)
TERM OF OFFICE	March 4, 1869–March 3, 1877
AGE AT INAUGURATION	46 years old
NUMBER OF TERMS	two
VICE PRESIDENTS	1st term: Schuyler Colfax (1823–1885); 2nd term: Henry Wilson (1812–1875)
FIRST LADY	Julia Boggs Dent Grant (1826–1902), wife (married Aug. 22, 1848)
CHILDREN	Frederick, Ulysses, Ellen, Jesse
GEOGRAPHIC SCENE	37 states
NEW STATES ADDED	Colorado (1876)
DIED	July 23, 1885, in Mount McGregor, N.Y.
AGE AT DEATH	63 years old
SELECTED LANDMARKS	Point Pleasant, Ohio (birthplace); Georgetown, Ohio (boyhood home); General Grant National Memorial, New York, N.Y. (grave)

Birthplace of Ulysses S. Grant (above). As a child Grant imagined becoming a farmer or a river trader.

BY THE END OF THE CIVIL WAR, Ulysses Simpson Grant was the highest ranking U.S. general since George Washington. He was a national hero, too. Grant's popular appeal helped him become President in the first post–Civil War national election. Mastery of military tactics did not prepare him for the world of politics, however. His administration is remembered more for its scandals than for its accomplishments.

As a child, Grant seemed an unlikely person to triumph on the battlefield. He disliked hunting, got sick in his father's tanning shop, and later resisted attending the U.S. Military Academy at West Point. Once there, however, Grant distinguished himself as a horseman and excelled at math. Within a few years, Grant was on active duty in the Mexican War. His subsequent attempts at civilian life yielded little financial success, and he was happy to return to the military when the Civil War began.

Grant entered the fighting as a brigadier general of Illinois troops in Missouri. His aggressive assault on Fort Donelson, Tennessee, during February 1862, gave the Union its first notable victory in the Civil War. Citizens boasted that his initials stood for "Unconditional Surrender," the terms he had set for the Southern rebels at the fort. When

The name of the nation's 18th President was accidentally changed from Hiram Ulysses Grant to Ulysses Simpson Grant when he was enrolled at the U.S. Military Academy. (His local congressman incorporated the maiden name of Grant's mother into his appointment recommendation by mistake.) Classmates nicknamed him "Uncle Sam," like the already popular patriotic character. Grant distinguished himself during the Civil War (above). By the end he was commander of all Union armies.

A scene from the Inauguration of Ulysses S. Grant (left). Passage of the 15th Amendment in 1870 permitted large numbers of African Americans to begin voting (above). In 1872 Victoria Claflin Woodhull became the first woman presidential candidate. She suggested that Frederick Douglass, the former slave, run as Vice President. He declined, and her third-party campaign fizzled. Grant won instead. Ulysses S. Grant was an expert handler of horses (bottom, left). While a student at West Point, he set a horse-jumping record that stood for 25 years. While President he was stopped for speeding in his horse-drawn carriage; Grant walked back to the White House after the officer confiscated his vehicle.

Northerners learned he had smoked a cigar during the assault, they sent him as many as 10,000 boxes of them to help guarantee future victories. (Thus developed Grant's custom of smoking some 20 cigars a day, a habit that probably helped cause his death.) Some called him "Butcher Grant" for the casualties that came with his victories, but Abraham Lincoln was impressed. "I cannot spare this man—he fights," he said. Lincoln named him commander of all Federal troops in March 1864. Grant, who was superstitious about retracing his steps, did not like to retreat. He persisted on the battlefield, and, supported by Union commanders fighting aggressively elsewhere, he wore down the Confederate side until it was forced to surrender.

After the embarrassing political arguments of Andrew Johnson's administration, voters were enthusiastic about electing Grant—the respected war hero—as their President. He was the only man to complete two presidential terms during the 76-year span between Andrew Jackson and Woodrow Wilson. Under Grant's leadership the government established the world's first national park (Yellowstone, founded in 1872), avoided war with Great Britain about Civil War damage claims, established the Department of Justice, and passed the 15th Amendment. This legislation granted voting rights regardless of "race, color, or previous condition of servitude" to all men. (Women did not gain voting rights until 1920.)

Ulysses S. Grant retired after an administration tainted by scandal (left). During his post-presidential years, Grant mixed quiet time (bottom right) with family, business, and travel. Grant found he had much in common with the Viceroy of China (above, seated at right) when they met during a world tour after his Presidency. Both leaders had defended their countries as generals during civil wars. Both liked to eat—the Viceroy hosted an eight-hour, 70-course dinner for his guest.

These accomplishments were overshadowed, however, by controversies. The federal government was unable to prevent white Southerners from using violence and political tricks to limit the rights of former slaves. The financial Panic of 1873 put millions of laborers out of work. Worst of all were the scandals of Grant's administration—from corrupt banking and currency deals to the stealing of federal liquor taxes by manufacturers and public officials. Although none of these crimes involved Grant directly, his reputation as a leader suffered.

Grant failed to win nomination for a third presidential term. (A constitutional amendment in 1951 limited a President to two elected terms of office, but no such barrier existed before then.) After leaving the White House, Grant, his wife, and teenage son embarked on a 30-month tour of the world. Along the way he met Queen Victoria in England and became the first person ever allowed to shake hands with a Japanese emperor. In 1880 he failed to win the Republican nomination for President. Grant invested in a family business venture during his retirement in New York City, but a dishonest business partner brought financial ruin to the project. Congress provided Grant with much-needed income by putting him back on the Army payroll as a general, although he was not on active duty.

At the suggestion of author and publisher Mark Twain, Grant tried to make even more money by writing his autobiography. Grant raced to complete the book before his life could be claimed by throat cancer. He finished only days before his death. The book became a bestseller and earned his family a small fortune. Grant and his wife, Julia, who died 17 years after him, are buried in the New York City landmark popularly known as Grant's Tomb.

"No terms except an unconditional and immediate surrender can be accepted."

Ulysses S. Grant,
during the assault of Fort Donelson, Tennessee,
February 16, 1862

Rutherford B. Hayes

19TH PRESIDENT OF THE UNITED STATES ★ *1877 – 1881*

NICKNAME	His Fraudulency
BORN	Oct. 4, 1822, in Delaware, Ohio
POLITICAL PARTY	Republican
CHIEF OPPONENT	Samuel Jones Tilden, Democrat (1814–1886)
TERM OF OFFICE	March 4, 1877–March 3, 1881
AGE AT INAUGURATION	54 years old
NUMBER OF TERMS	one
VICE PRESIDENT	William Almon Wheeler (1819–1887)
FIRST LADY	Lucy Ware Webb Hayes (1831–1889), wife (married Dec. 30, 1852)
CHILDREN	Sardis, James, Rutherford, Frances, Scott, plus three sons died young
GEOGRAPHIC SCENE	38 states
NEW STATES ADDED	none
DIED	Jan. 17, 1893, in Fremont, Ohio
AGE AT DEATH	70 years old
SELECTED LANDMARKS	Spiegel Grove National Historic Landmark, Fremont, Ohio (adult home, memorial library, museum, grave)

Lucy Hayes, shown with her children Fanny and Scott and a friend, was the first First Lady to finish college. She was nicknamed "Lemonade Lucy" for supporting temperance by serving soft drinks instead of alcohol at the White House.

RUTHERFORD BIRCHARD HAYES started his administration amid controversy. Politicians argued about how to count the national election returns. In the end, Hayes won office by one electoral vote, the narrowest presidential victory in history. He went on to bring dignity, honesty, and reform to the government.

Hayes came to the White House with a solid background of service to his country. He was born in Delaware, Ohio, graduated from Kenyon College in Ohio, and earned a law degree from Harvard University. In 1861 Hayes interrupted law practice in his home state to join the Union army. He rose to the rank of major general by the end of the Civil War and survived having four horses shot out from under him. Hayes declined to leave the battlefield after he was nominated for a seat in Congress. He wrote home that soldiers who campaigned for office "ought to be scalped" for deserting their posts. (These patriotic words assured his election.) Later he served three times as Ohio's governor.

Widespread ballot fraud, or illegal vote-casting, clouded the results of the popular and electoral voting in the 1876 presidential election. Victory belonged to the person with the greatest number of electoral votes, and Congress was left to determine the most accurate tally of them. The debate split along party lines and lasted for months. Finally, three days before the Inauguration, Congress confirmed Hayes as President. In exchange Republicans promised Democrats, who were concentrated in the South, that Reconstruction would end. The dealmaking earned Hayes the offensive nicknames of "His Fraudulency" and "Ruther*fraud* B. Hayes." As President, Hayes left scandal behind. He actually worked to increase the standards of behavior for civil servants, or government employees.

Having always planned to serve only one term, Hayes retired to Ohio where he took an active role in local and state causes. He died in 1893.

Alexander Graham Bell personally installed the first White House telephone while Rutherford B. Hayes was President. Another inventor, Thomas Edison, visited the First Family to demonstrate his new phonograph. The Hayes family held the first public Easter Egg Roll on the White House lawn.

Presidential Landmarks

★ *From Log Cabins to Libraries* ★

THE PRESIDENCY has led every Chief Executive to Washington, D.C. Even George Washington, who never lived there, visited the site of the nation's new capital as it was being planned and built. But all of the Presidents have left footprints in other parts of the country, too. Their birthplaces, homes, graves, museums, libraries, and memorials offer a trail of history for others to follow.

The oldest presidential landmarks lie along the eastern seaboard of the U.S. They remind us of the modest size of the new country and the role key states like Virginia and New York played in providing early national leaders. As citizens pushed the U.S. boundaries westward, new states, particularly in the Midwest, became an important homebase for Presidents. By the 20th century, the West Coast had begun to foster future Presidents, too.

The lives of some Presidents are commemorated at multiple sites. Abraham Lincoln probably lays claim to having more memorials than any other President, in part because he lived in and visited so many spots during his lifetime. Other Presidents leave little more than a gravesite behind. Birthplaces, boyhood homes, even adult residences can fall into disrepair or give way to new

(historical marker pictured)

WASHINGTON SLEPT HERE

"Monday, May 16th, 1791" wrote President George Washington in his diary as he recorded the date of his lodging in the Inn of Stephen Calfrey Pearce, 200 yards of this marker. Being forewarned, the Pearces had made lavish preparation for the entertainment of their distinguished guest and his party. Mrs. Pearce was famous for her cooking and Mr. Pearce for his story telling. The President enjoyed both immensely and praised gratefully the hospitality of the Inn Keepers who would accept no payment from the President of the United States.

The U.S. landscape is dotted with markers (top) and landmarks connected to the personal histories of the U.S. Presidents. See the accompanying map for a listing of key sites. Among those represented are (above, left to right) the tomb of James K. Polk in Nashville, Tenn., the Abraham Lincoln Presidential Library and Museum in Springfield, Ill., and the Franklin Delano Roosevelt Memorial in Washington, D.C.

Presidential Landmarks

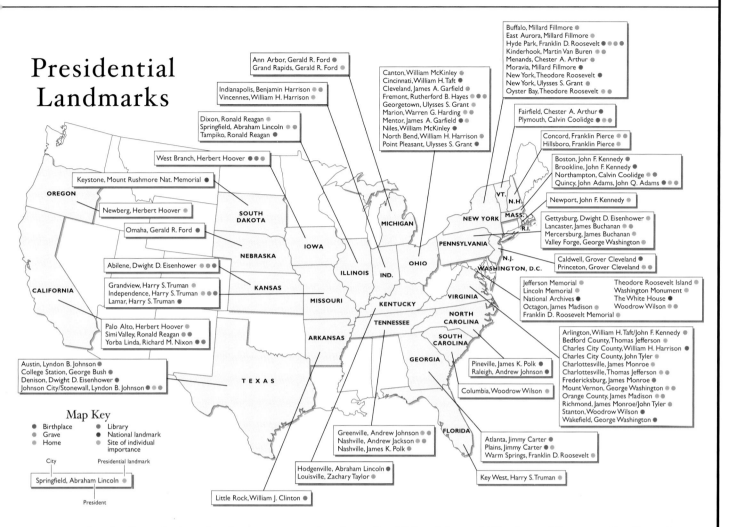

Ann Arbor, Gerald R. Ford ●
Grand Rapids, Gerald R. Ford ●

Indianapolis, Benjamin Harrison ● ●
Vincennes, William H. Harrison ●

Dixon, Ronald Reagan ●
Springfield, Abraham Lincoln ● ●
Tampiko, Ronald Reagan ●

West Branch, Herbert Hoover ● ● ●

Keystone, Mount Rushmore Nat. Memorial ●

Newberg, Herbert Hoover ●

Omaha, Gerald R. Ford ●

Abilene, Dwight D. Eisenhower ● ● ●

Grandview, Harry S. Truman ●
Independence, Harry S. Truman ● ● ●
Lamar, Harry S. Truman ●

Palo Alto, Herbert Hoover ●
Simi Valley, Ronald Reagan ● ●
Yorba Linda, Richard M. Nixon ● ●

Austin, Lyndon B. Johnson ●
College Station, George Bush ●
Denison, Dwight D. Eisenhower ●
Johnson City/Stonewall, Lyndon B. Johnson ● ● ●

Canton, William McKinley ●
Cincinnati, William H. Taft ●
Cleveland, James A. Garfield ●
Fremont, Rutherford B. Hayes ● ● ●
Georgetown, Ulysses S. Grant ●
Marion, Warren G. Harding ● ●
Mentor, James A. Garfield ● ●
Niles, William McKinley ●
North Bend, William H. Harrison ●
Point Pleasant, Ulysses S. Grant ●

Buffalo, Millard Fillmore ●
East Aurora, Millard Fillmore ●
Hyde Park, Franklin D. Roosevelt ● ● ●
Kinderhook, Martin Van Buren ● ●
Menands, Chester A. Arthur ●
Moravia, Millard Fillmore ●
New York, Theodore Roosevelt ●
New York, Ulysses S. Grant ●
Oyster Bay, Theodore Roosevelt ● ●

Fairfield, Chester A. Arthur ●
Plymouth, Calvin Coolidge ● ● ●

Concord, Franklin Pierce ● ●
Hillsboro, Franklin Pierce ●

Boston, John F. Kennedy ●
Brookline, John F. Kennedy ●
Northampton, Calvin Coolidge ● ●
Quincy, John Adams, John Q. Adams ● ● ●

Newport, John F. Kennedy ●

Gettysburg, Dwight D. Eisenhower ●
Lancaster, James Buchanan ●
Mercersburg, James Buchanan ●
Valley Forge, George Washington ●

Caldwell, Grover Cleveland ●
Princeton, Grover Cleveland ●

Jefferson Memorial ●   Theodore Roosevelt Island ●
Lincoln Memorial ●   Washington Monument ●
National Archives ●   The White House ●
Octagon, James Madison ●   Woodrow Wilson ●
Franklin D. Roosevelt Memorial ●

Arlington, William H. Taft/John F. Kennedy ●
Bedford County, Thomas Jefferson ●
Charles City County, William H. Harrison ●
Charles City County, John Tyler ●
Charlottesville, James Monroe ●
Charlottesville, Thomas Jefferson ● ●
Fredericksburg, James Monroe ●
Mount Vernon, George Washington ●
Orange County, James Madison ●
Richmond, James Monroe/John Tyler ●
Stanton, Woodrow Wilson ●
Wakefield, George Washington ●

Pineville, James K. Polk ●
Raleigh, Andrew Johnson ●

Columbia, Woodrow Wilson ●

Greenville, Andrew Johnson ● ●
Nashville, Andrew Jackson ● ●
Nashville, James K. Polk ●

Atlanta, Jimmy Carter ●
Plains, Jimmy Carter ● ●
Warm Springs, Franklin D. Roosevelt ●

Hodgenville, Abraham Lincoln ●
Louisville, Zachary Taylor ●

Key West, Harry S. Truman ●

Little Rock, William J. Clinton ●

Map Key

● Birthplace   ● Library
● Grave   ● National landmark
● Home   ● Site of individual
                        importance

● City   ● Presidential landmark

Springfield, Abraham Lincoln ●

President

construction before their value is ever recognized.

Some presidential landmarks are actually replicas of original structures. They may even be located on different ground than the first buildings. Most log cabin homes are copies, for example. The furnishings in landmark buildings may not be original either, although they may mimic known pieces of furniture, wallpaper designs, and so on. Even with these modifications, the sites help visitors imagine what life might have been like for the Presidents.

In 1940, while still President, Franklin D. Roosevelt began the tradition of creating presidential libraries. Every President since then has established a presidential library, either during or following his administration. Presidential libraries have also been established for two earlier Presidents, Abraham Lincoln

(in Illinois) and Herbert Hoover (in Iowa).

Presidential libraries may be located near important home sites, at academic institutions, or in major cities of importance to the President. These sites hold the presidential papers, or the important documents of a leader's administration. Historians and other visitors study the thousands of pages of paper that make up each collection. The libraries acquire other material from the personal, professional, and family history of the Presidents, too. Collections include everything from Dwight D. Eisenhower's military souvenirs to Presidents' favorite artworks to official gifts received while in office to Herbert Hoover's fishing gear. Staff members use these extensive holdings to create exhibits for the general public about the Presidents' lives.

James A. Garfield

20TH PRESIDENT OF THE UNITED STATES ★ *1881*

James A. Garfield.

NICKNAME	Preacher President
BORN	Nov. 19, 1831, near Orange, Ohio
POLITICAL PARTY	Republican
CHIEF OPPONENT	Winfield Scott Hancock, Democrat (1824–1886)
TERM OF OFFICE	March 4, 1881–Sept. 19, 1881
AGE AT INAUGURATION	49 years old
NUMBER OF TERMS	one (cut short by assassination)
VICE PRESIDENT	Chester A. Arthur (1829–1886)
FIRST LADY	Lucretia Rudolph Garfield (1832–1918), wife (married Nov. 11, 1858)
CHILDREN	Harry, James, Mary, Irvin, Abram, plus a son and a daughter died young
GEOGRAPHIC SCENE	38 states
NEW STATES ADDED	none
DIED	Sept. 19, 1881, in Elberon, N.J.
AGE AT DEATH	49 years old
SELECTED LANDMARKS	Lawnfield, Garfield National Historic Site, Mentor, Ohio (birthplace and replica homestead); Lake View Cemetery, Cleveland, Ohio

James A. Garfield became the second President to die by assassination, and the fourth to die in office. X-rays, surgery, and antibiotics might have saved him, had they been available.

JAMES A. GARFIELD, like William Henry Harrison, barely had a chance to establish himself as President before death removed him from office. He was shot by an assassin early in his term and died 79 days later.

Garfield was the last President born in a log cabin. His election followed notable service as an educator, soldier, and statesman. A graduate of Williams College in Massachusetts, Garfield returned to his home state of Ohio to be a college professor. Later he became a lawyer, Ohio state senator, Civil War colonel, and U.S. congressman. Garfield served 18 years in the House of Representatives before receiving his unexpected nomination for President in 1880. He became known as the "Preacher President" for his talents at public speaking.

As President, Garfield surprised legislators by how diligently he sought to end political corruption, or improper influence, especially among his own Republican Party. He refused to be bullied by powerful party leaders in the Senate when making political appointments; in the end, two senators resigned, and he got his own way. Garfield fought similar battles on a smaller scale at the White House. The place swarmed with job hunters. People expected to be rewarded with posts in Garfield's administration because they had supported the Republican Party.

One disappointed and mentally ill job hunter shadowed Garfield and his staff for weeks. He shot the President at a Washington, D.C., train station on July 2, 1881. Although Garfield survived the initial wound, the bullet could not be removed, and he died from complications two and a half months later. His assassin was tried and hanged. Reacting to Garfield's murder, lawmakers wrote new rules for how to fill many government posts. These jobs were to be given as a reward for talent and experience, not political favors.

James A. Garfield was the nation's first left-handed President. He was actually ambidextrous, or able to write with either hand. Friends said he could write Latin with one hand and Greek with the other hand—at the same time! Garfield had considered a career as a sailor until he fell overboard while working on a canal boat and caught a bad cold. A nonswimmer, he decided to teach instead.

Chester A. Arthur

21ST PRESIDENT OF THE UNITED STATES ★ *1881 – 1885*

NICKNAME	Elegant Arthur
BORN	Oct. 5, 1829, in Fairfield, Vt.
POLITICAL PARTY	Republican
CHIEF OPPONENT	none; succeeded Garfield
TERM OF OFFICE	Sept. 20, 1881–March 3, 1885
AGE AT INAUGURATION	51 years old
NUMBER OF TERMS	one (partial)
VICE PRESIDENT	none
FIRST LADY	Mary Arthur McElroy (1842–1917), sister
WIFE	Ellen Lewis Herndon Arthur (1837–1880), married Oct. 25, 1859
CHILDREN	Chester, Ellen, plus a son died young
GEOGRAPHIC SCENE	38 states
NEW STATES ADDED	none
DIED	Nov. 18, 1886, in New York, N.Y.
AGE AT DEATH	57 years old
SELECTED LANDMARKS	Fairfield, Vt. (reconstructed birthplace); Albany Rural Cemetery, Menands, N.Y.

Chester Arthur's wife died the year before he became President. His sister served as First Lady and helped him care for his younger child, 13-year-old Nell (above). "Elegant Arthur" changed clothes for each occasion of the day; he was said to own 80 pairs of pants.

MANY CITIZENS WERE AS SHOCKED at the thought of Chester Alan Arthur becoming President as they were by the shooting of his predecessor, James A. Garfield. Once again—as with John Tyler, Millard Fillmore, and Andrew Johnson—a Vice President chosen for political reasons instead of leadership skills became President.

Arthur had never been elected to public office until he became James Garfield's Vice President. Born in Vermont, Arthur was a graduate of Union College in New York and an attorney. In 1871 he was made collector of the port of New York City and was responsible for collecting import fees for goods arriving at the nation's busiest harbor. Arthur built his personal and political fortune there by using the "spoils system" and "machine politics." He awarded jobs, raises, and favorable regulations (the spoils) to employees and businesses who supported his political candidates with their votes and donations (the vote-buying "machine" that influenced elections). This favoritism led the *New York Times* to call his pre-White House career a "mess of filth."

Arthur was deeply shocked that Garfield had been shot by someone caught up in the greed of machine politics. As President, he angered old friends and surprised the nation by supporting passage of the Pendleton Act. This legislation created a Civil Service Commission to oversee the government's civilian (nonmilitary) workers. It established procedures to ensure that a core of basic federal jobs were filled by competitive exam, not presidential appointment. It also protected these employees from being fired because of their political views.

After Arthur learned that he suffered from a fatal kidney disease, he did not care if he was renominated for a second term (he was not). Arthur retired to New York City. He died 20 months later.

Chester Arthur visited Yellowstone National Park (right) in 1883. Arthur modernized the U.S. Navy by ordering the construction of four steel warships.

Grover Cleveland

22ND AND 24TH PRESIDENT OF THE UNITED STATES
1885 – 1889 ★ *1893 – 1897*

NICKNAME	Uncle Jumbo
BORN	March 18, 1837, in Caldwell, N.J.
POLITICAL PARTY	Democrat
CHIEF OPPONENTS	1st administration: James Gillespie Blaine, Republican (1830–1893); 2nd administration: President Benjamin Harrison, Republican (1833–1901)
TERM OF OFFICE	1st administration: March 4, 1885–March 3, 1889; 2nd administration: March 4, 1893–March 3, 1897
AGE AT INAUGURATION	1st administration: 47 years old; 2nd administration: 55 years old
NUMBER OF TERMS	two (nonconsecutive)
VICE PRESIDENTS	1st administration: Thomas Andrews Hendricks (1819–1885); 2nd administration: Adlai Ewing Stevenson (1835–1914)

The Clevelands aboard the presidential train

FIRST LADIES	Rose Elizabeth Cleveland (1846–1918), sister; Frances Folsom Cleveland (1864–1947), wife (married June 2, 1886)
CHILDREN	Ruth, Esther, Marion, Richard, Frances
GEOGRAPHIC SCENE	1st administration: 38 states; 2nd administration: 44 states
NEW STATES ADDED	Utah (1896)
DIED	June 24, 1908, in Princeton, N.J.
AGE AT DEATH	71 years old
SELECTED LANDMARKS	Caldwell, N.J. (birthplace); Westland (home) and Princeton Cemetery, Princeton, N.J.

GROVER CLEVELAND WAS THE FIRST DEMOCRAT to be elected President after the Civil War. Although he lost his reelection bid in 1888 to Benjamin Harrison, he returned to the White House four years later after winning a rematch in the 1892 election. Thus, Cleveland is the only President to serve two nonconsecutive terms of office. His disregard of popular and political opinion cost him reelection after each term.

Cleveland's political career developed rapidly; he went from county sheriff to U.S. President in only 11 years. Although born in New Jersey, he grew up in New York State, the son of a Presbyterian minister. His school years ended at age 16 with the death of his father. Eventually Cleveland studied law and entered into private practice in Buffalo, New York. His firm hand as the local sheriff led citizens to elect him mayor. Cleveland succeeded so well at ending corruption, waste, and scandal that he was nominated for governor of New York. He won by a landslide. His popularity in New York State made him a natural candidate for President in 1884.

Gossip and scandal fueled the presidential campaign. Republicans were delighted to discover that the bachelor Cleveland might have fathered a child. They chanted: "Ma, Ma, where's my Pa? Gone to the White House, ha, ha, ha!" However, the public seemed less concerned about Cleveland's private life than about the professional actions of his opponent. Democrats joked about "James Blaine, James Blaine the continental liar from the state of Maine." Cleveland claimed "Public Office Is a Public Trust." Republican "Mugwumps" (an Indian word meaning "big chief") deserted their own party's candidate and favored him instead. Cleveland narrowly won the race.

During his first administration, Cleveland vetoed more than twice as many pieces of legislation (413 total) as had all previous Presidents combined. As with Andrew Johnson two decades earlier,

---

Grover Cleveland, who weighed 250 pounds, was nicknamed "Uncle Jumbo." He was the first President since the Civil War who had not fought in that conflict. Cleveland avoided military service then by paying a Polish immigrant $150 to take his place. Although this practice was legal, it was not considered admirable. As a presidential candidate, Cleveland was criticized for avoiding combat.

Grover Cleveland's campaign banner (above) emphasized his party's ties to well-known Democratic Presidents of the past, such as Thomas Jefferson and Andrew Jackson. His two administrations were interrupted by the single term of Benjamin Harrison. Cleveland delivered his Inaugural Addresses from the East Portico of the U.S. Capitol (right).

critics called him "The Veto President." Children sang: "A fat man once sat in the President's chair, singing 'Ve-to,' 'Ve-to.'" Although Cleveland worked hard to hire loyal Democrats to fill government posts, other party members were often angered by his choices. He was more popular for his unexpected marriage, at age 49, to 21-year-old Frances Folsom, the daughter of a deceased friend.

During the election of 1888, Cleveland again won a greater share of the popular vote than his opponent. However, the Presidency went to Benjamin Harrison because he earned the most electoral votes. The story goes that the departing First Lady assured the White House staff that she and her husband would return after the next election. They did. Cleveland won by a sizable margin in both popular and electoral voting when he faced Harrison in 1892.

Grover Cleveland became the only President to marry at the White House (left) when he wed Frances Folsom during his first administration. The couple changed their wedding vows so Frances could pledge to "love, honor, and keep" her husband instead of agreeing to "love, honor, and obey" him. Their first child, nicknamed "Baby Ruth," had a candy bar named after her. Their second child, Esther (right), was the only child of a President born in the White House.

> "What is the use of being elected or reelected unless you stand for something?"
>
> Grover Cleveland, 1887

Grover Cleveland hunted with a rifle he nicknamed "Death and Destruction." The President was forced to take a break from outdoor recreation in 1893 after developing mouth cancer. To avoid media attention, Frances Cleveland arranged for doctors to operate on the President aboard a private yacht. Doctors removed the tumor and part of Cleveland's jaw, then inserted a rubber shape to take the place of the missing bone. They left no visible scars. Some two dozen years passed before news of the operation leaked out.

Public support of Cleveland began to fall soon after his reelection, however, with the start of a new round of economic hard times. The Panic of 1893 lasted for the rest of Cleveland's Presidency and brought widespread suffering. Cleveland argued with Congress over what, if anything, to do. Should the government issue more money, or less money, or should it do nothing? Should paper money continue to be worth a standard amount of gold? Should extra money be created in the form of silver coins? Was it better for the government to hoard precious metals or to share them? No one was quite sure how all the elements of national finance influenced one another, so it was hard to know what might help end the panic. Meanwhile, politicians gave little thought to the suffering of the nation's citizens. Some people joked that if a hungry man started eating grass on the White House lawn, Cleveland, instead of offering him food, would suggest he move to the backyard, where the grass was taller.

By the next election, Democrats were ready for a new candidate, and the public was ready for an entirely different party. Republicans, who had dominated the Presidency since the Civil War, became the favored party again. Except for Cleveland and Woodrow Wilson, Republicans controlled the White House from 1861 until 1933.

Cleveland retired to New Jersey and became a lecturer and trustee for Princeton University. His dying words, 11 years after leaving the White House, were: "I have tried so hard to do right."

The Clevelands (from left to right: Esther, Frances, Mrs. Cleveland, Ruth, Richard, and the former President) posed for a family snapshot on the porch of the President's retirement home in New Jersey. Frances outlived her husband by 39 years. She became the first widow of a President to remarry when she wed a professor in 1913.

Presidential Facts and Comparisons

★ A Look at the Stats ★

George Washington tried false teeth of silver, ivory, cow's teeth, and more. Contrary to legend, wood was never used.

FORTY-THREE MEN have served their nation as President in 44 administrations. (Grover Cleveland is counted twice—once for each of his two separate Presidencies.) The oldest President on taking office was Ronald Reagan, age 69; the youngest was Theodore Roosevelt, age 42. The nation's second oldest President, William Henry Harrison, served the shortest term in office—32 days. Franklin D. Roosevelt served the longest term; he was elected four times and was President for 12 years before dying in office at age 63.

Eight Presidents were born in Virginia, earning that state the nickname "Mother of Presidents." Many Presidents have come from Massachusetts, New York, and Ohio, too. In all, 23 Presidents were born in one of those four states. Some half-dozen Presidents were born in log cabins; Jimmy Carter was the first President born in a hospital. About half of the Presidents were sons of farmers.

Nine Presidents have failed to complete their terms of office. Eight died on the job. One, Richard Nixon, resigned from office because of political scandal.

During the course of the nation's history, the presidential salary has grown from $25,000 a year (for George Washington) to $400,000 a year today. Each President receives a significant expense allowance, too.

All but eight of the Presidents attended college; 31 were college graduates. More than half of all Presidents were members of the armed services, although not all witnessed combat. Eleven

Warren G. Harding throws out the first pitch of the baseball season. William Howard Taft began this presidential tradition in 1910.

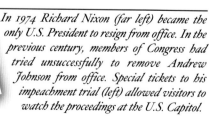

In 1974 Richard Nixon (far left) became the only U.S. President to resign from office. In the previous century, members of Congress had tried unsuccessfully to remove Andrew Johnson from office. Special tickets to his impeachment trial (left) allowed visitors to watch the proceedings at the U.S. Capitol.

Birthplaces of the Presidents

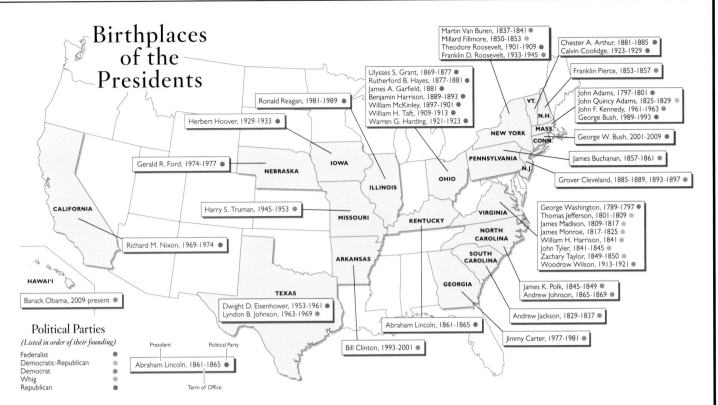

Martin Van Buren, 1837-1841 ●
Millard Fillmore, 1850-1853 ●
Theodore Roosevelt, 1901-1909 ●
Franklin D. Roosevelt, 1933-1945 ●

Chester A. Arthur, 1881-1885 ●
Calvin Coolidge, 1923-1929 ●

Franklin Pierce, 1853-1857 ●

Ulysses S. Grant, 1869-1877 ●
Rutherford B. Hayes, 1877-1881 ●
James A. Garfield, 1881 ●
Benjamin Harrison, 1889-1893 ●
William McKinley, 1897-1901 ●
William H. Taft, 1909-1913 ●
Warren G. Harding, 1921-1923 ●

John Adams, 1797-1801 ●
John Quincy Adams, 1825-1829 ●
John F. Kennedy, 1961-1963 ●
George Bush, 1989-1993 ●

George W. Bush, 2001-2009 ●

Ronald Reagan, 1981-1989 ●

Herbert Hoover, 1929-1933 ●

James Buchanan, 1857-1861 ●

VT.
N.H.
MASS.
NEW YORK
CONN.
PENNSYLVANIA
N.J.

Gerald R. Ford, 1974-1977 ●

NEBRASKA
IOWA
ILLINOIS
OHIO

Grover Cleveland, 1885-1889, 1893-1897 ●

CALIFORNIA

Harry S. Truman, 1945-1953 ●

MISSOURI
KENTUCKY

VIRGINIA
NORTH CAROLINA
SOUTH CAROLINA

George Washington, 1789-1797 ●
Thomas Jefferson, 1801-1809 ●
James Madison, 1809-1817 ●
James Monroe, 1817-1825 ●
William H. Harrison, 1841 ●
John Tyler, 1841-1845 ●
Zachary Taylor, 1849-1850 ●
Woodrow Wilson, 1913-1921 ●

Richard M. Nixon, 1969-1974 ●

ARKANSAS

HAWAI'I

Barack Obama, 2009-present ●

GEORGIA

James K. Polk, 1845-1849 ●
Andrew Johnson, 1865-1869 ●

Andrew Jackson, 1829-1837 ●

TEXAS

Dwight D. Eisenhower, 1953-1961 ●
Lyndon B. Johnson, 1963-1969 ●

Abraham Lincoln, 1861-1865 ●

Jimmy Carter, 1977-1981 ●

Bill Clinton, 1993-2001 ●

Political Parties
(Listed in order of their founding)

Federalist ●
Democratic-Republican ●
Democrat ●
Whig ●
Republican ●

President   Political Party

Abraham Lincoln, 1861-1865 ●

Term of Office

Presidents were former generals. Fourteen Presidents were first Vice President of the country. More than two dozen had served in the U.S. Congress. Seventeen were governors before becoming President. Twenty-six had studied law and became attorneys. Other prepresidential occupations include farmer, teacher, journalist, college professor, actor, engineer, and tailor.

Presidents have enjoyed hobbies including fishing, golf, and stamp collecting. Two played the piano (Harry S. Truman and Richard Nixon); two played the violin (Thomas Jefferson and John Tyler). Calvin Coolidge's instrument was the harmonica. Bill Clinton played the saxophone.

Most Presidents have been affiliated with Protestant churches, including 12 Episcopalians and 7 Presbyterians. Four Presidents, including Thomas Jefferson and Abraham Lincoln, listed no preferred religious affiliation. No one of non-Christian faith has yet served as President.

Some Presidents have enjoyed only brief retirements: James K. Polk died 103 days after his term ended. Herbert Hoover enjoyed the longest retirement: 31 years. Gerald R. Ford lived to be older than any other President: 93 years and 166 days. John F. Kennedy died at the youngest age: 46. Three Presidents died on Independence Day: John Adams, Thomas Jefferson, and James Monroe.

Gerald R. Ford is the only Eagle Scout to become a U.S. President. Folding the national flag (right) was one of his duties while camping with other Boy Scouts during his youth.

Benjamin Harrison

23RD PRESIDENT OF THE UNITED STATES ★ *1889 – 1893*

NICKNAME	Little Ben
BORN	Aug. 20, 1833, in North Bend, Ohio
POLITICAL PARTY	Republican
CHIEF OPPONENT	President Grover Cleveland, Democrat (1837–1908)
TERM OF OFFICE	March 4, 1889–March 3, 1893
AGE AT INAUGURATION	55 years old
NUMBER OF TERMS	one
VICE PRESIDENT	Levi Parsons Morton (1824–1920)
FIRST LADIES	Caroline Lavinia Scott Harrison (1832–1892), wife (married Oct. 20, 1853); Mary Scott Harrison McKee (1858–1930), daughter
SECOND WIFE	Mary Scott Lord Dimmick Harrison (1858–1948), married April 6, 1896
CHILDREN	Russell, Mary, Elizabeth
GEOGRAPHIC SCENE	38 states
NEW STATES ADDED	Montana, North Dakota, South Dakota, and Washington (1889); Idaho and Wyoming (1890)
DIED	March 13, 1901, in Indianapolis, Ind.
AGE AT DEATH	67 years old
SELECTED LANDMARKS	Indianapolis, Ind. (home); Crown Hill Cemetery, Indianapolis, Ind.

Harrison facing the latest round of office seekers

BENJAMIN HARRISON'S SINGLE TERM of office was sandwiched between the two presidential terms of Grover Cleveland. Harrison and Cleveland competed for the Presidency in the consecutive elections of 1888 and 1892. In both cases Cleveland won the popular vote. However, Harrison was awarded the Presidency in 1888 after receiving a majority of electoral college votes.

Harrison grew up in the shadow of another resident of the White House—his grandfather. "Little Ben" was a seven-year-old boy living in Ohio when William Henry Harrison became President. The younger Harrison went on to graduate from Ohio's Miami University and become an attorney in Indiana. He served one term in the U.S. Senate before being nominated for President.

Harrison, as was customary at the time, chose to run a low-key campaign. He spoke only to the crowds who were encouraged to gather at his home in Indianapolis. For one campaign stunt, 40,000 drummers from 11 states were organized to visit him. Harrison's well-financed campaign earned him victories in enough key states so that he topped his opponent in the electoral college. Cleveland's slim lead in popular votes—about 90,000—became irrelevant.

As President, Harrison authorized the first peacetime federal budget to reach the $1 billion mark. This money improved harbors, established naval fleets on both U.S. coasts, and helped pay the costs of building steamship lines. More states were added to the nation during Harrison's single administration than during any other Presidency.

Harrison lost his reelection bid to Cleveland. He returned to Indianapolis a widower, his wife having died of tuberculosis the previous year. He resumed his law practice and married his late wife's niece. He died of pneumonia five years later.

As a Union officer in the Civil War (above), Harrison fought in more battles in one month than his famous grandfather had in a lifetime. They are the only grandfather-grandson pair of Presidents.

AMERICA TAKES CENTER STAGE

★ *1897 – 1933* ★

circa 1890s

By the late 19th century, labor-saving inventions such as the mechanical washing machine were changing the way families handled routine household chores.

1903

Wilbur and Orville Wright made the first successful airplane flight—12 seconds long—on December 17. Only two dozen years later, Charles Lindberg would fly solo across the Atlantic.

1906

On April 18 an earthquake and subsequent fires leveled much of San Francisco. Neighboring communities were hit, too; 50 miles away the Santa Rosa Courthouse collapsed.

1912

The "unsinkable" Titanic went down on its first voyage after it struck an iceberg in the North Atlantic Ocean on April 14. More than 1,500 people died.

U.S. Presidents took firm control of the federal government at the start of the 20th century. They helped develop the United States into a global power, both economically and politically. The era featured fantastic advances in science, technology, transportation, and exploration. Leaders were challenged to expand the rights of citizens and curb the power of businesses. They struggled to cope with worldwide war and widespread economic suffering, too. Public opinion of federal policies played a central role in national elections.

1913–1920

Women intensified their efforts to gain suffrage, or voting rights. In 1920 an amendment finally granted all female U.S. citizens the right to vote.

1914–1918

U.S. forces entered World War I during 1917. Their presence helped win the war. Nearly 10 million people, including 100,000 Americans, died worldwide.

1920s

People celebrated increased peace and prosperity during the "Roaring Twenties." Flappers danced the Charleston as fashions, behaviors, and outlooks changed.

1930s

A decade of economic suffering followed the stock market collapse of October 1929. Citizens who had lost their jobs and even their homes sought free food in breadlines.

William McKinley

NICKNAME	Idol of Ohio
BORN	Jan. 29, 1843, in Niles, Ohio
POLITICAL PARTY	Republican
CHIEF OPPONENT	1st and 2nd terms: William Jennings Bryan, Democrat (1860–1925)
TERM OF OFFICE	March 4, 1897–Sept. 14, 1901
AGE AT INAUGURATION	54 years old
NUMBER OF TERMS	two (cut short by assassination)
VICE PRESIDENTS	1st term: Garret Augustus Hobart (1844–1899); 2nd term: Theodore Roosevelt (1858–1919)
FIRST LADY	Ida Saxton McKinley (1847–1907), wife (married Jan. 25, 1871)
CHILDREN	two daughters died young
GEOGRAPHIC SCENE	45 states
NEW STATES ADDED	none
DIED	Sept. 14, 1901, in Buffalo, N.Y.
AGE AT DEATH	58 years old
SELECTED LANDMARKS	National McKinley Birthplace Memorial, Niles, Ohio; McKinley Museum and McKinley National Memorial (grave), Canton, Ohio

When McKinley was Ohio's governor, each day at 3 p.m. he waved to his wife from his office window, and Ida McKinley waved back from their home across the street.

WILLIAM MCKINLEY WAS THE LAST CHIEF EXECUTIVE who fought in the Civil War. However, McKinley's witness of an earlier era did not stop him from pushing the nation and his office into modern times. He did everything from use telephones on a regular basis to expand the political influence of the United States around the globe. Early in his second term, McKinley became the fifth President to die in office, and the third one to be assassinated.

The state of Ohio sent five of her sons, including McKinley, to the White House in 28 years. (Two more followed him over the next 24 years.) As a youth, McKinley played Army games with friends or went fishing, ice skating, and horseback riding. He attended public schools where he excelled at speech making, and he studied briefly at Allegheny College in Pennsylvania. He served in the Civil War under future President Rutherford B. Hayes. Despite four years of duty, he escaped all injury and illness. Twice he won promotions for acts of bravery.

After the war McKinley took up the study of law and became an attorney. His final wartime rank of major remained his nickname among close friends for years.

"The Major" spent a dozen years in the U.S. House of Representatives and gained national notice for his McKinley Tariff legislation. Once implemented, however, this tax on imported goods brought unexpectedly high prices to consumer goods at home. Many Republicans, including McKinley and President Benjamin Harrison, lost their elected posts as a result. Nonetheless, McKinley persuaded Ohioans to elect him as their governor two years later. He served two terms before being nominated for President in 1896. McKinley

---

William McKinley (above, on election banner) was the only President between Andrew Johnson and Woodrow Wilson not to have facial hair. He liked to wear a red carnation in the buttonhole of his jacket. Ohio went so far as to make this bloom its official flower in honor of the "Idol of Ohio." McKinley liked cigars, too. Sometimes he broke one in two and chewed the halves instead of smoking the whole cigar.

defeated his opponent, William Jennings Bryan, in part because he spent five times as much money during the campaign as his rival. Bryan, a noted orator, traveled 18,000 miles around the country during a three-month-long speaking tour. McKinley, as Benjamin Harrison had done in 1888, ran a "front porch" campaign from his home in Ohio and relied on others to campaign for him nationally.

As President, McKinley focused on U.S. relations with foreign countries. He started with Spain. This European nation still ruled Cuba and other Caribbean islands near the United States as well as the Philippine Islands in the Pacific. Diplomatic talks gave way to war in 1898 after the suspicious destruction of the U.S. battleship *Maine* while it was anchored near Cuba. Future President Theodore Roosevelt rode to national fame at the head of the Rough Riders once the fighting began. Meanwhile, the U.S. Navy destroyed Spain's Atlantic and Pacific fleets during the four-month-long Spanish-American War.

Combat ended when Spain withdrew its claim to Cuba. Spain put Puerto Rico, Guam, and the Philippine Islands under U.S. control in exchange for a $20 million settlement.

Americans pledged to "Remember the Maine!" (top) by going to war with Spain soon after the ship's destruction. William McKinley helped lead the United States to victory in the Spanish-American War of 1898. Two years later, McKinley gathered with dignitaries to celebrate his second Inauguration (above).

Guam and the Philippines gave the United States a Pacific base from which to influence Asian affairs, particularly in China. McKinley further increased the U.S. presence in the Pacific by annexing, or taking over, the Hawaiian Islands. In addition he initiated plans to build the Panama Canal, linking the Atlantic and Pacific Oceans through Central America.

McKinley's first Vice President died in office. Theodore Roosevelt was nominated to fill the job during the election of 1900. Roosevelt talked himself hoarse while campaigning for "Four More Years of the Full Dinner Pail." Buoyed by a strong economy and public satisfaction with the outcome of the war, McKinley triumphed over Bryan again. This time he won by an even greater margin of support.

In the fall of 1901, barely six months into his second administration, McKinley attended the Pan-American Exposition in Buffalo, New York. During the events a lone assassin joined a crowd of spectators waiting to shake the President's hand. When McKinley reached out to greet him, the man fired two shots at the President from a hidden gun. McKinley died eight days later after developing gangrene from his wounds. The assailant, an unemployed laborer, said he was an anarchist, someone who disapproves of government organizations. He was convicted of murder and executed.

> "War should never be entered upon until every agency of peace has failed."
>
> William McKinley,
> First Inaugural Address, March 4, 1897

William McKinley often charmed strangers by presenting them with the carnation he wore on his jacket. Once, when two brothers were introduced to him, he carefully replaced the flower in his buttonhole with a fresh one so each boy could receive a bloom from the President. McKinley had just presented his lapel flower to a young girl when he was shot (right). The President died eight days later.

Theodore Roosevelt

26TH PRESIDENT OF THE UNITED STATES ★ *1901 – 1909*

NICKNAME	T.R.
BORN	Oct. 27, 1858, in New York, N.Y.
POLITICAL PARTY	Republican
CHIEF OPPONENTS	1st term: none, succeeded McKinley; 2nd term: Alton Brooks Parker, Democrat (1852–1926)
TERM OF OFFICE	Sept. 14, 1901–March 3, 1909
AGE AT INAUGURATION	42 years old
NUMBER OF TERMS	one, plus balance of William McKinley's term
VICE PRESIDENTS	1st term: none; 2nd term: Charles Warren Fairbanks (1852–1918)
FIRST LADY	Edith Kermit Carow Roosevelt (1861–1948), second wife (married Dec. 2, 1886)
FIRST WIFE	Alice Hathaway Lee Roosevelt (1861–1884), married Oct. 27, 1880
CHILDREN	Alice, Theodore, Kermit, Ethel, Archibald, Quentin
GEOGRAPHIC SCENE	45 states
NEW STATES ADDED	Oklahoma (1907)
DIED	Jan. 6, 1919, in Oyster Bay, N.Y.
AGE AT DEATH	60 years old
SELECTED LANDMARKS	New York, N.Y. (birthplace); Sagamore Hill National Historic Site (homestead) and Young's Memorial Cemetery, Oyster Bay, N.Y.; Theodore Roosevelt Island, Washington, D.C.; Mount Rushmore National Memorial, Keystone, S. Dak.

Theodore Roosevelt wrote more than 30 books.

THEODORE ROOSEVELT TOOK CHARGE of the White House after the assassination of William McKinley. He filled it with his own personality and vision. He was the first "accidental" President to later win outright election to the office. During his tenure he expanded the reach of the U.S. government into such areas as industry, labor, the environment, consumer rights, and foreign affairs.

Few Presidents, if any, could compete with the unique background that Roosevelt brought to the White House. He was the son of a wealthy New York family. Sickly and asthmatic, he was schooled at home. Finally "Teedie's" father encouraged him to improve his health through vigorous physical exercise. By the time he attended Harvard University he was fit enough to compete in the campus boxing program. Roosevelt graduated with honors, married, and became a member of New York's state assembly.

Then tragedy struck. Roosevelt's mother and wife both died from illnesses on Valentine's Day in 1884. Roosevelt took his grief to the western United States and worked as a cowboy and a rancher. Locals came to respect the eyeglasses-wearing "Four Eyes" as the East Coast "dude" whose strongest curse was "By Godfrey!" Roosevelt did not hesitate to punch out an offensive cowboy, fire a dishonest ranch hand, or capture thieves.

In the fall of 1886 Roosevelt returned to East Coast life. He remarried, took up writing, and reentered public service. He worked on the U.S. Civil Service Commission for Benjamin Harrison, headed the

Not since Thomas Jefferson had a President enjoyed as many talents and diverse interests as Theodore Roosevelt. He loved being active outdoors (above). Roosevelt would swim through shark-infested waters to explore a shipwreck or lead cross-country hikes on an unwavering straight course, taking each obstacle as a fresh challenge. After being wounded by an assassin during his 1912 presidential campaign, Roosevelt insisted on speaking for nearly an hour, dripping blood, before seeking medical care. The folded copy of his speech and his metal eyeglass case had slowed the path of the bullet and prevented the wound from being too severe.

New York City Police Board, and served as William McKinley's assistant secretary of the Navy. When the Spanish-American War broke out, Roosevelt recruited a volunteer company of cowboys, college football players, New York City police officers, and Native Americans. Roosevelt's "Rough Riders" became famous for their charge near San Juan Hill, in Cuba. Roosevelt was elected governor of New York after the war. In 1901 Roosevelt became Vice President and then President. He won outright election to the post in 1904.

Theodore Roosevelt posed with his Rough Riders atop San Juan Hill after their famous charge during the Spanish-American War.

> ## "Speak softly and carry a big stick; you will go far."
>
> Theodore Roosevelt's version of an African saying

Roosevelt's political background as an administrator prepared him to take aggressive charge of the office. He expanded the role of the national government in protecting the lives of its citizens. He went head to head with large corporations that had formed monopolies, called trusts, in railroad, beef, oil, tobacco, and other industries. Trusts had become so powerful from lack of competition that citizens and workers were suffering from high prices, low wages, and poor working conditions. Roosevelt became known as a "trustbuster" for breaking up these monopolies.

In other domestic affairs Roosevelt forced coal mine owners to settle labor disputes with 150,000 striking miners by threatening to have the government take control of the mines. He set aside vast areas of the country for conservation and resource development. He increased safety standards for the preparation of meat, other food products, and medicine.

In foreign policy Roosevelt outlined what became known as "Big Stick Diplomacy." He declared that the United States would serve as "an international police power" throughout the Western

Seven Rough Riders helped Theodore Roosevelt campaign to become governor of New York. At campaign stops (left), a bugler even sounded the cavalry charge. Roosevelt's second wife, Edith (below), served as his personal secretary when he was President. She gathered information to help her husband during the treaty negotiations that earned him a Nobel Peace Prize.

Theodore Roosevelt continued the work started by his predecessor for the construction of the Panama Canal, a waterway connecting the Atlantic and Pacific Oceans across Central America. He visited the construction site in 1906 (left). During his retirement years he spent seven months exploring the River of Doubt in the jungles of Brazil (right). He suffered periodically from malaria and other ailments during the trip and for the rest of his life.

Hemisphere of the globe if it felt threatened by other nations. He proved an effective mediator in disputes among other nations, too. He won the Nobel Peace Prize in 1905 for his role in negotiating an end to war between Russia and Japan.

Roosevelt, the youngest man ever to become President, was very much a family man when he entered the White House. His eldest daughter, Alice, was married there. His younger children grew up in its corridors and on its grounds. Once a son and his friends disrupted work at a nearby government building by using mirrors to bounce sunlight through the windows. When informed about the problem, Roosevelt, always playful, arranged for someone at the office building to send the boys a

message with signal flags: "Attack on this building must immediately cease...." A friend observed: "You must always remember that the President is about six."

Roosevelt left the White House in 1909. On an extended safari in Africa he collected hundreds of animals for the Smithsonian Institution. He made an unsuccessful attempt to regain the White House in 1912 by running as a third-party candidate for the Progressive, or Bull Moose, Party. Roosevelt's offer to raise a fighting force during World War I was refused, but all four of his sons joined the service. The combat death of his youngest son, Quentin, left Roosevelt shaken. With his health deteriorating, he died the following year.

Theodore Roosevelt (above with envoys of Japan and Russia) is known for being first at many things, both great and trivial. He was the first President to travel by car and submarine while in office. During his retirement years, he became the first President to ride in an airplane. He was the first President to have his initials become his nickname. He made the first overseas trip by a sitting President (to Panama). He was the first President and American to be awarded a Nobel Peace Prize. The teddy bear was named after Roosevelt by a toymaker who heard how he had spared the life of a bear cub during a hunting trip.

Kids in the White House

★ At Home in the Spotlight ★

THE FIRST RESIDENTS of the White House—John and Abigail Adams—were also the first occupants to bring children to the President's home. Their four-year-old granddaughter, Susanna, traveled with her grandmother to stay at the residence in 1800. A parade of children has continued to live there off and on ever since.

In 1806 Thomas Jefferson's grandson James became the first baby born in the President's home. Grover Cleveland is the only President to have one of his own children born in the White House. His daughter Esther was born there in 1893.

In 1861 the Lincolns were the first family to bring young children of their own to live in the White House. Among other antics, Tad Lincoln set up a White House refreshment stand, shot his toy cannon at the President's office door, and rode through a tea party in the East Room on a chair pulled by his pet goats.

Theodore Roosevelt brought six children with him to the White House in 1901. These youngsters roller-skated in the East Room, "sledded" down White House staircases on serving trays, and surrounded themselves with pets—including snakes, a badger, raccoons, pigs, parrots, baby bears, and a young lion. Their father noted: "I don't think that any family has ever enjoyed the White House more than we have."

The children of most Presidents are already

Theodore Roosevelt's youngest sons, Archie and Quentin, liked to join the daily roll call for the White House police (above). Willie and Tad Lincoln were an earlier pair of brothers who roamed freely in the President's home. They knew just how to cause chaos there by ringing various bells to call White House servants.

James A. Garfield's sons had pillow fights aboard velocipedes in the White House East Room (left). Quentin Roosevelt rode his pony, Algonquin (center), while growing up in the Executive Mansion. Once he brought his pet on the White House elevator so the pair could visit his brother, Archie, who was laid up with measles. The grandchildren of Benjamin Harrison took wagon rides behind a goat on the White House lawn (right).

grown up or are away in college by the time their parents move into the White House. Some of these young adults have been active campaigners for their fathers. In recent decades, four Presidents—John F. Kennedy, Jimmy Carter, Bill Clinton, and Barack Obama—have brought younger children with them to the White House. As parents they sheltered their children from public attention while encouraging them to "just be kids" at home. Caroline Kennedy rode the grounds on her pony, Macaroni, and Amy Carter played in her own tree house, for example. Since the days of Woodrow Wilson, Secret Service agents have acted as bodyguards for children of the Presidents—even out on dates! If the public spotlight ever gets too bright, presidential children can always find refuge back home in the White House.

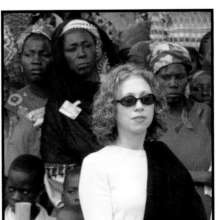

In 1971 Tricia Nixon became the eighth and most recent presidential daughter to marry at the White House; Maria Monroe was the first in 1820. John F. Kennedy, Jr., liked to hide under his father's desk in the Oval Office (left). Chelsea Clinton accompanied her parents on some of their official trips abroad (below, left). Even family pets earn notice, like Barney (below, right) who gained his own Web site during George W. Bush's presidency.

William Howard Taft

27TH PRESIDENT OF THE UNITED STATES ★ 1909–1913

NICKNAME	Big Bill
BORN	Sept. 15, 1857, in Cincinnati, Ohio
POLITICAL PARTY	Republican
CHIEF OPPONENT	William Jennings Bryan, Democrat (1860–1925)
TERM OF OFFICE	March 4, 1909–March 3, 1913
AGE AT INAUGURATION	51 years old
NUMBER OF TERMS	one
VICE PRESIDENT	James Schoolcraft Sherman (1855–1912)
FIRST LADY	Helen Herron Taft (1861–1943), wife (married June 19, 1886)
CHILDREN	Robert, Helen, Charles
GEOGRAPHIC SCENE	46 states
NEW STATES ADDED	New Mexico, Arizona (1912)
DIED	March 8, 1930, in Washington, D.C.
AGE AT DEATH	72 years old
SELECTED LANDMARKS	Cincinnati, Ohio (birthplace); Arlington National Cemetery, Arlington, Va.

William Howard Taft relaxed by playing golf.

WILLIAM HOWARD TAFT WAS ELECTED PRESIDENT in 1908 as Theodore Roosevelt's hand-picked successor. He lacked Roosevelt's charisma and administrative talent, however, and lost popularity as his term progressed. Taft was defeated during his reelection bid, a crowded and complex race that included a challenge by Roosevelt on a third-party ticket. Later, Taft served with distinction on the U.S. Supreme Court, the only man to be both a U.S. President and a Supreme Court justice.

Taft was the sixth Ohioan to become a U.S. President. His father, a lawyer and public servant, had served in the administrations of Ulysses S. Grant and Chester A. Arthur. Young Taft attended public schools and graduated second in his class from Yale University. By then "Big Bill" already weighed at least 225 pounds. Taft studied law, opened a practice, worked as a judge, and taught law.

In 1900 President William McKinley sent Taft to administer the Philippine Islands. He became governor of this new U.S. territory in the Pacific. Four years later Theodore Roosevelt made him secretary of war, responsible for the construction of the Panama Canal. Although Taft was eager to return to the bench as a judge, he turned down three opportunities to join the Supreme Court during these years. He felt he had to finish work assigned to him by Presidents instead.

Taft was encouraged by his wife, Helen, and Roosevelt to run for President in 1908. With some hesitation, he did. He won election easily because of his association with Roosevelt. Taft tried to continue the progressive reforms begun by his predecessor. In one term

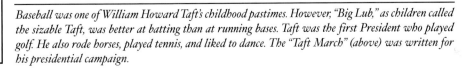

Baseball was one of William Howard Taft's childhood pastimes. However, "Big Lub," as children called the sizable Taft, was better at batting than at running bases. Taft was the first President who played golf. He also rode horses, played tennis, and liked to dance. The "Taft March" (above) was written for his presidential campaign.

Taft served as governor of the Philippines (left) and supervised the construction of the Panama Canal (right) before he became President. He was famous for installing an oversize bathtub in the White House (below) after getting stuck in its standard-size one. At 332 pounds he was the heaviest President ever.

of office he broke twice as many trusts as Roosevelt had done in eight years, including major monopolies in tobacco and petroleum. During Taft's administration, the federal government took control of railroad freight fares, established a parcel post delivery service, initiated a postal savings system, created the Department of Labor, and added new lands to the federal conservation program. Congress passed two amendments to the Constitution, too. One created the structure for a federal income tax; the other called for the direct election of U.S. senators by citizens. (Previously, state legislatures had elected senators.) Taft was the first person to be President of 48 states. Nearly 50 years would pass before the nation added Alaska and Hawaii, its last two states.

These accomplishments were overshadowed in the minds of others by Taft's shortcomings. His efforts to reduce the tariff, or tax, on imports divided his party into warring factions. Many leaders at home and abroad disapproved of his "Dollar Diplomacy," a program that substituted "dollars for bullets" in an effort to influence foreign policy. He was ridiculed for trivial things such as not remembering names, needing an oversize bathtub, and falling asleep at awkward moments. (Once he even slept through his own parade while riding in an open car through the streets of New York City.) Voters rejected his reelection bid more firmly than that of any other major candidate in history. He won 23 percent of the popular vote, and just 8 electoral votes. Even his former ally Roosevelt won more votes running on a third-party ticket.

"Political considerations have never weighed heavily with me."

William Howard Taft

"No one candidate was ever elected ex-President by such a large majority," joked William Howard Taft after losing his reelection bid to Woodrow Wilson. Taft and Wilson rode together to the U.S. Capitol when it was time for the new President to be inaugurated (left). Taft was the first former Chief Executive to become a trustee of the National Geographic Society (right); he wrote more than a dozen articles for its magazine.

After leaving the White House, Taft became a law professor at his alma mater, Yale University. Then, in 1921, President Warren G. Harding named him Chief Justice of the United States Supreme Court. Taft wrote 253 Court opinions during his nine years on the bench. Even more important than his rulings was the work he did persuading Congress to construct the Supreme Court building. (Previously, the Court met in a separate chamber of the U.S. Capitol building.)

Taft enjoyed his post so much that he remarked: "I don't remember that I ever was President."

Taft retired from the Supreme Court in 1930 when his health began to fail. He died a few weeks later. He was the first President to be buried in Arlington National Cemetery. His wife, Helen, was laid to rest beside him following her death 13 years later. John F. Kennedy and his wife, Jacqueline, are the only other presidential couple buried at Arlington.

"I have tried to do in each case what seemed to me the wisest thing."

William Howard Taft

Helen Taft (above) was the first President's wife to accompany her husband during his Inaugural Parade (left). As First Lady she coordinated the planting of ornamental Japanese cherry trees in the nation's capital. She took an active interest in government business, supported women's rights, and wrote a memoir about her years in the White House.

Presidents and the Supreme Court

★ *A Legacy That Lasts* ★

THE CRY "OYEZ! OYEZ! OYEZ!" opens each session of the U.S. Supreme Court. The President, with the approval of Congress, determines who will sit on the bench that holds the highest authority in the judicial branch of the U.S. government. Only 110 individuals have ever served on it. Because justices serve for life and are protected from firing and salary cuts, they are expected to weigh cases free from political pressures or other influences. Even so, they often reflect the beliefs and political backgrounds of the leaders who appoint them, giving Presidents a lasting legacy of influence long after they've retired from office.

The Supreme Court Building in Washington, D.C.

When a vacancy occurs on the Supreme Court, either because of death or retirement, the President nominates someone to fill the space. Nominees typically have had extensive and distinguished experience as attorneys, judges, or in political office. The Senate Judiciary Committee decides whether or not to recommend approval of a nominee by the full Senate. Most pass the test, but over the years about two dozen nominees have not.

With the exception of

The size and composition of the Supreme Court (above in 1892) has evolved since it formed in 1790 with six members. Membership ranged as high as 10 until Congress settled on its final size of nine members in 1869. The court met for 177 years before anyone other than white men joined its bench.

Jimmy Carter and three 19th-century Presidents, all other chief executives have appointed someone to the Supreme Court. George Washington holds the record for appointing the most justices: 10. Franklin D. Roosevelt appointed almost as many—nine—during his lengthy Presidency.

The Supreme Court opens its yearly term on the first Monday of October and continues to meet until early summer. It is asked to review some 10,000 cases each year; only about 100 are actually presented in front of the court. Whenever the justices gather to undertake official business, they shake hands as a reminder of their need to remain civil even when they disagree about the law.

The Supreme Court met inside the U.S. Capitol building for most of the first 145 years of its history. After former President William Howard Taft became its Chief Justice in 1921, he persuaded Congress to construct the court its own home. Taft died before he could see the opening of the Supreme Court Building in 1935.

In addition to issuing landmark decisions about

Former President William Howard Taft became the only man to serve as the nation's Chief Executive and sit on its Supreme Court when he was sworn in as its Chief Justice in 1921 (left). John Roberts (right, with President George W. Bush) became the court's newest Chief Justice in 2005. Of the 17 men who have served as Chief Justice, John Marshall held the post the longest: 34 years.

the law, members of the Supreme Court have twice helped determine the outcome of presidential elections. A commission made up of five Supreme Court justices and ten members of Congress voted 8 to 7 along party lines to hand victory to Republican candidate Rutherford B. Hayes following the election of 1876. More recently, in 2000, the Supreme Court ruled 5 to 4 in the case *Bush* v. *Gore,* also along party lines, in a decision that elevated George W. Bush to the Presidency. The court contributed to the ending of a Presidency, too, when its 1974 ruling forced Richard Nixon to release secret recordings that tied him to the Watergate scandal. The President resigned later that year.

The Supreme Court holds the final say in government disputes. Its decisions can only be overcome in three ways: the passage of improved legislation that respects the court's opinions, Constitutional amendment, or future rulings by the court.

The Supreme Court of 2003 included representation by two women and an African American: its first female justice Sandra Day O'Connor (seated), who served 1981-2006, Ruth Bader Ginsburg (standing), appointed in 1993, and Clarence Thomas, who replaced Thurgood Marshall, the court's first African American, in 1991.

Woodrow Wilson

28TH PRESIDENT OF THE UNITED STATES ★ *1913 – 1921*

NICKNAME	Professor
BORN	Dec. 29, 1856, in Staunton, Va.
POLITICAL PARTY	Democrat
CHIEF OPPONENTS	1st term: Theodore Roosevelt, Progressive (1858–1919) and President William Howard Taft, Republican (1857–1930); 2nd term: Charles Evans Hughes, Republican (1862–1948)

Wilson was reelected by being antiwar.

TERM OF OFFICE	March 4, 1913–March 3, 1921
AGE AT INAUGURATION	56 years old
NUMBER OF TERMS	two
VICE PRESIDENT	Thomas Riley Marshall (1854–1925)
FIRST LADIES	Ellen Louise Axson Wilson (1860–1914), first wife (married June 24, 1885); Margaret Woodrow Wilson (1886–1944), daughter; Edith Bolling Galt Wilson (1872–1961), second wife (married Dec. 18, 1915)
CHILDREN	Margaret, Jesse, Eleanor
GEOGRAPHIC SCENE	48 states
NEW STATES ADDED	none
DIED	Feb. 3, 1924, in Washington, D.C.
AGE AT DEATH	67 years old
SELECTED LANDMARKS	Staunton, Va. (birthplace); Columbia, S.C. (boyhood home); Woodrow Wilson House Museum and Washington National Cathedral (grave), Washington, D.C.

As PRESIDENT, WOODROW WILSON ushered important legislation through Congress. However, World War I became the greatest challenge of his two terms in office. When he failed to keep the United States out of the conflict, he used the nation's resources to help win it. He sought to secure lasting peace afterward with a new international governing body called the League of Nations.

Wilson grew up in the shadow of an earlier war—the Civil War. He was born in Virginia and raised in Georgia and the Carolinas. His first childhood memory was of hearing that Abraham Lincoln had been elected President and that war would follow. He watched Confederate troops march off to battle, saw soldiers die from their wounds, and, after the war, glimpsed Confederate General Robert E. Lee being paraded through Augusta, Georgia, under Union guard.

Wilson struggled with dyslexia, a learning disorder that delayed his mastery of basic skills in reading, writing, and math. He went on to graduate from the College of New Jersey (renamed Princeton University in 1896). Wilson practiced law, earned a graduate degree from Johns Hopkins University, and became a college professor. By 1902 he was president of Princeton University. Wilson stepped from

By 1917 intensified fighting in Europe (above) had forced Woodrow Wilson to change his first-term antiwar stance and enter the United States into World War I. Within 18 months some two million U.S. soldiers had joined the front lines and helped turn the tide of the Great War.

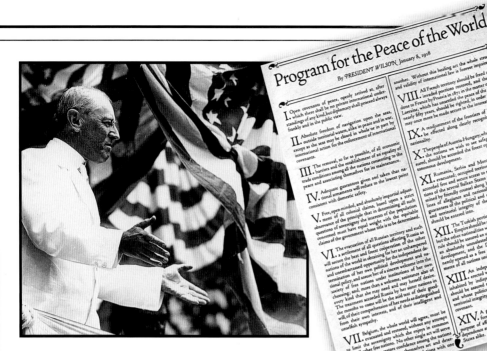

Program for the Peace of the World

By PRESIDENT WILSON, January 8, 1918

I. Open covenants of peace, openly arrived at, after which there shall be no private international understandings of any kind, but diplomacy shall proceed always frankly and in the public view.

II. Absolute freedom of navigation upon the seas, outside territorial waters, alike in peace and in war, except as the seas may be closed in whole or in part by international action for the enforcement of international covenants.

III. The removal, so far as possible, of all economic barriers and the establishment of an equality of trade conditions among all the nations consenting to the peace and associating themselves for its maintenance.

IV. Adequate guarantees given and taken that national armaments will reduce to the lowest point consistent with domestic safety.

V. Free, open-minded, and absolutely impartial adjustment of all colonial claims, based upon a strict observance of the principle that in determining all such questions of sovereignty the interest of the population concerned must have equal weight with the equitable claims of the government whose title is to be determined.

VI. The evacuation of all Russian territory and such a settlement of all questions affecting Russia as will secure the best and freest cooperation of the other nations of the world in obtaining for her an unhampered and unembarrassed opportunity for the independent determination of her own political development and national policy, and assure her of a sincere welcome into the society of free nations under institutions of her own choosing; and, more than a welcome, assistance also of every kind that she may need and may herself desire. The treatment accorded Russia by her sister nations in the months to come will be the acid test of their good will, of their comprehension of her needs as distinguished from their own interests, and of their intelligent and unselfish sympathy.

VII. Belgium, the whole world will agree, must be evacuated and restored, without any attempt to limit the sovereignty which she enjoys in common with all other free nations. No other single act will serve as this will serve to restore confidence among the nations in the law which they have themselves set and determined for the government of their relations with one

VIII. All French territory should be freed and the invaded portions restored, and the wrong done to France by Prussia in 1871 in the matter of Alsace-Lorraine, which has unsettled the peace of the world for nearly fifty years, should be righted, in order that peace may once more be made secure in the interest of all.

IX. A readjustment of the frontiers of Italy should be effected along clearly recognizable lines of nationality.

X. The peoples of Austria-Hungary, whose place among the nations we wish to see safeguarded and assured, should be accorded the freest opportunity of autonomous development.

XI. Rumania, Serbia and Montenegro should be evacuated; occupied territories restored; Serbia accorded free and secure access to the sea; and the relations of the several Balkan States to one another determined by friendly counsel along historically established lines of allegiance and nationality; and international guarantees of the political and economic independence and territorial integrity of the several Balkan States should be entered into.

XII. The Turkish portions of the present Ottoman Empire should be assured a secure sovereignty, but the other nationalities which are now under Turkish rule should be assured an undoubted security of life and an absolutely unmolested opportunity of autonomous development, and the Dardanelles should be permanently opened as a free passage to the ships and commerce of all nations under international guarantees.

XIII. An independent Polish State should be erected which should include the territories inhabited by indisputably Polish populations, which should be assured a free and secure access to the sea, and whose political and economic independence and territorial integrity should be guaranteed by international covenant.

XIV. A general association of nations must be formed under specific covenants for the purpose of affording mutual guarantees of political independence and territorial integrity to great and small States alike.

that post to the White House after brief service as governor of New Jersey. He was the top vote-getter in the crowded presidential race of 1912 that included President William Howard Taft and former President Theodore Roosevelt.

Wilson packed his first term of office with significant legislation. He established the Federal Reserve system that continues to control the nation's money supply today. In addition he reduced import taxes, established graduated income taxes, created a Federal Trade Commission to monitor business practices, supported labor practices such as strikes, discouraged the use of child labor, and promoted the eight-hour workday. He was the first President to hold periodic press conferences and to speak on the radio.

Wilson was reelected thanks to this record and because, as his campaign slogan put it, "He Kept Us Out of War." The Great War had begun in Europe in August 1914. The United States was drawn into the fight soon after Wilson's 1916 reelection. The war ended with a truce on November 11, 1918, a date celebrated as Armistice Day (and later renamed Veteran's Day).

Wilson became the first U.S. President to visit Europe while in office when he traveled to Paris to help establish terms for peace. The final treaty supported Wilson's idea of creating a League of Nations that would settle future disputes using words and economic influence, not weapons. Wilson could not persuade Congress to accept his plan, though, and the League formed without support from the United States. Nonetheless, in 1919 Wilson earned the Nobel Peace Prize for his efforts. The United Nations took the place of the League after World War II.

Wilson's first wife, Ellen, was a talented artist. As First Lady she worked to improve housing for residents in the nation's capital. Two of the Wilsons' three daughters were wed in White

The son of a Presbyterian minister, Woodrow Wilson thought it was God's will that he had become President. He devoted himself to ending World War I (center) as if it were a charge from heaven. Wilson's "Fourteen Points" for lasting peace (top, center), outlined in January 1918, formed the basis for peace settlements after the war ended. Wilson campaigned so intensely (top, left and top, right) for U.S. support of the treaty that his health suffered.

U.S. citizens helped secure a victory in World War I (above) by taking part in a nationwide rationing program during the war. Woodrow and Edith Wilson (right) set a positive example for others by going without gas on Sundays, meat on Mondays, and wheat on Tuesdays. They even let sheep roam on the White House lawns so they could "mow" the grass naturally, saving gas and labor. Nationwide sacrifices helped make scarce resources available to U.S. soldiers overseas. The war proved deadly and expensive to nations everywhere. Nearly 10 million soldiers died worldwide in a conflict that cost more than $300 billion.

House ceremonies during his first term of office. Wilson was devastated when Ellen became ill and died in 1914. He even told friends he would welcome being assassinated. The following spring Wilson was introduced to a widow. He liked her so much at first sight that he invited her to stay for tea at the White House. He married his new friend, Edith, before the end of the year.

Wilson, who had suffered for years from minor strokes, had a major stroke in October 1919, which ended his campaign to win congressional support for the League of Nations. Edith took charge of her husband's recovery. She kept details of her husband's health a secret, overruled the idea that he should resign, and controlled what official business could be brought to his attention. Although her boldness drew criticism then—and still does among historians— it helped Wilson complete his Presidency.

Wilson's retirement was relatively brief, and his health remained poor. He died in 1924, six months after the death of his successor, Warren G. Harding. Both Woodrow and Edith Wilson are buried at the Washington Cathedral. He is the only President buried in the nation's capital.

"The world must be made safe for democracy."

Woodrow Wilson,
Request that Congress declare war on Germany, April 2, 1917

Presidents at War

★ Serving as the Commander in Chief ★

During wartime, U.S. Presidents take on the added responsibility of Commander in Chief for the nation's armed forces. Two of the country's earliest Presidents took this duty literally. During the Whiskey Rebellion of 1794, George Washington rode at the head of more than 10,000 soldiers to silence protests over a new federal tax on liquor. Likewise, when the British threatened the nation's capital near the end of the War of 1812, James Madison actually took command of scattered troops in an attempted defense.

Since then many wartime Presidents have visited troops near combat zones, even at the risk of being in harm's way. Most participate in debates about military strategy, too. All Presidents at least direct the nature of the fight by choosing military commanders. They often play a role in shaping the peacetime that follows war, too.

Ironically some of the nation's most prominent wartime leaders had no personal combat experience themselves. Woodrow Wilson and Franklin D. Roosevelt, for example, grew up during peacetime. In all, 12 U.S. Presidents never served in the military. Others include John Adams and John Quincy Adams (who were foreign diplomats instead of soldiers during the Revolutionary War), Grover Cleveland (who paid someone else to take his place during the Civil War, a legal option at the time), and Bill Clinton (who pursued his education, not military service, during the Vietnam War). Even Abraham Lincoln, one of the most important commanders in chief, had served in the military for just a few months during a frontier Indian war.

Commanders in Chief through the centuries of the Presidency: George Washington (top) led federal troops during the Whiskey Rebellion of 1794. During the Civil War of the 1860s, Abraham Lincoln (above left) began the practice of visiting battlefront troops. During the 20th century, Woodrow Wilson (above, right at far right) worked with leaders from France, Great Britain, and Italy to draft the peace treaty that ended World War I.

Nonetheless, wartime service is often seen as a measure of fitness for presidential candidates. Those with little or no experience may be criticized, particularly if it appears that service was deliberately avoided. Those with more experience are often more favorably received. A number of Presidents have gained election, in part at least, because of famous military performances. They include George Washington, Andrew Jackson, Ulysses S. Grant, Theodore Roosevelt, and Dwight D. Eisenhower. Ironically most of these leaders presided over periods of national peace after they were elected.

Presidential popularity tends to rise during times of national crisis. Approval ratings soared for Franklin D. Roosevelt after the bombing of Pearl Harbor, for Jimmy Carter during the early months of the Iran hostage crisis, and for George W. Bush following the 2001 terrorist attacks on U.S. soil. Such popularity inevitably falls if conflicts remain unresolved or if presidential leadership becomes questioned.

If presidential elections occur during times of war, voters often choose to "stay the course" instead of changing leaders. Such was the case for Franklin D. Roosevelt; he was reelected twice during World War II. George W. Bush was also returned to the White House in 2004 with the help of wartime support. On the other hand, if a wartime leader is perceived to be failing as Commander in Chief, that issue alone can end a Presidency. For example, wartime unpopularity forced Lyndon B. Johnson to cancel his 1968 reelection bid.

Wartime Presidents often choose to reduce Constitutional freedoms in the name of national defense. At the outset of the Civil War, for example, Abraham Lincoln jailed potential traitors and restricted freedom of speech. During World War II, Franklin D. Roosevelt authorized the detention in restricted camps of more than 100,000 Japanese American citizens. Concerns over terrorist threats prompted George W. Bush to permit greater surveillance of U.S. residents. Not all Presidents have chosen this tack, however. James Madison insisted during the War of 1812 that civil liberties like free speech remain unchecked in order to demonstrate the nation's commitment to liberty.

President Harry S. Truman's decision to have the Enola Gay *(top) drop an atomic bomb on Japan during World War II continues to be much-debated. Eleanor Roosevelt (above, left), often visited World War II troops on behalf of her husband. Vietnam anti-war protests (above, center) affected the popularity of two U.S. Presidents, Lyndon B. Johnson and Richard Nixon. George W. Bush visited troops abroad and at home (above, right) during the Iraq War.*

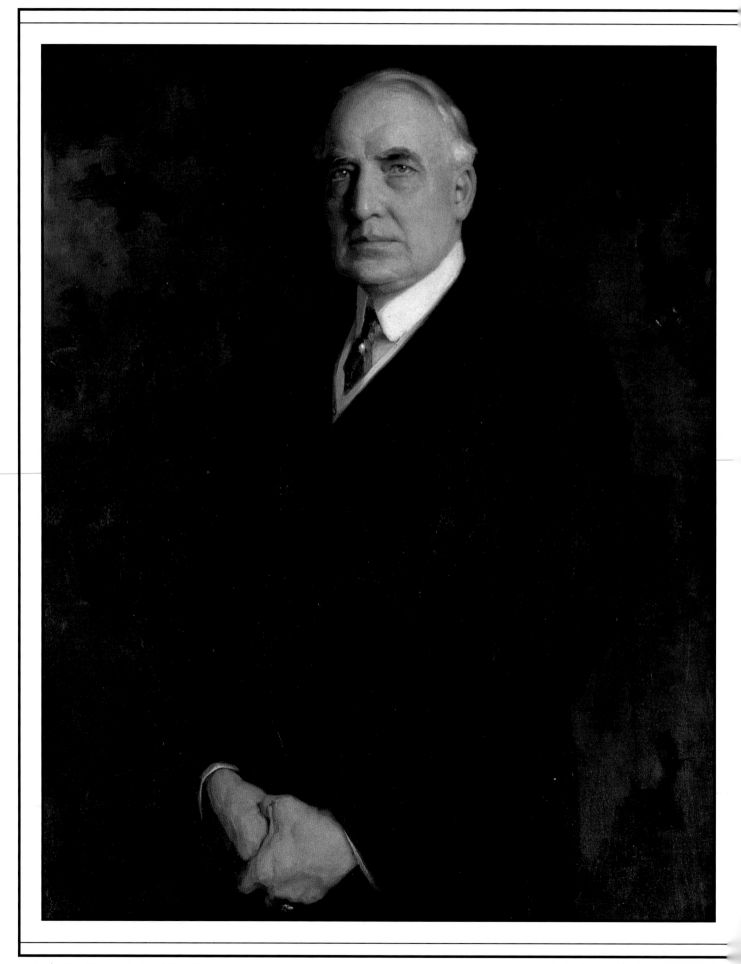

Warren G. Harding

29TH PRESIDENT OF THE UNITED STATES ★ 1921 – 1923

NICKNAME	Wobbly Warren
BORN	Nov. 2, 1865, in Caledonia (now Blooming Grove), Ohio
POLITICAL PARTY	Republican
CHIEF OPPONENT	James Middleton Cox, Democrat (1870–1957)
TERM OF OFFICE	March 4, 1921–Aug. 2, 1923
AGE AT INAUGURATION	55 years old
NUMBER OF TERMS	one (cut short by death)
VICE PRESIDENT	Calvin Coolidge (1872–1933)
FIRST LADY	Florence Kling De Wolfe Harding (1860–1924), wife (married July 8, 1891)
CHILDREN	none
GEOGRAPHIC SCENE	48 states
NEW STATES ADDED	none
DIED	Aug. 2, 1923, in San Francisco, Calif.
AGE AT DEATH	57 years old
SELECTED LANDMARKS	Harding Home and Museum and Harding Memorial (grave), Marion, Ohio

Warren G. Harding delivered his Inaugural Address through a new invention: a megaphone that magnified his voice.

WHEN HE WAS A YOUNG MAN, Warren Gamaliel Harding's friends thought he "looked like a President." Harding's presidential profile helped carry him to the White House, but it did not prepare him for the challenges of the job. Harding became the sixth President to die in office when his health failed him at midterm. His death came just as major scandals about his administration were coming to light.

Harding was born in Ohio. After graduating from Ohio Central College in Iberia, he became a newspaper publisher in the nearby town of Marion. He went on to serve in the state legislature, as lieutenant governor and governor of Ohio, and as a U.S. senator during his climb to prominence in the Republican Party. His habit of changing his mind earned him the nickname "Wobbly Warren." Harding's nomination to the party ticket of 1920 followed much behind-the-scenes, late-night deal making by party leaders, many of whom were heavy smokers. This strategy became known as the "smoke-filled room" approach to politics.

The complex responsibilities of being President began to trouble Harding midway into his term. So did hints of illegal behavior within his administration. In early 1923 an important Harding appointee fled the country because of criminal activity on the job. One of the man's coworkers committed suicide soon after. Then the private secretary of Harding's scandal-plagued attorney general killed himself over a different scheme. Speculation over these events was interrupted when Harding, his health already weakened, began a cross-country trip to visit the U.S. territory of Alaska. He died suddenly during the trip while staying in San Francisco.

Warren G. Harding's Presidency is consistently ranked among the worst in U.S. history because of its widespread corruption. The greatest scandal—the Teapot Dome affair—came to light after his death. Apparently without the President's knowledge, a Harding Cabinet member had granted oil-drilling rights on federal lands like Wyoming's Teapot Dome. The man received sizable illegal payments and even a herd of cattle from oil company officials in exchange.

Warren G. Harding was elected President with the greatest landslide in a century. He earned 60 percent of the popular vote in the first election in which women were able to vote nationwide.

Calvin Coolidge

30TH PRESIDENT OF THE UNITED STATES ★ *1923 – 1929*

NICKNAME	Silent Cal
BORN	July 4, 1872, in Plymouth, Vt.
POLITICAL PARTY	Republican
CHIEF OPPONENTS	1st term: none, succeeded Harding; 2nd term: John W. Davis (1873–1955), Democrat and Robert M. La Follette (1855–1925), Progressive
TERM OF OFFICE	Aug. 3, 1923–March 3, 1929
AGE AT INAUGURATION	51 years old
NUMBER OF TERMS	one, plus balance of Warren G. Harding's term
VICE PRESIDENTS	1st term: none; 2nd term: Charles Gates Dawes (1865–1951)
FIRST LADY	Grace Anna Goodhue Coolidge (1879–1957), wife (married Oct. 4, 1905)
CHILDREN	John, Calvin
GEOGRAPHIC SCENE	48 states
NEW STATES ADDED	none
DIED	Jan. 5, 1933, in Northampton, Mass.
AGE AT DEATH	60 years old
SELECTED LANDMARKS	Plymouth, Vt. (birthplace, homestead); Northampton, Mass. (library, homestead); Plymouth Notch Cemetery, Plymouth, Vt.

Vermont-born Calvin Coolidge never lost his fondness for making maple syrup.

CALVIN COOLIDGE'S HIGH STANDARD OF CONDUCT restored trust in the Presidency following the sudden death of his predecessor, Warren G. Harding. Coolidge was a calm, frugal presence in the White House during the extravagance and waste of the Roaring Twenties.

The plain style of Coolidge's Presidency had its roots in his simple New England childhood. His favorite chore, as a red-headed youth in rural Vermont, was making maple syrup. He went on to graduate from Amherst College, become a lawyer, and hold more than a dozen elected posts—including governor of Massachusetts—before rising from Vice President to President in 1923.

Coolidge cooperated with investigations into the Harding scandals. He removed corrupt staff members, and he chose reliable replacements for their posts. He followed a simple strategy: "When things are going along all right, it is a good plan to let them alone." This notion inspired the slogan "Keep Cool With Coolidge" during his successful election campaign in 1924.

Coolidge was nicknamed "Red" (for his red hair), "Cal" (short for Calvin), and "Silent Cal" (because he spoke little). His habit of expressing himself with few words was famous. Once a dinner guest told Coolidge she had bet she could get three words of conversation out of him. All he replied was: "You lose." He advised his successor, Herbert Hoover, on how to handle talkative visitors: "If you keep dead still, they will run down in three or four minutes."

Coolidge retired to Massachusetts in 1929. He wrote, served as a trustee for the National Geographic Society, and worked in the insurance industry before his death in 1933. Frugal with words to the end, Silent Cal left behind a will to his estate that was only 23 words long.

Calvin Coolidge was the last President who met with everyone who visited the White House to see its chief resident (above). Several hundred people often called each day. He prided himself on his speed at working through a crowd. Once, he shook hands with 1,900 visitors in only 34 minutes.

Herbert Hoover

31ST PRESIDENT OF THE UNITED STATES ★ *1929 – 1933*

NICKNAME	Chief
BORN	Aug. 10, 1874, in West Branch, Iowa
POLITICAL PARTY	Republican
CHIEF OPPONENT	Alfred Emanuel Smith, Democrat (1873–1944)
TERM OF OFFICE	March 4, 1929–March 3, 1933
AGE AT INAUGURATION	54 years old
NUMBER OF TERMS	one
VICE PRESIDENT	Charles Curtis (1860–1936)
FIRST LADY	Lou Henry Hoover (1874–1944), wife (married Feb. 10, 1899)
CHILDREN	Herbert, Allan
GEOGRAPHIC SCENE	48 states
NEW STATES ADDED	none
DIED	Oct. 20, 1964, in New York, N.Y.
AGE AT DEATH	90 years old
SELECTED LANDMARKS	Newberg, Oreg. (boyhood home); Hoover Institution, Stanford University, Palo Alto, Calif.; Herbert Hoover National Historic Site (including birthplace, presidential library, museum, and grave), West Branch, Iowa

Herbert Hoover directed European relief efforts (above, Poland in 1946) before and after his Presidency. During World War I Finnish citizens used "hoover" as a new verb meaning "to help."

WHEN THE STOCK MARKET CRASHED in October 1929 only a few months after Herbert Clark Hoover had taken office—the President found himself responsible for a different nation from the one he had planned to lead. The Great Depression that followed proved unstoppable and cost him the opportunity for a second term.

Hoover was a successful businessman, scientist, and public servant before becoming President. Born in Iowa and orphaned at age nine, he majored in geology at Stanford University. Hoover then began traveling the globe for the mining industry. While living in London, he received his first public service assignment—evacuating 120,000 Americans from Europe at the start of World War I. Later he helped direct relief efforts for European victims of the war. He went on to serve as secretary of commerce for Warren G. Harding and Calvin Coolidge.

Hoover carried 40 of the 48 states during the 1928 election. Although he had questioned some of the financial policies that led to the stock market crash of 1929, no one anticipated how serious the Great Depression that followed it would become. No economic collapse before or since has been so far-reaching, long lasting, or severe. A desperate public blamed Hoover for their troubles and, in 1932, voted in large numbers for the Democratic candidate, Franklin D. Roosevelt.

Two U.S. Presidents called Hoover back from retirement to perform national service. He organized post–World War II food relief in Europe for Harry S. Truman, and he evaluated government efficiency for Truman and again for Dwight D. Eisenhower. Hoover lived longer after leaving the White House than any other President—31 years. He died in 1964 at the age of 90.

Herbert Hoover became a multimillionaire during his years as a geologist. He refused to be paid for his public service. Hoover acted more aggressively than any previous President to end hard times after the stock market crashed in 1929 (above). Despite his efforts, suffering continued to spread.

SEEKING STABILITY IN THE ATOMIC AGE

★ *1933 – 1981* ★

1933

Germany revoked the citizenship of physicist Albert Einstein during his 1933 visit to the United States. Among the ideas proposed by this scientific genius was the concept of an atomic bomb.

1945

World War II ended with the explosion of two atomic bombs in Japan, including an attack on Hiroshima on August 6. Nuclear weapons have never again been used in combat.

1946

The first programmable electronic computer weighed 30 tons and used some 18,000 bulky vacuum tubes to transfer information. By 1952 computers were calculating election results.

1957

Racial tensions mounted in Little Rock, Arkansas, after the governor ignored the 1954 Supreme Court ruling, Brown v. Board of Education, *on the integration of public schools.*

The challenges faced by Presidents increased in complexity as the 20th century progressed. Leaders struggled to fight wars, end poverty, preserve democracy, extend equality, survive energy shortages, and heal national wounds. They led citizens through the tragedies of presidential deaths and scandals, too. Much of the era was dominated by the uneasy balance of power between the rivals of the atomic age—the United States and the Soviet Union. Presidents sought to offset the troubles of the times with hopes for a promising future.

1967

Widespread protest of U.S. involvement in the Vietnam War developed during the late 1960s and early 1970s. Young people were among the most visible demonstrators.

1969

On July 20, humans set foot on the moon for the first time. A series of Apollo lunar missions carried 12 U.S. astronauts to the moon six times from 1969 to 1972.

1970s

After the first successful human heart transplant in 1967, scientists tried to perfect the procedure during the 1970s. Medical advances in the 1980s extended the survival rate of patients.

1976

U.S. citizens celebrated the 200th anniversary of the nation's Declaration of Independence with ceremonies, parades, and fireworks.

Franklin D. Roosevelt

32ND PRESIDENT OF THE UNITED STATES ★ 1933 – 1945

NICKNAME	FDR
BORN	Jan. 30, 1882, in Hyde Park, N.Y.
POLITICAL PARTY	Democrat
CHIEF OPPONENTS	1st term: President Herbert Clark Hoover, Republican (1874–1964); 2nd term: Alfred Mossman Landon, Republican (1887–1987); 3rd term: Wendell Lewis Willkie, Republican (1892–1944); 4th term: Thomas Edmund Dewey, Republican (1902–1971)
TERM OF OFFICE	March 4, 1933–April 12, 1945
AGE AT INAUGURATION	51 years old
NUMBER OF TERMS	four (cut short by death)
VICE PRESIDENTS	1st & 2nd terms: John Nance Garner (1868–1967); 3rd term: Henry Agard Wallace (1888–1965); 4th term: Harry S. Truman (1884–1972)
FIRST LADY	Anna Eleanor Roosevelt Roosevelt (1884–1962), wife (married March 17, 1905)
CHILDREN	Anna, James, Elliott, Franklin, John, plus a son died young
GEOGRAPHIC SCENE	48 states
NEW STATES ADDED	none
DIED	April 12, 1945, in Warm Springs, Ga.
AGE AT DEATH	63 years old
SELECTED LANDMARKS	Franklin D. Roosevelt National Historic Site (includes home that was birthplace, childhood, and adult home; presidential library; museum; grave), Hyde Park, N.Y.; Little White House State Historic Site, Warm Springs, Ga.; FDR Memorial, Washington, D.C.

TWO GOOD TERMS DESERVE ANOTHER

NOT SINCE THE DAYS OF ABRAHAM LINCOLN did a President face such challenges as those met by Franklin Delano Roosevelt. During what became the longest Presidency in U.S. history, Roosevelt led the nation out of the Great Depression and saw it safely through the darkest days of World War II. His wife, Eleanor, was an equal partner in his political career.

Franklin D. Roosevelt was the second member of his extended family to become President of the United States. His path to the White House included many of the same political and personal steps taken decades earlier by Theodore Roosevelt, a fifth cousin. Franklin was born at his family's estate in Hyde Park, New York. He called this spot home for most of his life. Roosevelt was his parents' only child. His mother and father took seven weeks to agree upon his name. As was the custom of the era, Roosevelt was clothed in dresses and kilts until age eight. His parents took him on extended trips abroad and had him tutored at home until his teen years.

After graduating from Harvard University in 1904, Roosevelt attended Columbia Law School. He passed the bar exam and took up the practice of law. By then he had already married a distant relative, Anna Eleanor Roosevelt, known as Eleanor. The cousins had met for the first time in 1902, the year Eleanor

Franklin D. Roosevelt was the only person to serve three full terms as U.S. President and be elected to a fourth. He was encouraged during his childhood (top) to pursue public service as an adult. He began courting his distant cousin, Eleanor Roosevelt (above), while a student at Harvard University.

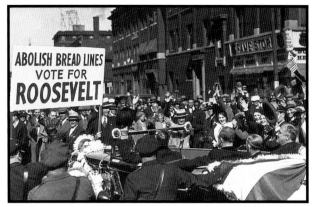

ABOLISH BREAD LINES
VOTE FOR
ROOSEVELT

"I pledge you, I pledge myself, to a new deal for the American people."

Franklin D. Roosevelt,
Democratic nomination acceptance speech, July 2, 1932

Franklin D. Roosevelt had the longest Presidency in U.S. history. He took office in 1933 after promising to end the Great Depression (left). When challenges continued at home and started abroad with World War II, voters were reluctant to switch leaders. He died in office in 1945. The 22nd Amendment, which became law in 1951, prohibits anyone from serving more than two terms as President. It was written by lawmakers who were uncomfortable with Roosevelt's extended term of office.

turned 18 and Franklin was 20. At their wedding in 1905 the bride was given away by President Theodore Roosevelt, her uncle.

In 1910 Franklin D. Roosevelt joined the New York Senate. A few years later Woodrow Wilson named him assistant secretary of the Navy. He ran unsuccessfully for the U.S. Senate in 1914 and left the Navy in 1920 to campaign as the running mate of the Democratic presidential nominee, James M. Cox. Illness sidelined his political career in 1921 when he was stricken suddenly with polio. Roosevelt went from being active and robust one day to being unable to walk two days later. Eleanor encouraged her husband to fight for his recovery. Although he never regained active use of his legs, Roosevelt learned how to stand on leg braces and take limited steps with the assistance of others. Within three years he was practicing law again. Before the decade was out he had become governor of New York.

When Roosevelt ran for President in 1932, the nation was staggering under the burden of the Great Depression—the greatest economic crisis in its history. One-fourth of all workers were unemployed. Countless families had gone broke because of bank failures. More than a million homeless hoboes sought food and work as they roamed the country. Displaced families tacked together shacks in temporary settlements they nicknamed Hoovervilles—after President Herbert Hoover.

The grim national scene prompted voters to flock to Roosevelt and his promise of a "new deal for the American people." He earned 57 percent of the popular vote and won the electoral votes of all but six states. In the three presidential elections that followed, Roosevelt continued his streak of majority victories, earning 61 percent, 55 percent, then 53 percent of the vote.

"While it isn't written in the Constitution, nevertheless it is the inherent duty of the federal government to keep its citizens from starvation," Franklin D. Roosevelt observed. As President he enacted sweeping legislation, including the Social Security Act (being signed at left).

"The only thing we have to fear is fear itself."

Franklin D. Roosevelt,
First Inaugural Address, March 4, 1933

Franklin D. Roosevelt used radio to connect with the American people in the days before television came into widespread use. His series of "fireside chats" (left), delivered in his reassuring voice, inspired the nation to face the day's challenges. He even used radio to build ties with French citizens. In 1942 he addressed them in their own language to announce the U.S. invasion of occupied French territories in North Africa. Roosevelt became the first President to appear on television, with a 1939 broadcast from the New York World's Fair.

As President, Roosevelt took charge of ending the Depression. Where Hoover had hesitated to interfere, Roosevelt plunged in. The beginning of his Presidency was famous for its rush of legislation and was later referred to as Roosevelt's Hundred Days. During this period, he signed 14 bills in all. Among other things, these new laws restored confidence in the banking industry, employed young men through a Civilian Conservation Corps, launched the construction of dams and power plants in the Tennessee River Valley, aided farmers, established loan programs, and improved working conditions. Later, Roosevelt established the Securities and Exchange Commission to help prevent future financial panics in the stock market. He created the Social Security system, too. This cornerstone program for public welfare assured that senior citizens would have retirement incomes and that the unemployed would receive temporary support while they sought new jobs. Many of these New Deal programs endure as essential elements of the American way of life.

In 1932 voters had been asked to "Kick Out Depression With a Democratic Vote." Four years later they agreed overwhelmingly to "Follow Through With Roosevelt." In 1940 they supported Roosevelt's third presidential campaign because he pledged that unless the U.S. was attacked, he would stay out of the war that was spreading around the globe. The next year Japan bombed U.S. naval bases at Pearl Harbor, Hawaii. Roosevelt predicted that the date, December 7, would "live in infamy," and he asked Congress to declare war on Japan. Declarations against Germany and Italy followed. For the rest of his life, the world would be at war.

Franklin D. Roosevelt met with other Allied leaders from World War II in Tehran, Iran, in 1943 (left). Roosevelt befriended "Big Three" ally Joseph Stalin, premier of the Soviet Union (seated at left), by poking fun at their companion Winston Churchill, prime minister of Great Britain (seated at right). He joked about the British, Churchill's cigars, even his moods. Soon the stern-faced Stalin was laughing along, smiling, while Roosevelt playfully called him "Uncle Joe."

Roosevelt's mother was a central figure in his family life along with his wife, Eleanor, and their five children (left). After her husband's death, Eleanor (right) became known as the First Lady of the World for her work with the United Nations. She was part of the first U.S. delegation to that body, chaired its Commission on Human Rights, and helped write its International Declaration of Human Rights. She was the first President's wife to fly abroad.

During World War II Roosevelt took seriously his role as Commander in Chief. He plotted military strategy, appointed key field commanders, and authorized the secret development of the atomic bomb. He formed partnerships with Winston Churchill from Great Britain and, later, with Joseph Stalin of the Soviet Union. The "Big Three" discussed strategies for war and peace, including Roosevelt's idea for starting the United Nations. In 1944, with war raging full tilt, Roosevelt agreed to serve for a fourth term as President. Voters decided not to "change horses in midstream" and returned him to the White House once more.

During the early years of her husband's Presidency, Eleanor Roosevelt tried to broaden the reach of the New Deal to African Americans, working women, children, labor unions, and immigrants. She wrote a daily national newspaper column and met weekly with women reporters. When war took center stage, she shifted her focus to it. Eleanor toured factories, launched battleships, and visited troops around the world. She represented her husband beyond the nation's capital, while he concentrated on military strategy.

In the spring of 1945, Franklin Roosevelt made a visit to the "Little White House," his retreat at Warm Springs, Georgia. Twelve years had passed since his first Inauguration, and it was almost three months since his fourth. (Beginning in 1937, Presidents were inaugurated on January 20 instead of March 4.) Other commitments kept Eleanor from making the trip, but among those joining the

"We look forward to a world founded upon four essential human freedoms
...freedom of speech
...freedom of...worship
...freedom from want
...freedom from fear."

Franklin D. Roosevelt,
State of the Union Address, January 6, 1941

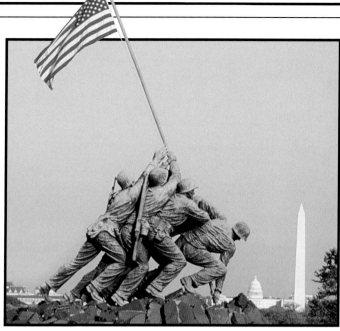

U.S. soldiers fought battles around the globe after the United States joined the fighting of World War II in 1941. U.S. servicemen were part of the Allied forces who stormed the coast of Normandy, France, on D-Day, June 6, 1944 (left), in their march to free Europe from German control. Conquest of Pacific islands, including Japan's Iwo Jima in early 1945, helped turn the tide of battle in the Pacific. Later this battle was recalled in a famous public statue (right).

President was Lucy Page Mercer Rutherford. More than 30 years earlier, while she served as Eleanor's secretary, Lucy had fallen in love with Franklin. Although Franklin ended their affair after it was discovered by his wife, he and Lucy secretly renewed their friendship later on. During their

visit to Georgia, Roosevelt suddenly fell ill while being sketched for a portrait. He reached for his head and observed: "I have a terrific headache." He was having a stroke. Roosevelt never spoke again and died within hours.

The nation was plunged into grief. Roosevelt was the only President whom many adults had ever known, and he had helped them survive some of the country's toughest challenges. Roosevelt's combination as "Dr. New Deal" and "Dr. Win the War" had cured the Great Depression. Within months of his death, World War II would end, too. His pattern of federal involvement in national issues became the norm for future leaders. In 1997 Roosevelt became the fourth President ever—and the only 20th-century one—to be recognized with a national monument in Washington, D.C.

The sudden death of Franklin D. Roosevelt in 1945 stunned U.S. citizens. This musician (left) wept over the death of the President. Tears fell as he played at Roosevelt's memorial service. Roosevelt's lasting importance was recognized with the opening of the Franklin Delano Roosevelt Memorial in 1997. Eleanor Roosevelt is recognized at the structure, too. The monument overlooks the cherry-tree-lined Tidal Basin in Washington, D.C. It offers views of the other three presidential memorials. These honor George Washington, Thomas Jefferson, and Abraham Lincoln.

The First Ladies

★ *Partners, Hostesses, and Advocates* ★

S<small>O FAR</small> every President of the United States has been a man. However each of these men has partnered with a woman to help him with his duties. Most of the women have been wives of Presidents. Occasionally—either because of poor health or lack of interest—a President's wife has declined to serve as First Lady. If a wife is unavailable, daughters, other female relatives, or family friends are asked to step in.

Early on, these presidential partners were addressed with titles such as "Lady," or "Mrs. President." The term "First Lady" became popular by the early 20th century; it recalled the woman's role in the home that is first in importance to the nation.

For more than 100 years the chief duty of the First Lady was to serve as hostess at White House events. However, many of these women, such as Dolley Madison, were more than gracious entertainers; they were shrewd students of politics, too. They knew just how to soothe upset guests and encourage support of their husbands.

Early First Ladies came to the White House with the same background in domestic life as other women of their day. Until the mid-19th

A variety of roles have occupied First Ladies during their partnerships with U.S. Presidents. Louisa Adams (below, right) kept her husband, John Quincy Adams, company in 1828 by winding silk from her own silkworms while he worked nearby. Lucretia Garfield (below, left) helped in the kitchen during 1881. Edith Wilson (far left) stepped in to deal with administrative details in 1919 after a stroke left her husband partially paralyzed. Critics charged that she had become too involved in presidential matters, but her work helped her husband complete his term.

Times change: Entertaining was the focus for First Lady Martha Washington (top, left). Two centuries later Hillary Rodham Clinton (top, right) added political office to the options for First Ladies by winning a seat in the U.S. Senate at the end of her husband's administration. In 2008 she sought the Presidency itself. Mamie Eisenhower (far left) dressed in style for her husband's Inaugural Ball.

century, few had even attended school. Abigail Fillmore was the first President's wife to have held a job of her own (as a school teacher).

When time and interests permit, First Ladies devote attention to national issues and causes. Eleanor Roosevelt expanded the role of the President's wife during her 12 years as First Lady. Because her husband's mobility was limited by polio, she traveled and spoke extensively on his behalf. She pursued her own interests, too—from civil rights to family welfare to benefits for laborers.

In recent decades each First Lady has chosen a program to support. Jacqueline Kennedy established the President's home as a national museum. Lady Bird Johnson supported efforts to beautify the capital city and its monuments. Pat Nixon encouraged national volunteer efforts. Betty Ford spoke out on behalf of handicapped children. Rosalynn Carter took up the cause of the mentally ill, while Nancy Reagan campaigned against illegal drugs, and Barbara Bush promoted the cause of literacy. Hillary Clinton took strong stands on national health care and the welfare of children in this nation and abroad. Laura Bush brought her long-standing interest in literacy to the job of First Lady. Each woman has helped focus national attention on issues that might otherwise have been neglected.

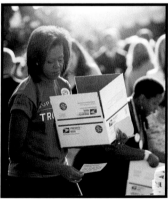

Snapshots (from left to right) show many roles assumed by First Ladies. Eleanor Roosevelt visits with mine workers. Jacqueline Kennedy, who revived interest in White House history, poses in the newly restored residence. Laura Bush stands shoulder-to-shoulder with members of the armed services in a show of wartime support. First African-American First Lady Michelle Obama helps mail postcards to American soldiers serving in the Iraq War.

Harry S. Truman

33RD PRESIDENT OF THE UNITED STATES ★ *1945 – 1953*

NICKNAME	Give 'Em Hell Harry
BORN	May 8, 1884, in Lamar, Mo.
POLITICAL PARTY	Democrat
CHIEF OPPONENT	1st term: none, succeeded Roosevelt; 2nd term: Thomas Edmund Dewey, Republican (1902–1971)
TERM OF OFFICE	April 12, 1945–Jan. 20, 1953
AGE AT INAUGURATION	60 years old
NUMBER OF TERMS	one, plus balance of Franklin D. Roosevelt's term
VICE PRESIDENTS	1st term: none; 2nd term: Alben William Barkley (1877–1956)
FIRST LADY	Elizabeth (Bess) Virginia Wallace Truman (1885–1982), wife (married June 29, 1919)
CHILDREN	Margaret
GEOGRAPHIC SCENE	48 states
NEW STATES ADDED	none
DIED	Dec. 26, 1972, in Independence, Mo.
AGE AT DEATH	88 years old
SELECTED LANDMARKS	Lamar, Mo. (birthplace); Grandview, Mo. (family farm); Key West Little White House Museum, Key West, Fla.; Harry S. Truman National Historic Site (adult home) and Harry S. Truman Library and Museum (and grave), Independence, Mo.

Harry S. Truman's whistle-stop campaign of 1948

WHEN HARRY S. TRUMAN BECAME PRESIDENT after the sudden death of Franklin D. Roosevelt, he was stunned. "I felt like the moon, the stars, and all the planets had fallen on me," he said. Issues such as the use of atomic weapons, tensions with the Soviet Union, and war in Korea dominated his administration.

Truman was no stranger to challenge when he became President. He grew up on a farm in Missouri, and tight family finances made him the only 20th-century President who did not attend college. Truman's meandering career included work as a railroad timekeeper, a farmer, a World War I artillery captain, and a clothing store owner. He entered politics in 1922 as a local administrator; eventually he spent ten years in the U.S. Senate. In 1944 President Franklin D. Roosevelt persuaded Senator Truman to join his fourth-term reelection ticket.

Only months after becoming Vice President, Truman found himself taking the presidential oath of office because President Roosevelt had died. Soon after that, World War II ended in Europe. Truman decided to use a secret weapon — the atomic bomb — to stop the intense fighting that continued with Japan. He hoped this plan would spare the lives of U.S. troops by ending the war quickly and avoiding the need to invade Japan. Thousands of Japanese died instantly in nuclear attacks at Hiroshima and Nagasaki before Japan agreed to stop fighting. Worldwide casualties by the end of the war topped 10 million people, including more than 400,000 Americans.

International events dominated Truman's Presidency. He

Harry S. Truman married Elizabeth "Bess" Wallace when he was 35 (above); the couple met in Sunday school when he was six. Truman's middle initial did not stand for a middle name; his parents used the letter to honor their own fathers, each of whom had a name that started with "S."

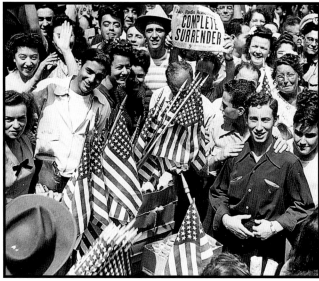

Harry S. Truman met with Allied leaders in July 1945 (left). Celebrations marked the end of World War II (right). The nation enjoyed a postwar boom during Truman's Presidency. Thousands of returning veterans earned free college educations through the G.I. Bill of Rights. Couples who had put off marriage during the war were wed in record numbers and started a "baby boom" of soaring births.

supported the creation of the United Nations and favored the formation of Israel. He used the Marshall Plan to rebuild war-torn Europe and helped form the North Atlantic Treaty Organization (NATO) to fortify the security of western Europe, the U.S., and Canada. In particular, he sought to discourage the expanding influence of the Soviet Union and its political system of communism. Communism—a program of government control over citizens, industries, and finances—was at odds with the U.S. system

of democracy, freedom, and market-based capitalism. A Cold War—one with limited fighting but much hostility, mistrust, and stockpiling of nuclear weapons—developed between the United States, the Soviet Union, and their allies.

As tensions grew between the two "blocs" of countries, Truman committed the United States to "support free peoples who are resisting" conquest. When the Soviet Union lowered its so-called Iron Curtain of restricted access to West Berlin, Truman organized a massive airlift of supplies into the city. When war broke out between communist North Korea and independent South Korea in 1950, Truman developed an international army through the United Nations to "contain" the spread of communism. When anticommunist citizens asked for U.S. assistance in Vietnam, Truman sent aid.

A fear of communism at home developed at the same time as these international worries. U.S. Senator Joseph McCarthy exploited this anxiety by conducting congressional investigations of suspected communists. Among those who eventually joined his efforts

Harry S. Truman took delight in an election-eve headline that mistakenly announced the victory of his opponent in 1948. His whistle-stop campaign effort helped clinch his victory. It took him to six million people during a 31,000-mile train journey. "Give 'em hell, Harry!" yelled supporters, when Truman criticized the uncooperative Congress.

After World War II, Germany and its capital city of Berlin were divided in half; the Soviet Union assumed control over eastern sections, and the U.S., France, and Great Britain oversaw western territories. When the Soviet Union cut off access to West Berlin in June 1948, Western allies delivered necessary supplies to stranded residents (above). Planes landed as often as every few minutes during the Berlin airlift. The Soviet blockade lasted until May 1949.

was a future President, Senator Richard M. Nixon. McCarthy's Red Scare (named after the symbolic communist color) lasted until 1954, when other senators shut down his hearings.

Truman won election in his own right in 1948. As President he tried to extend Roosevelt's New Deal of federal programs with his own 21-point Fair Deal, but most proposals failed to take hold. His efforts to integrate all races in the armed forces met with both favor and controversy.

> ### "The buck stops here."
>
> A presidential motto
> on Harry S. Truman's desk

Challenged by so many difficult issues, Truman left the White House with the lowest approval rating for a President up to that time. In later years respect for Truman's handling of tough times increased; since 1962 historians have consistently ranked him among the top ten Presidents.

Truman and his wife retired to Independence, Missouri. Bess Truman lived to age 97—longer than any other First Lady. She died in 1982, ten years after her husband.

Harry S. Truman knew nothing about the development of the atomic bomb until after he became President near the end of World War II. As President he followed the war's progress by visiting the White House war room (left). After the war Truman supported the European recovery plan devised by Secretary of State George C. Marshall (right). The Marshall Plan shared $12 billion over three years with such countries as England, France, and West Germany. It boosted the American economy and helped create democracies throughout Europe. "Peace, freedom, and world trade are indivisible," noted Truman.

Pollsters and Polling

★ *Sizing Up Public Opinion* ★

ONE OF the first recorded public opinion surveys—conducted in 1824 by a newspaper in Pennsylvania—suggested that Andrew Jackson would win the election. He did not. (His strong showing among voters failed to earn him the support he needed in the electoral college.) Informal measures of public opinion, often called straw polls, continue to this day. So do complex polls conducted by professional researchers, although even these efforts can lead to false predictions.

George Gallup, political pollster

The scientific research methods used by modern pollsters originated in 1935 through the work of statisticians such as George Gallup and Elmo Roper. They competed in 1936 with *Literary Digest,* a magazine known for its respected polls, to predict whether or not Franklin D. Roosevelt would be reelected for a second term of office. Gallup and Roper each predicted victory for Roosevelt, while *Literary Digest* forecast that Alfred Landon would win. Landon, in fact, lost decisively, establishing Gallup and

Roper's reputations as pollsters.

Analysis of the *Literary Digest* poll revealed unintended bias in the magazine's choice of whom to survey. By targeting people listed as owners of cars and telephones, they had inadvertently surveyed individuals who matched the more affluent background of Republican voters. Instead, Gallup and Roper deliberately had interviewed people chosen to represent the mix of the overall population.

Over the years pollsters have worked to improve the accuracy of their results. They learned to survey a large number of people, often 1,000 or more individuals. They worked to create questions free from unintended pressures on how best to answer them. Pollsters tried to account for people who might give misleading answers, too. Someone who objected to candidates for personal reasons—such as their gender or race—might be reluctant to admit that prejudice to an interviewer, for example. Polling results typically include a margin of error percentage that can be applied to the surveys' results.

Even so, pollsters still make mistakes.

The 1948 presidential race provides one famous example. Pollsters uniformly predicted a victory by Republican challenger Thomas E. Dewey. Instead Harry S. Truman won by two million votes. The polling firms concluded that, because they had stopped polling several weeks before Election Day, they had missed late-breaking trends among voters.

Today polling is a constant for the election season. Some organizations conduct daily tracking polls that ask the same question of new samples of respondents over and over in an effort to chart a candidate's level of support over time. Other polls measure voter opinions at specific moments during the campaign season, such as after a presidential debate or major political event.

Polling continues even on Election Day with pollsters interviewing voters after they've cast their ballots. These so-called exit polls help news organizations predict the outcome of the day's voting even as the ballots are still being counted. Only after the final tallies are in can pollsters breathe a sigh of relief—or begin to investigate what went wrong this time and identify how to improve their methods for the next election season.

Pollsters use written questionnaires (above, a 1944 Gallup survey), make phone calls, and stop people on the street in their efforts to predict support for presidential candidates. The accuracy of polls is put to the test on Election Day (left, citizens cast their ballots) when these forecasts are measured up against the final results.

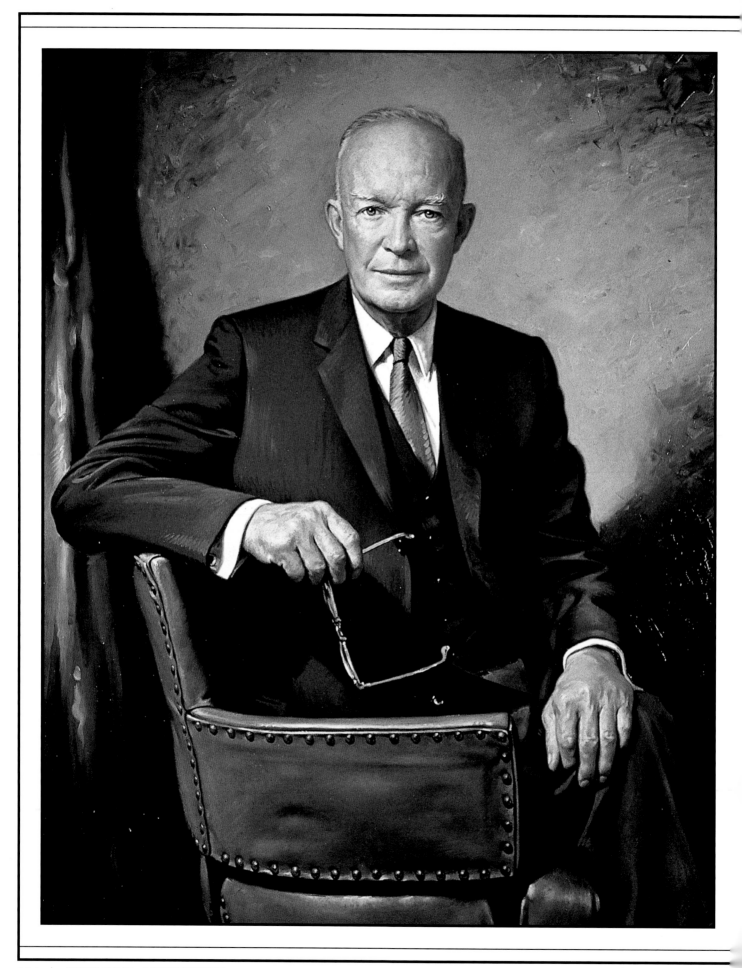

Dwight D. Eisenhower

34TH PRESIDENT OF THE UNITED STATES ★ *1953 – 1961*

NICKNAME	Ike
BORN	Oct. 14, 1890, in Denison, Tex.
POLITICAL PARTY	Republican
CHIEF OPPONENT	1st and 2nd terms: Adlai Ewing Stevenson, Democrat (1900–1965)
TERM OF OFFICE	Jan. 20, 1953–Jan. 20, 1961
AGE AT INAUGURATION	62 years old
NUMBER OF TERMS	two
VICE PRESIDENT	Richard M. Nixon (1913–1994)
FIRST LADY	Marie (Mamie) Geneva Doud Eisenhower (1896–1979), wife (married July 1, 1916)
CHILDREN	John, plus a son died young
GEOGRAPHIC SCENE	48 states
NEW STATES ADDED	Alaska, Hawaii (1959)
DIED	March 28, 1969, in Washington, D.C.
AGE AT DEATH	78 years old
SELECTED LANDMARKS	Eisenhower Birthplace State Historical Park, Denison, Tex.; Eisenhower National Historic Site, Gettysburg, Pa. (retirement home); Eisenhower Center (including presidential library, museum, family home, grave), Abilene, Kans.

The Eisenhowers on their wedding day

LIKE GENERALS GEORGE WASHINGTON AND ULYSSES S. GRANT, General Dwight David Eisenhower became President thanks to his popularity as a war hero. Eisenhower—the man who helped bring victory to Europe during World War II—sought to keep peace at home and abroad after becoming President. His moderate political views earned the Republican Party new respect.

Although born in Texas, Eisenhower was raised in Abilene, Kansas, where his father worked in a creamery. He learned lessons about war and peace at an early age while growing up there with five brothers. The boys, all of whom took turns using the nickname "Ike," never hesitated to come to blows among themselves or with others when arguments arose. Even as a youngster, Eisenhower enjoyed studying military history. He went on to graduate from the U.S. Military Academy at West Point and take up a career in the Army. Later that year he met Marie "Mamie" Doud; the couple married soon after.

For the next 26 years, Eisenhower's Army duties took him to bases throughout the United States as well as to the Panama Canal Zone and the Philippines. Along the way he finished first in his class at officer training school and did desk duty at war offices in Washington, D.C. Much to his regret he missed out on World War I combat; he was instead assigned to train others to fight.

By the time of World War II, however, Eisenhower's leadership skills and organizational talents earned him key military appointments. He commanded the combined Allied forces that overran

Dwight D. Eisenhower played football at West Point (above) until a knee injury ended his athletic career. His skills as a military leader helped carry him to the White House years later.

Dwight D. Eisenhower served as supreme commander of all Allied forces during the World War II campaigns that liberated North Africa and Europe from German and Italian occupation forces. In June 1944 Eisenhower urged members of the U.S. 101st Airborne Division (left) to accomplish their mission during the impending D-Day invasion of France. Later on, Eisenhower toured so many countries as President—27 in all—that his travels were written up in NATIONAL GEOGRAPHIC.

enemy troops in North Africa, Sicily, Italy, and northern Europe. Before the end of the war, he had risen to the Army's highest rank— five-star general. One soldier who spotted the rows of stars on Eisenhower's uniform exclaimed: "Cripes! The whole Milky Way!"

After the war, Eisenhower served as chief of staff for the Army, president of Columbia University, and commander of international troops in Europe. As early as 1943, people had suggested that Eisenhower run for President with either political party. Happy with Army life, he dismissed the idea.

Finally, in 1952, he agreed to run for President as a Republican. Eisenhower faced the same opponent that year and four years later—Adlai Stevenson. Eisenhower's signature grin, victory wave, and record of wartime service encouraged voters to proclaim: "We like Ike!" They proved it by awarding Eisenhower a sizable majority of votes in each election.

Challenges from the Truman administration carried over into Eisenhower's Presidency. Peace talks finally ended the fighting in Korea in 1953. The conflict had killed or wounded more than three million people, including 34,000 Americans. Relations

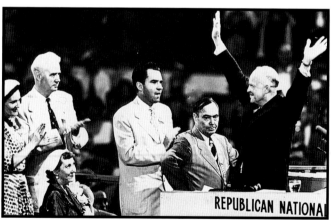

Republicans reclaimed the White House after a 20-year absence thanks to the popular appeal of party nominee Dwight D. Eisenhower (left and right). During his Presidency "Ike" authorized construction of the nation's interstate highway system and collaborated with Canada to create the St. Lawrence Seaway linking the Great Lakes with the Atlantic Ocean. By the end of his administration, citizens could chant: "Ike is nifty, Ike is nifty; started out with 48; ended up with 50," because Alaska and Hawaii had joined the Union.

President-elect Eisenhower visited U.S. troops in Korea during 1952 (left) as part of his efforts to end U.S. military involvement there. Senator Joseph McCarthy continued to inflame U.S. fears of communism at home until his high-profile congressional hearings (right) were shut down in 1954. The domino theory—the idea that communism could spread from one vulnerable country to the next like a row of tumbling dominoes—led the President to develop his Eisenhower Doctrine. This policy fostered increased U.S. assistance of anticommunist efforts in Vietnam during his administration.

with the Soviet Union remained tense. Although Eisenhower urged the Soviets to consider nuclear disarmament, or the reduction of atomic weapons, neither side seemed willing to trust the other. In 1957 the Soviets launched the world's first satellite, Sputnik. Americans feared it might be armed with nuclear weapons. Three years later the Soviets were equally alarmed when they captured a U.S. pilot flying a U-2 spy plane over their country.

At home, Eisenhower worked to make the United States live up to its ideals of freedom and equality. "There must be no second-class citizens in this country," he wrote. The President sent federal troops to Little Rock, Arkansas, to enforce the Supreme Court's *Brown* v. *Board of Education* ruling. This landmark decision called for public schools to be desegregated, or open to children of all races. He also bolstered civil rights by signing new voting laws.

In 1961 Eisenhower and his wife retired to a farm they had purchased in 1950 near Gettysburg, Pennsylvania. Because Eisenhower's career had kept them forever on the go (they moved 28 times during their marriage), this was the first home they ever owned. Although several heart attacks threatened the former President's health, he enjoyed writing his memoirs, playing golf, painting landscapes, and keeping a finger in politics. He died in 1969. Mamie died 10 years later.

Black children and white children in the U.S. were routinely educated in separate schools (left) when Dwight D. Eisenhower became President. Dwight and Mamie Eisenhower (above) were a popular presidential couple. Mamie acted as a traditional hostess during her years as First Lady. She restored the custom, discontinued during World War II, of holding an annual White House Easter Egg Roll. Eisenhower changed Franklin D. Roosevelt's name for the presidential retreat in Maryland from Shangri-La to Camp David in honor of their grandson.

John F. Kennedy

35TH PRESIDENT OF THE UNITED STATES ★ *1961 – 1963*

NICKNAME	JFK
BORN	May 29, 1917, in Brookline, Mass.
POLITICAL PARTY	Democrat

John F. Kennedy sits perched on a scooter with mother, Rose, and siblings Eunice, Kathleen, Rosemary, and Joe, Jr.

CHIEF OPPONENT	Richard M. Nixon (1913–1994)
TERM OF OFFICE	Jan. 20, 1961–Nov. 22, 1963
AGE AT INAUGURATION	43 years old
NUMBER OF TERMS	one (cut short by assassination)
VICE PRESIDENT	Lyndon B. Johnson (1908–1973)
FIRST LADY	Jacqueline Lee Bouvier Kennedy (1929–1994), wife (married Sept. 12, 1953)
CHILDREN	Caroline, John, plus a son died young
GEOGRAPHIC SCENE	50 states
DIED	Nov. 22, 1963, in Dallas, Tex.
AGE AT DEATH	46 years old
SELECTED LANDMARKS	Brookline, Mass. (birthplace); Hammersmith Farm, Newport, R.I. ("summer White House"); Sixth Floor Museum, Dallas, Tx.; John F. Kennedy Library and Museum, Boston, Mass.; Arlington National Cemetery, Arlington, Va.

JOHN FITZGERALD KENNEDY WAS ELECTED by the narrowest popular voting margin in history and served as President for only about 1,000 days before he was assassinated. Yet he remains a central figure of the American Presidency. His eloquent calls for peace, justice, and national service inspired action among countless citizens during his lifetime and continue to influence others today.

After his death the Kennedy administration was compared to Camelot, the legendary ancient realm of the fair-minded King Arthur. Kennedy's birth to a privileged family made the perfect place to begin the comparison. His father hoped one of his four sons would become President; eventually three of them campaigned for that office. John (nicknamed Jack) attended prestigious schools and graduated with honors from Harvard University. Although plagued by a string of childhood illnesses, he was athletic, playful, and handsome. A decorated World War II naval officer, Jack took up the family's presidential hopes after his older brother, Joseph, died in combat.

Kennedy met Jacqueline Bouvier during his six years as a U.S. congressman from Massachusetts. Jackie was sophisticated, charming, and beautiful. The pair were married in 1953, soon after Jack became a U.S. senator. Kennedy sought the Democratic presidential nomination in 1960. "We stand today on the edge of a New Frontier,"

John F. Kennedy became a World War II hero after the patrol torpedo boat under his command (left) was destroyed by a Japanese warship (right). Kennedy swam with the surviving crew members to safety several miles away, towing along one injured sailor by clamping the man's life jacket strap in his teeth. When asked later how he became a hero, Kennedy replied: "It was easy—they sank my boat."

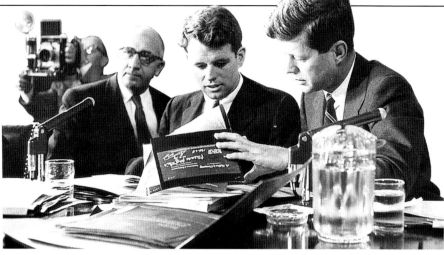

John F. Kennedy's family moved into the White House (left) a few weeks after his Inauguration. His wife, Jacqueline, was an active First Lady while mothering their young children, Caroline and John. Jackie promoted the performing arts and helped foster the Camelot image of the Kennedy Presidency. John F. Kennedy included his brother Bobby (above, center) among his closest advisers while President.

he proclaimed after winning the nomination. Kennedy narrowly defeated Richard Nixon in a tight race. Illegal voting in key states like Texas and Illinois may have helped seal his victory. Kennedy is the only Catholic to be elected President.

Conflicts in the Cold War dominated much of Kennedy's Presidency. First, the U.S. government secretly tried to overthrow Cuba's new communist dictator, Fidel Castro, by helping Cuban exiles invade their homeland at the Bay of Pigs. U.S. involvement proved embarrassing when the mission failed. Then tensions flared when the Soviet Union built a wall dividing East from West Berlin

in Germany. Next the two superpowers narrowly avoided nuclear war during the Cuban missile crisis, a tense standoff resulting from the U.S. discovery of Soviet warheads in Cuba. Secretly Kennedy fought the spread of communism elsewhere by continuing U.S. support of anticommunists in Vietnam. Publicly he urged Americans to win the "space race" against the Soviets by sending astronauts to the moon and back. Cold War tensions eased somewhat in 1963 after the two nations signed a treaty banning most nuclear testing.

Civil rights, including the freedom for all races to vote, was a dominant issue, too. At first Kennedy

Both the Soviet Union and the United States increased their military arsenals (left) during the early years of John F. Kennedy's administration. Cold War tensions were reduced shortly before Kennedy's death when he signed a nuclear-test-ban treaty (right) with the United States, the Soviet Union, and the United Kingdom, outlawing atomic explosions in the atmosphere, space, and underwater.

John F. Kennedy visited coal miners (left) as part of his presidential campaign in 1960. Near the end of Kennedy's administration more than 200,000 people took part in a March on Washington to commemorate the 100th anniversary of Abraham Lincoln's Emancipation Proclamation. Martin Luther King, Jr., delivered his famous "I have a dream" speech (right) to mark the occasion.

relied on the Justice Department, headed by his younger brother Robert (Bobby), to aid this cause. Later the President publicly supported racial equality. Much of the civil rights legislation Kennedy favored became law in tribute to him after his assassination.

Kennedy was shot and killed on November 22, 1963, while touring Dallas, Texas, in a presidential motorcade. More than a hundred nations sent representatives to his funeral in Washington, D.C. Anyone who could find a television "attended" the event, too. All were moved by the solemn processions, by Jackie's dignity, and by the composure of their children. Hearts broke as three-year-old John-John saluted his father's coffin.

The identity of Kennedy's assassin remains a subject of speculation. Gunman Lee Harvey Oswald was charged with the death but was himself murdered before he could be tried. Repeated investigations have failed to confirm theories that others may have helped Oswald kill the President.

The Camelot image of the Kennedy years endures, even as new facts emerge about the era (such as the extent of the covert, or secret, support his administration gave to anticommunists in Vietnam, and his extramarital affairs while in office). Jack's brother Bobby became a U.S. senator; he was assassinated in 1968 while running for President. His youngest brother, Edward (Teddy), is a U.S. senator; he sought his party's nomination for President in 1980. Jackie remarried five years after her husband's death. She died from cancer in her mid-60s and was buried beside Jack at Arlington National Cemetery.

> "Ask not what your country can do for you— ask what you can do for your country."

John F. Kennedy,
Inaugural Address, January 20, 1961

John F. Kennedy was the youngest man ever elected President. (Teddy Roosevelt was the youngest President by succession, not election.) Kennedy was also the youngest one to die, when an assassin shot him in a motorcade (left) just three years after his election. Jacqueline Kennedy modeled her husband's funeral after Abraham Lincoln's. Kennedy's casket even lay in state at the U.S. Capitol on the same platform that was used for Lincoln.

Presidents Who Died in Office

★ The Mysterious Twenty-Year Curse ★

EIGHT OF the nation's Presidents have died before completing their terms of office. Half of these men were victims of illnesses; the others were assassinated. Oddly, seven of these deaths have occurred in a regular pattern. The winner of every five elections from 1840 to 1960 has died before completing his final term. This circumstance has been called the 20-year jinx or the 20-year curse.

President Kennedy lies in state, 1963.

The first President to die in office was William Henry Harrison. He died on April 4, 1841, exactly one month after his Inauguration, from complications of a cold. Abraham Lincoln's first term began 20 years after Harrison's. Lincoln died on April 15, 1865,

within a week of the end of the Civil War, after being shot by a supporter of the defeated South.

Twenty years after Lincoln's first election, James A. Garfield took office. Garfield was shot on July 2, 1881, by a deranged former political supporter. He died two and a half months later.

President William McKinley was shot 20 years afterward. Early in his second term, a disgruntled factory worker fired on him in a receiving line. McKinley died eight days later, on Sept. 14, 1901.

The next two sitting Presidents to die five terms apart were victims of natural causes. Warren G. Harding died suddenly on Aug. 2, 1923. Doctors think he may have had a heart attack. Franklin D. Roosevelt was killed by a stroke, a brain injury caused by improper blood flow in the head. He died a few months into his fourth term of office on April 12, 1945.

John F. Kennedy, the last President to die in office, and on a 20-year cycle, was assassinated on Nov. 22, 1963, in Dallas, Texas.

Zachary Taylor was the only President who

The nation mourned the death of Abraham Lincoln after the Civil War by hanging ribbons (far left) in their windows to honor "the late lamented President Lincoln." His body was drawn through the nation's capital in a solemn funeral procession (left) before traveling home to Illinois for burial.

In 1881 Alexander Graham Bell tried to find the bullet lodged in James A. Garfield by an assassin (left). Bell's early metal detector failed, and Garfield died of blood poisoning. Presidential deaths make front-page news (above).

died in office outside of the 20-year death cycle. He died from cholera on July 9, 1850.

Ronald Reagan finally broke the 120-year history of cyclical presidential deaths. Even so, his life was threatened by an assassination attempt in 1981. Prompt modern medical attention saved his life.

Other assassination attempts were made against Presidents Andrew Jackson, Harry S. Truman, and Gerald Ford. An assassin threatened President-elect Franklin D. Roosevelt, too. No Vice Presidents have been assassinated, but seven have died in office.

Often the bodies of fallen Presidents—even those who die after their terms are over—"lie in state." During this honor the coffin of the deceased is temporarily displayed on a platform, and visitors file past the casket in tribute. Sometimes the coffin lid is open to show the body inside; other times it is closed and covered with the U.S. flag. Seven Presidents have lain in state in the White House East Room; ten others have rested in the rotunda of the U.S. Capitol. Ronald Reagan was the first President to receive this honor (in 2004) since the death of Lyndon B. Johnson in 1973.

The death of a President brings shock and sorrow to the entire nation, not just to relatives. Mourners bade farewell to William McKinley as his coffin was loaded onto his funeral train (left). John F. Kennedy's family observed his funeral procession (right) while millions of citizens watched via live television broadcast.

Lyndon B. Johnson

36TH PRESIDENT OF THE UNITED STATES ★ *1963 – 1969*

NICKNAME	LBJ
BORN	Aug. 27, 1908, near Stonewall, Tex.
POLITICAL PARTY	Democrat
CHIEF OPPONENTS	1st term: none, succeeded Kennedy; 2nd term: Barry Morris Goldwater, Republican (1909–1998)
TERM OF OFFICE	Nov. 22, 1963–Jan. 20, 1969
AGE AT INAUGURATION	55 years old
NUMBER OF TERMS	one, plus balance of John F. Kennedy's term
VICE PRESIDENTS	1st term: none; 2nd term: Hubert Horatio Humphrey (1911–1978)
FIRST LADY	Claudia Alta (Lady Bird) Taylor Johnson (1912–2007), wife (married Nov. 17, 1934)
CHILDREN	Lynda, Luci
GEOGRAPHIC SCENE	50 states
DIED	Jan. 22, 1973, near San Antonio, Tex.
AGE AT DEATH	64 years old
SELECTED LANDMARKS	Lyndon B. Johnson National Historical Park, Stonewall, Tex., and Johnson City, Tex. (includes visitor center, reconstructed birthplace, school, boyhood home, Johnson Settlement, "Texas White House," LBJ Ranch, and grave); Lyndon Baines Johnson Library and Museum, University of Texas, Austin, Tex.

LBJ and Lady Bird by the U.S. Capitol

LYNDON BAINES JOHNSON CHANNELED ENERGY from the nation's grief over the sudden death of John F. Kennedy into creating a living memorial to the slain leader. Johnson called this legacy the Great Society. He envisioned a nation that offered opportunity, prosperity, and fairness to all citizens. His tireless efforts for this cause brought considerable improvement to the lives of racial minorities and the poor. These accomplishments became overshadowed, however, by escalating U.S. involvement in an increasingly controversial war in Vietnam.

"No words are sad enough to express our sense of loss," President Johnson observed two days after the funeral of John F. Kennedy. "No words are strong enough to express our determination to continue the forward thrust of America that he began." Johnson, a veteran politician, was uniquely prepared to lead that effort.

The son of a farmer and legislator, Johnson grew up in rural Texas. His childhood mixed hard times with breaks for marble games, endless chores with a memorable visit to the Alamo. After finishing high school, he drifted around California for two years doing odd jobs. Later he enrolled at Southwest Texas State Teachers

Lyndon B. Johnson became the only U.S. President to take the oath of office on an airplane when he was sworn in aboard Air Force One (above) two hours after the assassination of John F. Kennedy. The plane was preparing to take him back to Washington, D.C., along with Kennedy's body. Johnson was flanked by his wife on one side and Kennedy's widow (at right) on the other. Jacqueline Kennedy still wore the clothes stained during the shooting of her husband.

Lyndon B. Johnson gathered to celebrate his Inauguration in 1965 with family and his new Vice President, Hubert H. Humphrey. The Cold War had figured prominently in his reelection. Voters were troubled when Johnson's opponent spoke about the reasonableness of using nuclear weapons in a war. Democrats attacked this "hawkish," or warlike, position with a television commercial that shifted from the scene of a child playing with a daisy to the exploding mushroom cloud of a nuclear bomb.

College; he graduated in 1930. Johnson met his future wife, Claudia "Lady Bird" Taylor, while working for a U.S. congressman. Her nickname gave the couple the same initials after they were married. In future years, their daughters, their Texas ranch, and even a family dog bore names that yielded the trademark L.B.J. initials.

Johnson was elected to the House of Representatives six consecutive times beginning in 1937. He received a Silver Star for World War II service while on leave from Congress. He earned the nickname "Landslide Lyndon" in 1948 when he won his first U.S. Senate seat by nothing like a landslide—just 87 votes. He was reelected overwhelmingly six years later. In 1960 Kennedy asked the influential senator to be his running mate. (He had just defeated Johnson in a spirited contest for their party's presidential nomination.) Johnson's southern background helped secure their victory that fall.

After Kennedy was assassinated three years later, Johnson suggested the nation create an improved Great Society as a way of commemorating the slain President. Using skills from his years as a powerful U.S. senator, Johnson influenced Congress to pass sweeping laws. Among other things, this legislation secured fair voting rights for minorities, funded education programs, battled poverty and crime, encouraged fair housing practices, strengthened access to health care, aided environmental cleanup and conservation, and established federal services such as the Public Broadcasting Service. No President has ever been more successful at ushering legislation through Congress.

Johnson won outright election to the Presidency in the midst of this burst of legislation. Voters agreed to go "All the Way With LBJ" in 1964. He truly was "Landslide Lyndon" by then, earning 16 million more votes than his opponent. This edge gave him 61 percent of the popular vote.

The Vietnam War undercut Johnson's domestic triumphs. Before his administration was over, the United States had dropped more tons of bombs over the divided countries of North and

As President, Lyndon B. Johnson (above, at left) declared a "war on poverty." He worked two shifts a day, sleeping a few hours at night and napping in his pajamas between shifts during the day. Johnson was famous for giving "the treatment"—intense verbal and physical communication—to anyone whose support he needed. "You really felt as if a St. Bernard had licked your face for an hour, had pawed you all over," explained one recipient. Few could resist his pitch.

"Let this session of Congress be known as the session which did more for civil rights than the last hundred sessions combined."

Lyndon B. Johnson, State of the Union Address, January 8, 1964

Race relations and civil rights were a dominant issue during the Presidency of Lyndon B. Johnson. Johnson sought to end practices of discrimination such as segregated schools and waiting rooms (left) by signing new legislation to protect human rights regardless of race (center). He appointed the first African American to the Supreme Court in 1967—Thurgood Marshall (right). His emphasis on Civil Rights kindled a shift in the South to the Republican Party.

South Vietnam than it had used in Europe during all of World War II. Yet, despite these efforts, North Vietnamese communists were more committed than ever in the fight to reunite North with South. Widespread opposition developed to the war among U.S. citizens, particularly as the growing level of their nation's involvement became fully known.

Public protests about the Vietnam War forced Johnson to abandon thoughts of running for reelection in 1968. Instead, he pledged to seek peace between the North and South Vietnamese. His efforts were unsuccessful; the two sides had difficulty even agreeing what shape to make their negotiating table.

In 1969 Johnson retired with Lady Bird to the LBJ Ranch near Johnson City, Texas. He wrote his memoirs, managed his farm, and regretted the bitter end of his Presidency. Johnson had had a severe heart attack years earlier while a U.S. senator; he suffered two more during his retirement. The last one proved fatal. After lying in state at the U.S. Capitol, President Johnson's body was buried at his family ranch. In the decades following her husband's death, Lady Bird Johnson worked tirelessly for her favorite causes. She died in 2007 at the age of 94.

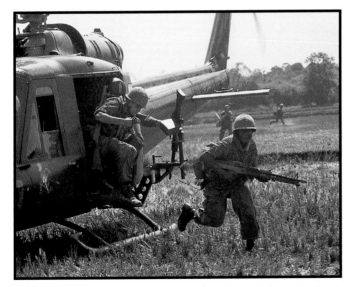

Sticking with the Cold War instincts of earlier Presidents, Lyndon B. Johnson insisted that the Vietnam War had to be won to prevent the spread of communism throughout Southeast Asia. Secretly he sent more and more aid to anticommunist South Vietnam until, by the end of his Presidency, more than half a million U.S. soldiers were on duty there.

The Johnsons enjoyed the beauty of the hill country in their native Texas (above). During their years together in the White House, Lady Bird promoted legislation to limit unsightly billboards along highways. She encouraged better landscaping of public areas in the nation's capital and elsewhere, too. Later she promoted the study and cultivation of wildflowers around the country.

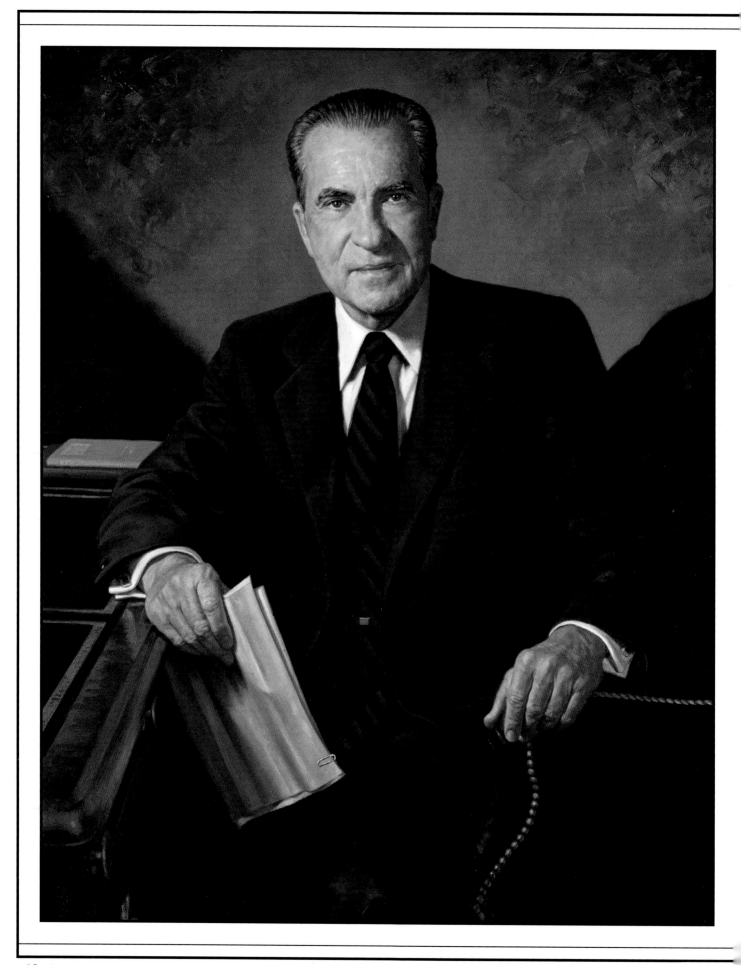

Richard Nixon

37TH PRESIDENT OF THE UNITED STATES ★ *1969 – 1974*

NICKNAME Tricky Dick

BORN Jan. 9, 1913, in Yorba Linda, Calif.

POLITICAL PARTY Republican

CHIEF OPPONENTS 1st term: Hubert Horatio Humphrey, Democrat (1911–1978) and George Corley Wallace, American Independent (1919–1998); 2nd term: George Stanley McGovern, Democrat (1922–present)

TERM OF OFFICE Jan. 20, 1969–Aug. 9, 1974

AGE AT INAUGURATION 56 years old

NUMBER OF TERMS two (cut short by resignation)

VICE PRESIDENTS 1st term and 2nd term (partial): Spiro Theodore Agnew (1918–1996); 2nd term (balance): Gerald R. Ford (1913–2006)

FIRST LADY Thelma Catherine (Pat) Ryan Nixon (1912–1993), wife (married June 21, 1940)

CHILDREN Patricia, Julie

GEOGRAPHIC SCENE 50 states

DIED April 22, 1994, in New York, N.Y.

AGE AT DEATH 81 years old

SELECTED LANDMARKS Richard Nixon Library and Birthplace (includes museum and grave), Yorba Linda, Calif.

Richard Nixon vacationed in Florida with his wife, daughters, and future son-in-law before embarking on his 1968 presidential campaign.

RICHARD MILHOUS NIXON WAS FORCED TO RESIGN from office after the public learned how he had encouraged the use of illegal activity to support his administration. He is the only U.S. President to resign, and the only one to leave office alive without completing his term. The importance of Nixon's official accomplishments in office are diminished by his serious abuses of presidential power.

Throughout his long political career, Nixon made much of his humble origins. He grew up in Southern California where his family struggled against threats of poverty and ill health. Two of his four brothers died by the time he was 20. Nixon paid for his education at nearby Whittier College by working long hours as manager of the vegetable section in his father's grocery store. Later he graduated from Duke University Law School in North Carolina and opened a law practice back home. He met his future wife, Thelma "Pat" Ryan, when they acted together in a local play. He served as a noncombat naval officer in the Pacific during World War II.

Nixon won seats in the U.S. House in 1946 and the U.S. Senate in 1950. By then, people were calling him "Tricky Dick" because of "dirty tricks" (including illegal campaign funding and sensational character attacks) he used to get elected. He won notice for his part in Senator Joseph McCarthy's "Red Scare" search for communists. Then Nixon became Dwight D. Eisenhower's Vice President. He lost the 1960 presidential race to John F. Kennedy and the 1962 California governor's race before being elected President in 1968.

Richard Nixon, who served in the U.S. Navy during World War II (above), contributed to a growing public mistrust of government during his Presidency. The more often he used his trademark phrase, "Let me make one thing perfectly clear," the less sure citizens became that they were hearing the truth. This "credibility gap" had begun after World War II as the public realized government actions did not always match government claims.

Richard Nixon spoke with astronauts in space (left) after their successful landing on the moon, July 20, 1969. Nixon toured the country with enthusiasm whether he was campaigning or appearing as President (right). Nixon's career was the subject of more than 50 cover stories for Time *magazine. During his administration the nation's voting age was lowered from 21 to 18 by Constitutional amendment.*

In the White House at last, Nixon was eager to mark his place in history. At home he tried to improve welfare, protect the environment, and reduce crime. He fought double-digit inflation caused by large military budgets and energy shortages. He often ignored or stretched laws that met with his disapproval (from those that regulated wiretapping procedures to those that funded Native American education programs). Federal courts often overruled him.

Abroad Nixon improved relations between the United States and the communist nations of China and the Soviet Union. He made celebrated trips to each country, and he signed new agreements limiting the spread of nuclear weapons. Although Nixon entered the White House with a pledge to end the Vietnam War, the task proved difficult. Even as more troops came home, fighting spread to nearby countries. North Vietnam took control of South Vietnam in 1975, two years after the nations made "peace" and U.S. troops had withdrawn. Many Americans were bitter about the war's costs: 58,000 U.S. lives and $110 billion.

Nixon expanded on his use of "dirty tricks" while President. He and other staff members broke laws in their efforts to discover embarrassing information about his rivals and enemies (a list of more than 40,000 names). They hired people to commit burglaries and tap phones in their search for "dirt."

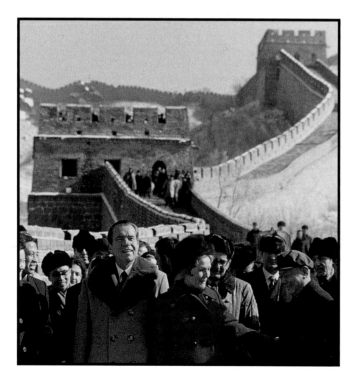

In 1972 Richard Nixon became the first U.S. President to visit China. Nixon helped dissolve hostilities between the two nations by meeting with communist leaders and visiting landmarks like the Great Wall (left). Three months later he met with communist leaders in the Soviet Union.

They silenced their helpers with "hush money," spent federal campaign funds improperly, made illegal use of government records, and filed false income tax reports.

In 1972 Nixon's associates hired men to burglarize Democratic Party offices at the Watergate building in Washington, D.C. (They hoped to gain insider information there that would help Nixon be reelected later that year.) The Watergate scandal that ended Nixon's Presidency began after the burglars were caught. The investigation of the break-in did not progress quickly enough, though, to prevent Nixon's landslide reelection in 1972.

For more than two years Nixon and others tried to hide their involvement in the crime. They denied that Nixon was involved in planning the caper or its cover-up. Newspaper reporters and members of Congress led increasingly intense investigations into possible crimes. Eventually the Supreme Court forced Nixon to release secret tape recordings he had made of his White House conversations. The tapes confirmed that Nixon had lied about his innocence in

"Pat" Nixon earned her nickname for being born near St. Patrick's Day. She traveled widely as First Lady and promoted volunteer work. Daughters Julie (left) and Tricia were married after their father's election.

planning illegal activities and covering them up.

On August 9, 1974, Nixon resigned from office. Otherwise he faced the likelihood of impeachment by the House of Representatives and removal from office through a trial in the U.S. Senate. More than 20 other people, including top White House staff members, a former attorney general, and a former secretary of commerce were found guilty of crimes, fined, and/or sent to jail. Nixon's first Vice President, Spiro Agnew, had resigned from office in an earlier scandal involving bribery and income tax evasion. After Agnew's successor, Gerald Ford, became President, he spared Nixon from prosecution by pardoning him for any crimes he may have committed.

Nixon lived another two decades. He and his wife eventually settled in the New York City area. He died in 1994. Historians have rated Nixon's Presidency as one of the worst in U.S. history. Classified documents from his administration continue to be made public, allowing scholars to further evaluate his reputation and legacy.

"Those who hate you don't win unless you hate them. And then you destroy yourself."

Richard M. Nixon, parting speech, August 9, 1974

Richard Nixon announced his plans to resign from office during a televised address in August 1974 (left). Scandals resulting from the bungled burglary two years earlier of offices in the Watergate building (right) had led citizens to call for his removal from office (center). Nixon had defused an earlier scandal with another emotional television appearance. In 1952 he preserved his spot as Vice President on Dwight D. Eisenhower's ticket by denying, during a televised speech, his illegal use of campaign funds. His remarks became known as the "Checkers speech" because he admitted that the family dog, Checkers, had been a political gift.

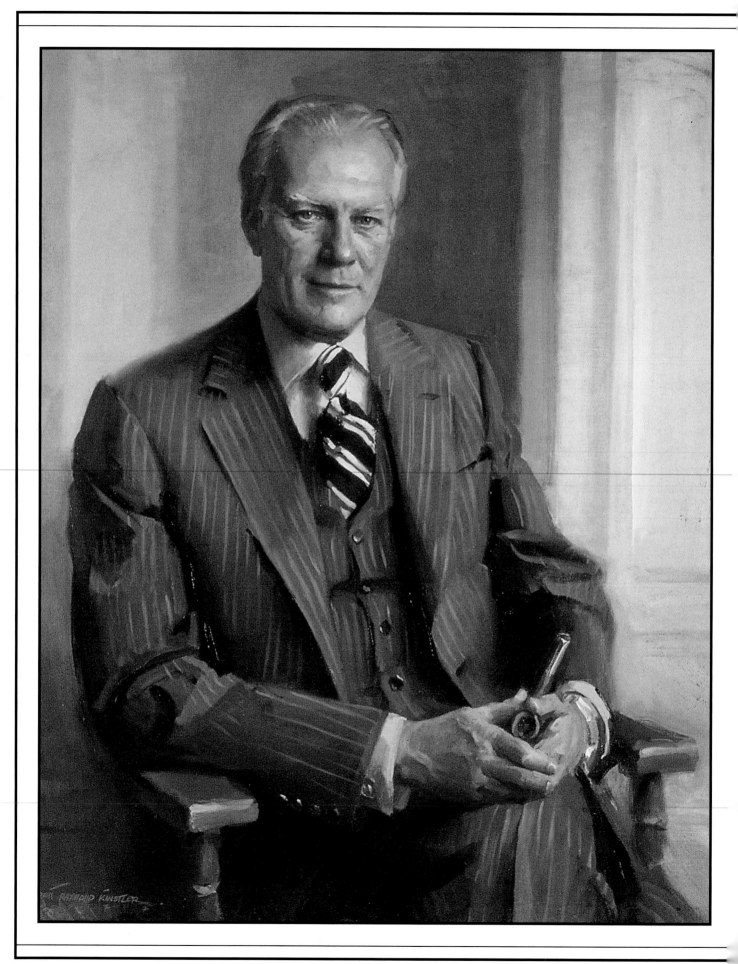

Gerald R. Ford

38TH PRESIDENT OF THE UNITED STATES ★ *1974 – 1977*

Gerald R. Ford

NICKNAME	Jerry
BORN	July 14, 1913, in Omaha, Nebr.
POLITICAL PARTY	Republican
CHIEF OPPONENT	none, succeeded Nixon
TERM OF OFFICE	Aug. 9, 1974–Jan. 20, 1977
AGE AT INAUGURATION	61 years old
NUMBER OF TERMS	one (partial)
VICE PRESIDENT	Nelson Aldrich Rockefeller (1908–1979)
FIRST LADY	Elizabeth (Betty) Bloomer Warren Ford (1918–present), wife (married Oct. 15, 1948)
CHILDREN	Michael, John, Steven, Susan
GEOGRAPHIC SCENE	50 states
DIED	Dec. 26, 2006
AGE AT DEATH	93 years old
SELECTED LANDMARKS	Omaha, Nebr. (birthplace); Gerald R. Ford Library, Ann Arbor, Mich.; Gerald R. Ford Museum (and grave), Grand Rapids, Mich.

Gerald R. Ford rejected offers to play professional football after college and went to law school instead. Years later, Lyndon B. Johnson joked that Ford had "played football too long without a helmet." Ford replied by showing up at a public event with an old helmet that no longer fit. "Heads tend to swell in Washington," he joked.

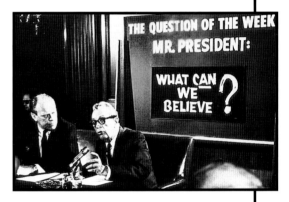

Gerald Rudolph Ford is the only President never elected to the offices of President or Vice President. He was promoted to both roles during the turbulent political changes of the early 1970s. In the wake of President Richard Nixon's resignation, Ford worked to restore the confidence of citizens in their Chief Executive.

Ford came to the Presidency after serving 25 years as one of Michigan's representatives to Congress. A native of Nebraska, he was a graduate of the University of Michigan and Yale University Law School. During World War II, he earned ten battle stars for combat duty in the Navy. He married Elizabeth "Betty" Bloomer Warren, a former professional dancer, in 1948.

Ford, who joined Congress in 1949, became Vice President in 1973. He was appointed to the post by then President Nixon after Vice President Spiro T. Agnew was forced by scandals to resign from office. When the scandal-plagued Nixon himself resigned in disgrace some eight months later, Ford became President. "This is an hour of history that troubles our minds and hurts our hearts," Ford noted. Yet he praised the soundness of the nation for its successful transfer of power from Nixon to himself. "Our Constitution works; our great Republic is a government of laws and not of men. Here the people rule," he said.

With words like these and with honest behavior, Ford began restoring citizen trust in the government. His efforts to resolve other challenges—such as double-digit inflation, high unemployment, and economic recession—were less successful. Ford drew criticism, too, for granting Nixon a full pardon for crimes committed while President. In a close contest in 1976, Ford lost his chance to gain outright election. He went on to live longer than any other President.

Public distrust of the Presidency (above) carried over from Nixon's term in office to Ford's. The U.S. celebrated the 200th anniversary of the signing of the Declaration of Independence during Ford's Presidency.

The Electoral College

★ Gatekeepers of the Presidency ★

IN MOST COUNTRIES, national elections are straightforward affairs. Eligible voters have the opportunity at a specified time to mark their preference on a ballot of various choices. Victors are declared based on the tabulated results.

Citizens of the United States participate in a more complex, two-step process. The outcome of the Presidency rests not, as is often thought, with the votes cast on Election Day. In fact these votes only determine the membership of an electoral college that is charged by the U.S. Constitution with selecting the President and Vice President of the United States.

Each state has as many members in the electoral college as it has U.S. Senators and Representatives (*see map*). The District of Columbia has electoral votes, too, even though it lacks full representation in Congress. The first electoral college had 69 members. Today there are 538. In order to

Electoral Votes by State

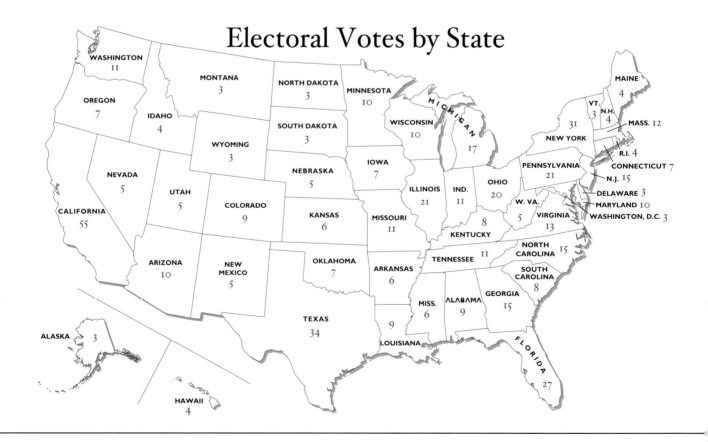

WASHINGTON 11
MONTANA 3
NORTH DAKOTA 3
MINNESOTA 10
MAINE 4
OREGON 7
IDAHO 4
SOUTH DAKOTA 3
WISCONSIN 10
MICHIGAN 17
VT. 3
N.H. 4
31
MASS. 12
NEW YORK
NEVADA 5
WYOMING 3
NEBRASKA 5
IOWA 7
R.I. 4
PENNSYLVANIA 21
CONNECTICUT 7
N.J. 15
UTAH 5
COLORADO 9
ILLINOIS 21
IND. 11
OHIO 20
DELAWARE 3
MARYLAND 10
CALIFORNIA 55
KANSAS 6
MISSOURI 11
W. VA. 8
VIRGINIA 13
WASHINGTON, D.C. 3
KENTUCKY
5
ARIZONA 10
NEW MEXICO 5
OKLAHOMA 7
ARKANSAS 6
TENNESSEE 11
NORTH CAROLINA 15
SOUTH CAROLINA 8
GEORGIA 15
MISS. 6
ALABAMA 9
TEXAS 34
LOUISIANA 9
FLORIDA 27
ALASKA 3
HAWAII 4

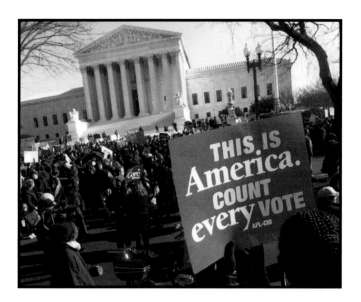

become President, a candidate must win a majority, at least one more than half, of all electoral votes, or 270.

The founding fathers established the electoral college to assure that the President and Vice President would be selected by an elite group of learned and well-qualified individuals, fairly distributed among the states. At the time, few people had the right to vote, and members of the electoral college were either appointed by governors or selected by state legislatures. The earliest members of the electoral college voted independently, based on their individual judgements.

During the 1820s, as voting rights began to expand, states started to entrust citizens with the selection of electors. Then as now, voters expressed preferences for their state's electors (who usually go unnamed) by their selection of a presidential candidate. Victory within each state goes to the electors who represent the political party of the victorious candidate. This "winner-take-all" formula is used today by most states and the District of Columbia. Maine and Nebraska allocate electoral votes in proportion to the support received by various candidates within each congressional district.

Members of the electoral college vote during separately held state meetings on an appointed day in December, and their votes are tabulated in front of a joint session of Congress in early January. If controversies arise, members of Congress are empowered to intervene. Otherwise the selection process for President and Vice President is complete.

Thus every presidential election has two sets of results, the popular vote and the elec-

toral college vote. In most cases, the winner of the popular vote is victorious in the electoral college, as well. However four of the nation's 55 presidential elections have brought victory to men who failed to win the popular vote.

Three of these elections occurred during the 19th century. Inconclusive voting by the electoral college in 1824 prompted the House of Representatives to award the Presidency to John Quincy Adams. Rutherford B. Hayes became President following the election of 1876 when disputes over the selection of electors forced Congress to refer the decision to a special commission. In 1888 Benjamin Harrison defeated Grover Cleveland without dispute in the electoral college yet failed to win a majority of popular votes.

The long absence of further discrepancies between popular and electoral voting led many to view the electoral college as a largely ceremonial body. In the election of 2000, though, ballot irregularities in Florida left the choice of that state's electors in doubt. Five weeks of debate followed. Action by the U.S. Supreme Court led Florida's deal-changing votes to fall by default to George W. Bush. He became President despite having lost the popular election by more than 500,000 votes.

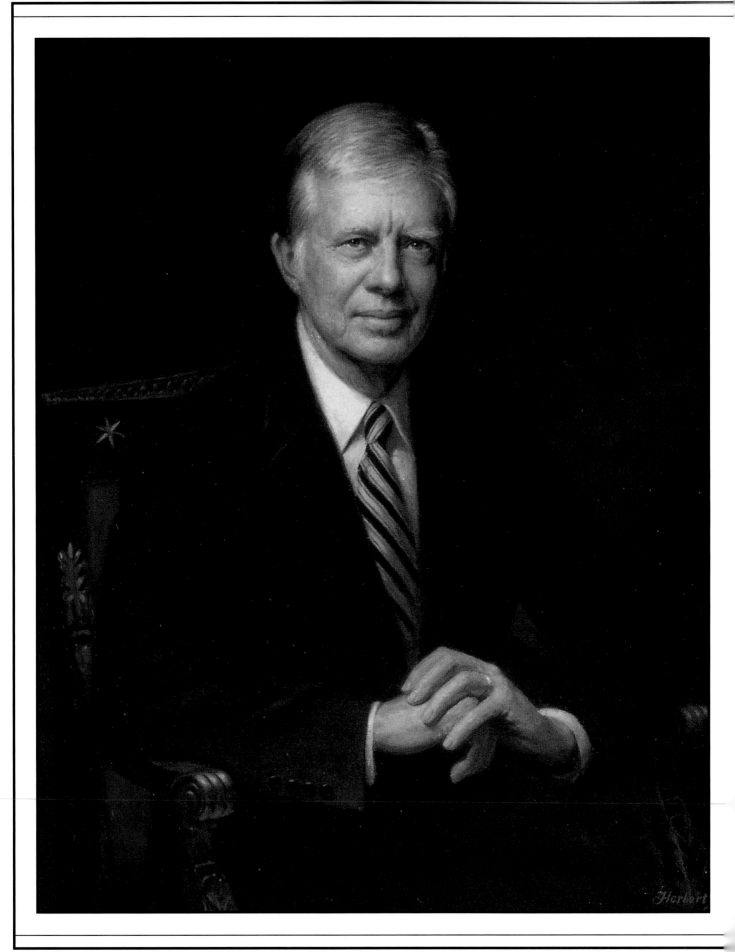

Jimmy Carter

39TH PRESIDENT OF THE UNITED STATES ★ *1977 – 1981*

Jimmy Carter

NICKNAME	Jimmy
BORN	Oct. 1, 1924, in Plains, Ga.
POLITICAL PARTY	Democrat
CHIEF OPPONENT	President Gerald R. Ford, Republican (1913–2006)
TERM OF OFFICE	Jan. 20, 1977–Jan. 20, 1981
AGE AT INAUGURATION	52 years old
NUMBER OF TERMS	one
VICE PRESIDENT	Walter Frederick (Fritz) Mondale (1928–present)

The Carters on their wedding day

FIRST LADY	Rosalynn Smith Carter (1927–present), wife (married July 7, 1946)
CHILDREN	John, James, Donnel, Amy
GEOGRAPHIC SCENE	50 states
SELECTED LANDMARKS	Plains Nursing Center, Inc., Plains, Ga. (birthplace); Jimmy Carter National Historic Site, Plains, Ga.; The Carter Center and the Jimmy Carter Library, Atlanta, Ga. (includes a museum)

JAMES EARL CARTER, JR., WAS THE FIRST PERSON elected President from the Deep South since Zachary Taylor in 1848. Economic troubles at home combined with other challenges from abroad (including citizens being taken hostage in Iran) cost him his bid for a second term of office. Carter returned to the world stage after his Presidency ended, serving as an advocate for international peace. In 2002 he became the third U.S. President to win a Nobel Peace Prize.

Carter liked his nickname, "Jimmy," so much that he was sworn in as President by that name. As a child growing up in the Deep South, Carter had been known by another nickname, too: "Hot," short for "Hot Shot." Carter helped with chores on his father's sizable peanut farm, attended schools segregated by race, and played with children both black and white. He graduated 59th out of the 820 students in his class at the U.S. Naval Academy at Annapolis. He married the best friend of one of his sisters and took up a career in the U.S. Navy.

After his father's sudden death in 1953, Carter left the Navy and his post as a nuclear submarine engineer to manage the family farm.

Jimmy Carter (above) was nicknamed "Jimmy Cardigan" after he wore a sweater instead of a suit when he addressed the nation during a televised fireside chat in 1977. Carter dispensed with other formal precedents, too. Bands stopped playing "Hail to the Chief" for his public entrances. He sent his daughter, Amy, to public schools. Sometimes he even carried his own suitcase and stayed at private homes when he traveled.

Jimmy Carter broke with precedent during his Inaugural Parade in 1977. Instead of riding in a motorcade, he walked from the U.S. Capitol toward the White House with his daughter, Amy; his wife, Rosalynn; and other family members. As First Lady, Rosalynn sat in on Cabinet meetings, represented the nation abroad, and spoke out in favor of mental health care.

"Let us create together a new national spirit of unity and trust."

Jimmy Carter, Inaugural Address, January 20, 1977

Carter was elected, in part, because voters liked the fact that he was an "outsider"—someone who was not part of national politics and the recent Watergate scandals. Being an "outsider" turned into a drawback after Carter became President. Because he ignored the political strategies of Congress, legislators on Capitol Hill regularly refused to pass his bills. The economy did not cooperate either. Years of extravagant government spending and a new wave of energy shortages sent price inflation higher than ever. Citizens were literally stranded at empty gas pumps in their search for gasoline.

Although these issues proved troublesome to solve, Carter took other significant action. He pardoned citizens who had illegally avoided fighting in the Vietnam War, appointed people from diverse backgrounds to key posts, reduced the rules that governed national transportation systems, increased protection of the environment, and promoted research about alternative forms of energy. He also established a Department of Energy and a separate Department of Education.

Carter emphasized respect for human rights in his relations with other nations. He withheld U.S. foreign aid from countries with unjust governments. Carter arranged for Panama to assume control of the canal that the United States had built through its territory years before. He expanded relations with China. He tried to further limit the spread of nuclear weapons. He organized international protests, including a controversial boycott of the 1980 summer Olympics in Moscow, after the Soviet Union invaded nearby Afghanistan.

Carter's greatest foreign policy challenge

Later he served in the Georgia Senate. As governor of the state during the early 1970s, Carter criticized racial discrimination, the practice of favoring whites over blacks and other races. Carter entered the presidential race of 1976 almost completely unknown to the rest of the country. His tireless campaigning won him the Democratic Party nomination and, in what became a tight race, the Presidency.

The popularity of nuclear energy suffered during the Carter Presidency after a serious accident occurred in 1979 at the Three Mile Island nuclear power plant near Harrisburg, Pennsylvania (left). Jimmy Carter encouraged scientists to develop new forms of energy using such renewable resources as the sun and the wind.

Jimmy Carter helped negotiate important treaties between Egyptian President Anwar Sadat and Israel's Prime Minister Menachem Begin in 1978 (left). Their Camp David Accords were reached with Carter's help at the presidential retreat in Maryland. These agreements renewed hopes for peace in the Middle East, a region that had been torn apart by wars and terrorism. The most difficult challenge Carter faced in his Presidency was the Iranian hostage crisis. Fifty-two Americans were held prisoner by Iranian militants (right) for 444 days. They were finally set free after Carter left office in January 1981.

began in 1979 when angry Iranians stormed the U.S. Embassy in Tehran and captured its occupants. They held 52 Americans as hostages for the rest of Carter's Presidency. All efforts to free the prisoners were unsuccessful.

As President, Carter's popularity ranged from very high to very low. It shifted depending on the state of the economy, the status of the hostage crisis, and his success at restoring confidence in government. He lost his reelection bid by a wide margin.

Just 56 years old when he left office, Carter began an active retirement life that continues today. He has written more than 20 books, for example, many of them bestsellers. His greatest focus, however, has been devoted to the Carter Center, which he founded in Atlanta, Georgia, with his wife, Rosalynn, soon after his presidency ended.

Working through the center, Carter helps negotiate peace agreements between nations, works with others to verify that countries have fair elections, and directs efforts to improve health in developing lands. These and his other efforts to increase world peace earned him the Nobel Peace Prize in 2002. Only two other Presidents—Theodore Roosevelt and Woodrow Wilson—have been so honored. Carter is the only one to receive Nobel recognition for post-presidential achievements.

Jimmy Carter, who was only 56 years old at the end of his Presidency, went on to distinguish himself in the decades that followed as a peacemaker and moderator of democratic elections. His career of retirement service earned him the Nobel Peace Prize in 2002 at age 78.

FOOTPRINTS ON THE GLOBAL FRONTIER

★ *1981 – Present* ★

1986

U.S. space shuttle missions were halted for more than two years after the Challenger *blew apart on January 28. All seven crew members died.*

1989

Berlin citizens marked the end of the Cold War by tearing down the wall that had divided their city into separate zones. East united with West to embrace democracy.

1990

South African officials released Nelson Mandela from his 27-year imprisonment. When they ended apartheid—a system that oppressed the black majority—Mandela was elected president soon after.

1995

The bombing of the Murrah Federal Building, in Oklahoma City on April 19 shocked the nation. Two American members of an anti-government militia movement were responsible.

The Cold War gave way near the end of the 20th century to a new frontier of shifting global alliances. The Soviet Union dissolved. The European Union expanded. Trade, population, even disease became more mobile. Although some nations moved closer to peace, old hatreds erupted elsewhere—often fueled by religious differences. Threats of terrorism began to rise among angry groups of outsiders. Nations sought to collaborate, compromise, and compete on a planet whose population is more connected and interdependent than ever.

2001

On September 11 members of the Al Qaeda terror network crashed hijacked jets into the World Trade Center in New York City and other targets. The towers were destroyed and more than 2,700 people died.

2006

The release of the documentary film An Inconvenient Truth *focused national and international attention on the consequences of global warming for the health of the planet.*

2007

As the Iraq War entered its fourth year, the U.S. sent a surge of additional troops to help subdue growing unrest and violence within the country. By then more than 3,000 U.S. soldiers had died.

2008

Declining real estate values, unstable home mortgage finances, and risky investment strategies triggered worldwide economic panic in financial markets and prompted government intervention.

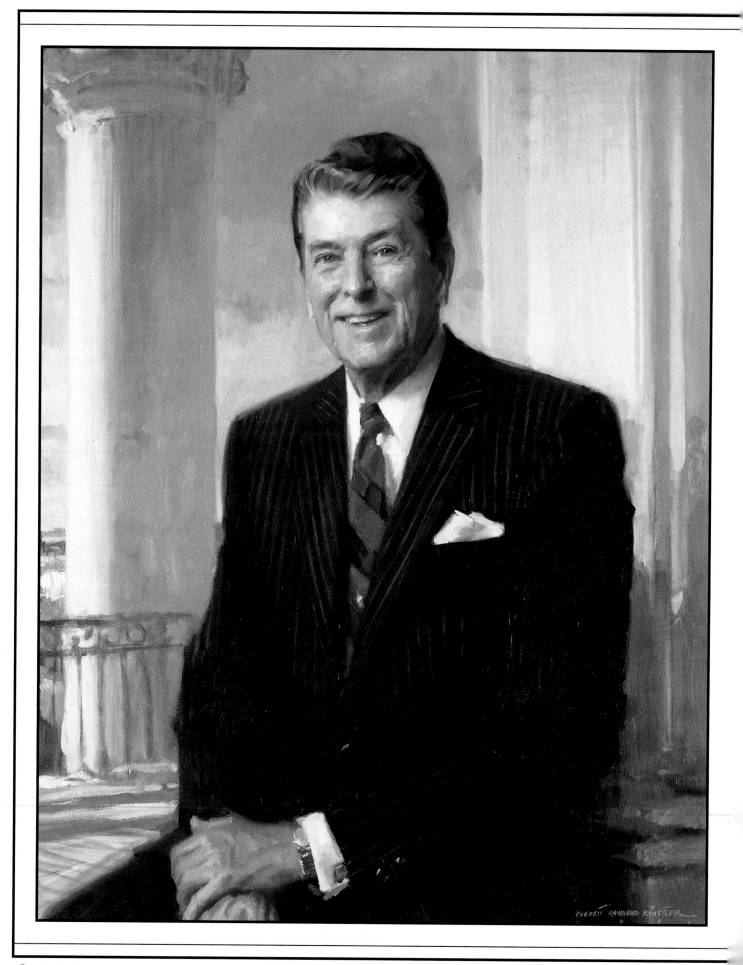

Ronald Reagan

40TH PRESIDENT OF THE UNITED STATES ★ *1981 – 1989*

NICKNAME	Dutch
BORN	Feb. 6, 1911, in Tampico, Ill.
POLITICAL PARTY	Republican
CHIEF OPPONENTS	1st term: President Jimmy Carter, Democrat, (1924–present) and John Bayard Anderson, Independent (1922–present); 2nd term: Walter Frederick (Fritz) Mondale, Democrat (1928–present)
TERM OF OFFICE	Jan. 20, 1981–Jan. 20, 1989
AGE AT INAUGURATION	69 years old
NUMBER OF TERMS	two
VICE PRESIDENT	George Bush (1924–present)
FIRST LADY	Nancy Davis Reagan (1921–present), wife (married March 4, 1952)
FIRST WIFE	Jane Wyman (1914–2007), married Jan. 24, 1940; divorced July 18, 1949
CHILDREN	Maureen, Michael, Patricia, Ronald
GEOGRAPHIC SCENE	50 states
DIED	June 5, 2004, in Los Angeles, Calif.
AGE AT DEATH	93 years old
SELECTED LANDMARKS	Tampico, Ill. (birthplace); Dixon, Ill. (boyhood home); Ronald Reagan Presidential Library and Center for Public Affairs, Simi Valley, Calif.

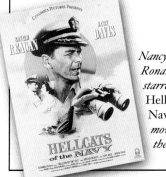

Nancy Davis and Ronald Reagan starred together in Hellcats of the Navy, *the last movie either of them made.*

RONALD WILSON REAGAN WAS THE OLDEST person to become President, at age 69. Yet this former Hollywood actor and governor of California brought a youthful optimism to his work. The "Great Communicator" strengthened support for the Republican Party and filled federal courts with conservative judges. He helped force the end of the Cold War, too, though at an economic cost that haunted future Presidents.

Reagan ended his presidential career near the end of the 20th century, but he was born during a simpler era when the century was just beginning. He grew up in small towns in northern Illinois, particularly Dixon. His family called him "Dutch," short for "fat little Dutchman." He enjoyed playing sports and was a popular actor at the public schools he attended and at Eureka College in Eureka, Illinois.

After graduation he worked as a radio sports announcer in the Midwest. In 1937 Reagan moved to Hollywood. He made 53 movies and hosted two television shows during the next three decades. Even his World War II service involved making training films for the armed forces. Reagan "lived" so many lives through the parts he played in movies that he sometimes got them mixed up later on with his own story. (He recalled combat scenes from movies, for example, as if they were events from of his own service during World War II.) Reagan married two Hollywood actresses. He is the only President who had a marriage (his first one) end in divorce.

Reagan's experiences as a union labor leader in Hollywood, public speaker, and political volunteer helped interest him in running for office. Although he had grown up loyal to the Democratic Party, he began supporting Republicans during the Eisenhower era. He officially joined the Republican Party in 1962. In

Nancy Davis met her future husband, Ronald Reagan, when both of them were acting in Hollywood. They married three years later (above). Nancy Reagan appeared in a total of 11 films. As First Lady she encouraged children to "Just Say No" to illegal drugs.

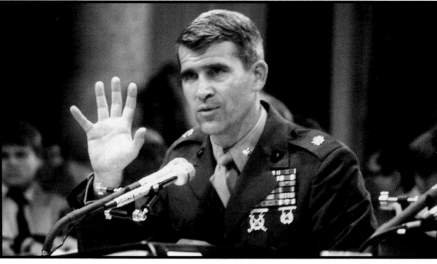

In 1983 the United States entered into combat for the first time since the Vietnam War by invading the Caribbean island of Grenada (left). Ronald Reagan ordered the invasion after American residents there seemed threatened by an unexpected change of national leadership. The Reagan administration drew criticism because of the Iran-contra scandal: secret foreign policy dealings by high-level government officials, including Lieutenant Colonel Oliver North (above), that contradicted official policy.

1966 Californians elected him to the first of two terms as governor. Reagan sought his party's presidential nomination twice (in 1968 and 1976) before earning it in 1980. Citizens voted "yes" to elect Reagan as President because they generally answered "no" to his query about their lives during the Carter Presidency: "Are you better off than you were four years ago?" He was reelected four years later.

In an effort to improve the economy, Reagan cut taxes, reduced federal spending in some areas, and increased government spending on defense by $1.5 trillion over seven years. He proposed the first trillion-dollar federal budget. His economic program came to be known as "Reaganomics." It suggested that if economic benefits such as tax cuts were made to the wealthy, these savings would "trickle down" and help less affluent citizens. This vision of "supply-side economics" became a cornerstone of the modern Republican Party. Although

Challenges of the job: Ronald Reagan fired 13,000 air traffic controllers in 1981 when they went out on strike (left). An assassin attempted to shoot the President a few months after he took office (right). Reagan reassured those around him with his good humor. "If I had had this much attention in Hollywood, I'd have stayed there," he joked to the hospital staff. Prompt emergency care saved his life.

Like all Presidents, Ronald Reagan appointed officials (left), federal judges, and Supreme Court judges. He put new judges in half of the nation's federal court seats, and he placed three new judges on the nation's highest court, including its first woman judge, Sandra Day O'Connor. By being able to select so many judges, Reagan was able to shape the opinions of the federal courts to reflect his own vision for the judiciary system. Ronald Reagan's plan of increased spending on national defense put a strain on the U.S. economy and added to the national debt. His program was even tougher on the Soviet Union. America's old Cold War foe simply could not afford to keep up in the military arms race anymore. Mikhail Gorbachev, a new, more moderate Soviet leader, sought to limit the use of nuclear weapons. The two leaders (right) signed an agreement in 1987 that reduced stockpiles of nuclear missiles for the first time.

inflation and unemployment eventually improved during his administration, new problems developed. The collapse of the savings and loan industry, sizable annual budget deficits, and a growing national debt, for example, became costly concerns that would take years for future Presidents to solve.

The Reagan administration bred its share of scandals. The greatest one, the Iran-contra scandal, involved illegal sales of arms to the Middle Eastern nation of Iran. Profits from the sales were secretly diverted to support rebel forces in Nicaragua, a country in Central America. Upper level administrators encouraged the activity. Other charges of illegal behavior forced the resignations of Reagan's secretary of labor, the attorney general, and senior staff members at the Environmental Protection Agency, the Central Intelligence Agency, the Defense Department, and the Department of Housing and Urban Development.

Reagan remained popular despite the scandals and criticisms of his Presidency. Some credited this success to his Hollywood looks and his skill as the "Great Communicator." Others called him the "Teflon President," because, just like the non-stick pan surface, nothing bad ever "stuck" to his image.

Reagan was 77 years old when he retired with his wife, Nancy, to Los Angeles. In 1994 he was diagnosed with Alzheimer's disease, an illness that affects memory, and he led an increasingly secluded life. His death ten years later prompted tributes on both coasts. After lying in state at the U.S. Capitol and receiving the honor of a state funeral, his body was flown home to California for a sunset burial.

> ## "What I'd really like to do is go down in history as the President who made Americans believe in themselves again."
>
> Ronald Reagan, 1981

Ronald Reagan's death in 2004 brought the nation its first presidential state funeral in more than 20 years. At one point during the week-long series of events, his casket was moved by horse-drawn caisson (left) to the U.S. Capitol for public viewing. Burial took place on the grounds of Reagan's presidential library in Simi Valley,

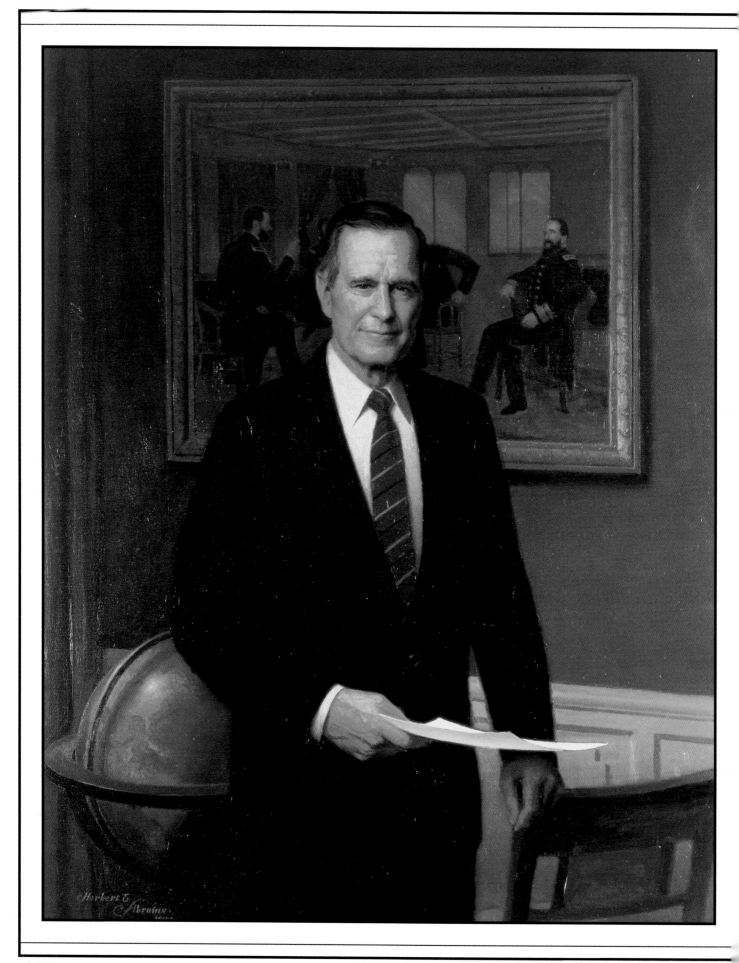

George Bush

NICKNAME	Poppy
BORN	June 12, 1924, in Milton, Mass.
POLITICAL PARTY	Republican
CHIEF OPPONENT	Michael Stanley Dukakis, Democrat (1933–present)
TERM OF OFFICE	Jan. 20, 1989–Jan. 20, 1993
AGE AT INAUGURATION	64 years old
NUMBER OF TERMS	one
VICE PRESIDENT	James Danforth (Dan) Quayle, III (1947–present)
FIRST LADY	Barbara Pierce Bush (1925–present), wife (married Jan. 6, 1945)
CHILDREN	George, Robin (died young), John, Neil, Marvin, Dorothy
GEOGRAPHIC SCENE	50 states
SELECTED LANDMARKS	George Bush Presidential Library, Texas A&M University, College Station, Tex.

George Bush played baseball for Yale University. He was named after a grandfather, George Herbert Walker, who was known as "Pop." Bush was called "Little Pop" or "Poppy" into his adulthood.

GEORGE HERBERT WALKER BUSH presided over a continued shift in Republican Party thinking towards conservative viewpoints. U.S. armed forces took part in two military actions, including the Persian Gulf War, during a Presidency that witnessed the collapse of the Soviet Union. A sagging economy undercut Bush's war-time popularity by the time of his reelection bid.

Bush brought years of varied government experience and a distinguished personal background with him to the White House. The son of a wealthy U.S. senator, Bush attended elite private schools. He enlisted in the military after high school and became the Navy's youngest pilot. Bush earned a Distinguished Flying Cross as a Navy bombing pilot in the Pacific during World War II. After the war he graduated with honors from Yale University.

Bush worked in the oil business in Texas for 18 years before seeking his first public office. He lost a 1964 U.S. Senate bid, but he gained a seat in the U.S. House of Representatives two years later. After two terms he made a second unsuccessful run for the Senate. For the next ten years he was appointed by Republican Presidents Richard M. Nixon and Gerald R. Ford to a series of prominent posts: U.S. ambassador to the United Nations, chairman of the Republican National Committee, top U.S. diplomat in China, and director of the Central Intelligence Agency.

Bush eyed the Vice Presidency in 1968 and 1974, and he sought the Republican presidential nomination in 1980. Instead, he earned eight years of experience as Ronald Reagan's Vice President before gaining the Presidency himself in 1988.

George Bush married Barbara Pierce (above) while on leave from World War II service. The couple had met two years before during an earlier shore leave. Both claim to have fallen in love at first sight.

U.S. combat success in the Persian Gulf War (above, soldiers wear protective gear) pushed George Bush's approval rating to a high of 89 percent, but a sagging economy undercut his popularity by the time he sought reelection in 1992.

"Out of these troubled times... a new world order can emerge: a new era, freer from the threat of terror, stronger in the pursuit of justice, and more secure in the quest for peace."

George Bush, September 12, 1990

Bush inherited from Reagan a national and world scene that was in transition. Most notable was the rapid transformation of the Soviet Union from a Cold War superpower into a splintered collection of former communist states. First Poland, then East Germany, Czechoslovakia, Hungary, Yugoslavia, Bulgaria, Albania, and, finally, the Soviet Union

In 1989 the Exxon Valdez oil tanker ran aground off the shore of Alaska. The accident resulted in the largest oil spill in the nation's history. Almost 11 million gallons of oil polluted more than 1,000 miles of shoreline and killed hundreds of thousands of birds and animals. The disaster destroyed the local fishing industry despite an extensive and costly cleanup effort (above).

itself, rejected the Communist form of government. The Soviet Union dissolved, and Russia emerged as its most powerful descendant. Most of the momentum for these changes came from within the region itself, but the Bush administration supported these moves toward democracy. The only remaining strongholds of communism by the end of the Bush Presidency were China, Cuba, Laos, North Korea, and Vietnam.

In 1989 Bush ordered U.S. troops to invade Panama. Their mission was to seize Manuel Noriega, the country's military leader, and bring him to the United States so he could stand trial on charges of drug trafficking. He was captured four days later. (Eventually he was tried, convicted, and imprisoned for his illegal activity.) The invasion

The hair of Barbara Bush turned to a distinctive silver at an unexpectedly early age following the death of her three-year-old daughter to leukemia. She and her husband lived in more than two dozen homes in 17 cities before moving into the White House. As First Lady, Barbara Bush promoted literacy and other education programs. Entertainers were among those attending the third national literacy awards she hosted at the White House (above).

George Bush poses with his four sons (left, from left to right: Neil, John, George W., and Marvin). Two sons followed their father into politics. John, called "Jeb," served as governor of Florida from 1999 to 2007. Jeb's older brother, George W., was elected governor of Texas in 1994 and put the Republican Party back in the White House in the tight presidential race of 2000. Commander in Chief George Bush reviews a ceremonial guard in 1989 (right).

caused significant property damage, left 500 Panamanians dead, and cost the lives of 23 Americans.

A year later the U.S. took part in combat again. Iraq's 1989 invasion of neighboring Kuwait, a tiny oil-rich nation on the Persian Gulf, provoked worldwide outrage. The United States led an international fight in the region several months later that liberated Kuwait and severely damaged Iraq's military defenses. Iraq's leader, Saddam Hussein, remained in command of his nation, but other governments agreed to enforce sanctions, or restrictions, on Iraq until the nation could prove it no longer possessed weapons of mass destruction. The war, which lasted only a few months, cost more than $60 billion, a sum that many nations helped pay. The United States lost 148 lives during the war; Iraqi deaths may have been as high as 100,000.

These international events often overshadowed domestic policy during the Bush administration. Nonetheless, the President worked to rescue the bankrupt savings and loan industry, fought rising unemployment, signed a new Clean Air Act, and agreed to legislation that promoted equal rights of access for the disabled. Enormous budget deficits continued to swell the national debt. They forced Bush to break his 1988 campaign promise—"Read my lips: No new taxes." This change and a worsening economy cost Bush his reelection bid in 1992. Voters gave him the lowest support at the polls earned by any sitting President since William Howard Taft. This loss was tempered by the election of Bush's son, George W., in 2000. Many administrators from the first Bush Presidency returned to serve under the son.

Four years after retiring to Texas, George Bush made news by making his first parachute jump since World War II. This time it was just for fun.

In the President's Shadow

★ *Security, the Media, and Presidential Perks* ★

Today's Presidents may share the same residence as their predecessors, but their work and lifestyles are vastly different. The first Presidents handled much of their own paperwork, for example. They met freely with citizens who dropped by the White House, too. As the nation and its government grew in size, so did the complexity of the job for its Presidents.

Now Presidents travel by jet and limousine, not horse and buggy. The size of their staffs has grown from a handful to hundreds. The cost of running the White House has kept a parallel pace. The risks and realities of presidential assassinations have tightened the Presidents' freedom of movement. Gone are the days when John Quincy Adams could walk alone from the White House to the Potomac River and swim there in the nude.

Now more than two dozen secret service agents take turns guarding the President and his family members around the clock. Other staff members help manage the President's busy calendar, write many of his speeches, and advise the President on everything from foreign policy to party politics.

As a result, today's Presidents are more isolated than ever before from ordinary life. William Henry Harrison once strolled beyond the White House gates to do a little grocery shopping. Ulysses S. Grant took off by himself

Secret service agents began guarding the life of the U.S. President following the assassination of William McKinley in 1901. Since then they've done everything from protecting the presidential limousine (left) to supervising ordinary movements of the President and family members (right). Whether the Chief Executive wants to buy flowers for the First Lady, browse through a music store, or go for a jog, secret service agents assure that the outing is safe and sound.

Today Presidents may travel by jet on Air Force One (previous page), helicopter aboard Marine One (below) or limousine in a presidential motorcade (above), among other options. Members of the news media stay nearby, whether on the road or back at the White House (at right with Ronald Reagan in the press briefing room).

on speeding buggy rides. But no President sets foot beyond the grounds of the White House today just on a whim or all alone.

However, even as the lives of Presidents have become more controlled, their activities have grown in national visibility. Expanding media coverage by newspapers, radio, television, and the Internet assures that the public knows more than ever about what a President says and does. All major news outlets assign one or more people to cover the President's activities. There are some 2,000 members of this presidential press corps.

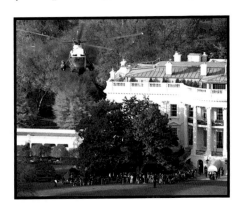

This many reporters could not possibly follow every single move of the President. Instead small groups of them—a few dozen or so at a time—take turns with the work. They are called the press pool because they pool, or collect their reports, then share them with everyone in the press corps.

One representative of each day's press pool writes an eyewitness summary of the day's events. These reports are filled with colorful details so that other reporters will be able to visualize and write vivid news accounts.

Additional members of the pool make still photos, video footage, and audio recordings to share with the press corps. The reports of the press pool form the basis for the hundreds of news stories seen by the public.

Today's Presidents balance the demands and scrutiny of their jobs with many impressive perks, or benefits. For starters, they receive an annual salary of $400,000. (George Washington earned $25,000 a year.) They have free housing at the White House as well as at the presidential retreat of Camp David, in nearby Maryland.

These homes offer many luxuries that cushion the impact of their isolation. Presidents may enjoy swimming, bowling, horseback riding, skeet shooting, and woodland walks without ever leaving home. They can screen movies in a private theater and read the latest books in a private library, too.

When it's time to travel, Presidents may choose between a fleet of limousines, a jet named Air Force One, a helicopter, a yacht, even a bullet-proof train car. Yet at the end of the day, they tread the same stairs to bed as have all the Presidents since John Adams.

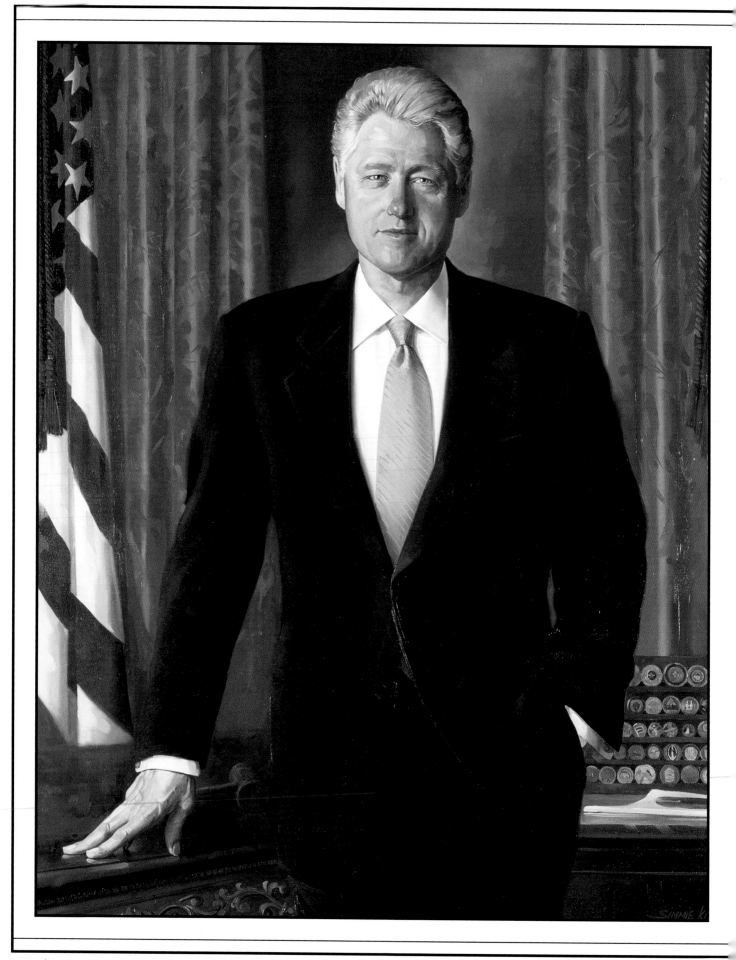

Bill Clinton

42ND PRESIDENT OF THE UNITED STATES ★ *1993 – 2001*

NICKNAME	Comeback Kid
BORN	Aug. 19, 1946, in Hope, Ark.
POLITICAL PARTY	Democrat
CHIEF OPPONENTS	1st term: President George Bush, Republican (1924–present) and Henry Ross Perot, Independent (1930–present); 2nd term: Robert Joseph Dole, Republican (1923–present) and Henry Ross Perot, Reform (1930–present)
TERM OF OFFICE	Jan. 20, 1993–Jan. 20, 2001
AGE AT INAUGURATION	46 years old
NUMBER OF TERMS	two
VICE PRESIDENT	Albert Gore, Jr. (1948–present)
FIRST LADY	Hillary Diane Rodham Clinton (1947–present), wife (married Oct. 11, 1975)
CHILDREN	Chelsea
GEOGRAPHIC SCENE	50 states
SELECTED LANDMARKS	Presidential Center and Library, Little Rock, Ark., Home, Fayetteville, Ark.

WILLIAM JEFFERSON CLINTON BROUGHT THE DEMOCRATIC PARTY its first two-term Presidency since the era of Franklin Delano Roosevelt. Clinton earned respect internationally for his leadership and work for world peace. At home he balanced the federal budget for the first time in decades and reduced the national debt. These professional successes were undercut by bitter partisan political fighting over real and alleged scandals. Impeached by the House of Representatives on charges of misconduct, Clinton was tried and acquitted by the U.S. Senate.

Clinton was the first U.S. President born after World War II. He grew up in Hot Springs, Arkansas, where he did well in school. As a youth, Clinton joined the Boy Scouts, sang in the church choir, and raced to complete crossword puzzles. Later he graduated from Georgetown University in Washington, D.C., and studied as a prestigious Rhodes Scholar at England's Oxford University before turning his attention to law. He met his future wife, Hillary Rodham, while the two of them were law students at Yale University.

After graduating, Clinton taught law at the University of Arkansas and took up politics. By 1978, at age 32, he had become the

Bill Clinton's 1963 handshake with President John F. Kennedy helped cement his childhood ambition to be President. Clinton was known until age 16 by the birth name he shared with his natural father, William Jefferson Blythe, who died before Bill was born. Later, he adopted his stepfather's last name.

During his youth Bill Clinton played the saxophone in a jazz trio called The Three Blind Mice; sunglasses completed the musicians' attire. During presidential elections he performed twice on nationally televised talk shows. Clinton jammed with other musicians at a White House jazz festival (above).

Throughout his Presidency Bill Clinton tried to foster peaceful relations in the Middle East. In meetings with Israeli and Palestinian leaders (far left), Clinton sought to improve understanding between people of different religions. With Boris Yeltsin (left), Clinton worked to reduce arms and improve international relations.

nation's youngest governor. Although unseated in the next election, Clinton became known as the "Comeback Kid" after he regained his post in 1982. He went on to serve four consecutive terms as governor of Arkansas. As a presidential candidate in 1992, Clinton portrayed himself as a moderate Democrat, one who understood the perspective of a majority of Americans. Clinton and his vice presidential nominee, Al Gore, became the youngest national ticket ever elected; they were the first all-Southern ticket since the Jackson administration of 1828. The two men were reelected four years later, making Clinton one of only five Presidents in the century to complete two terms of office.

As President, Clinton (helped by a booming economy) began balancing the federal budget for the first time in four decades. He created free trade between the United States, Canada, and Mexico

with the North American Free Trade Agreement (NAFTA), and he normalized U. S. trade relations with China. As his Presidency progressed, Clinton wielded increasing influence over efforts to end hostilities at trouble spots in the Middle East, Europe, and elsewhere.

Clinton lived up to his image as the "Comeback Kid" during a Presidency that was challenged by party politics, international instability, and personal scandal. He battled with Congress over how to manage the budget, taxes, health care, and trade while he labored to define the role of the United States as a peacemaker in a post–Cold War world. Frequently Clinton found himself trying to focus attention on the nation's business even as investigators probed into his handling of administrative and personal matters.

In 1998 Kenneth Starr, an independent prosecutor, accused Clinton of breaking laws to conceal a romantic relationship with a White House intern. The House of Representatives considered Starr's charges and voted to impeach the President, or recommend that he be tried by the Senate and removed from office. They accused Clinton of lying under oath and using illegal means to keep his

During the last six years of Bill Clinton's administration, Kenneth Starr (near left) led a series of investigations into possible illegal behavior by the President (far left) and associates. These proceedings became ensnared in bitter partisan, or political party, disputes. Republicans accused Democrats of hiding the truth, while Democrats accused Republicans of trying to undermine the Clinton Presidency with false charges.

Bill Clinton remained active in retirement, whether campaigning on behalf of his wife's 2008 presidential bid (left) or collaborating with former President George Bush to raise funds for disaster relief (right, accepting Liberty Medals in 2006 for their efforts). During his Presidency, Clinton worked to improve relations with Russia and to promote peace and human rights in such places as the Middle East, Northern Ireland, Haiti, Bosnia, and Kosovo.

affair a secret. Clinton was acquitted by the U.S. Senate during the trial that followed in 1999. He and Andrew Johnson are the only two Presidents to be impeached and tried by Congress.

Clinton succeeded at broadening the Democratic Party base of support during his Presidency. Many past supporters of the Republican Party, particularly a wide variety of voters from middle-income levels, sided with the Democrats instead. However the taint of personal scandal surrounding Clinton by the end of his administration limited how effectively he could support the presidential bid of his own Vice President in 2000.

Hillary Clinton assumed a broader range of responsibilities as First Lady than any other President's wife since Eleanor Roosevelt. She headed an effort to reform the nation's health care system, traveled extensively on behalf of her husband, promoted children's rights, and wrote a weekly newspaper column. She protected the privacy of her teenage daughter, Chelsea, and supported her husband during the scandals that plagued his Presidency. She became the first First Lady to seek and win elected office by running for the U.S. Senate during the final year of her husband's Presidency. In 2008 Senator Clinton made an unsuccessful bid to become the Democratic Party presidential nominee.

> "There is nothing wrong with America that cannot be cured by what is right with America."

Bill Clinton,
First Inaugural Address, January 20, 1993

Bill Clinton shared the spotlight during the celebration of his Inauguration in 1997 with his daughter, Chelsea, and wife, Hillary. During his second term, opinion polls showed that most citizens supported Clinton's performance as President even though the House of Representatives was recommending he be removed from office.

George W. Bush

43RD PRESIDENT OF THE UNITED STATES ★ *2001 – 2009*

NICKNAME	Dubya (W.)
BORN	July 6, 1946, in New Haven, Conn.
POLITICAL PARTY	Republican
CHIEF OPPONENTS	1st term: Albert Arnold Gore, Jr., Democrat (1948–present) Ralph Nader, Green (1934–present); 2nd term: John Kerry, Democrat (1943–present); Ralph Nader, Green (1934–present)
TERM OF OFFICE	Jan. 20, 2001–Jan.20, 2009
AGE AT INAUGURATION	54 years old
NUMBER OF TERMS	two
VICE PRESIDENT	Richard Bruce Cheney (1941–present)
FIRST LADY	Laura Welch Bush (1946–present), wife (married November 5, 1977)
CHILDREN	Jenna, Barbara (twins)
GEOGRAPHIC SCENE	50 states

Two future Presidents were captured in this family snapshot from 1955. George Bush, the nation's 41st Chief Executive, holds his young son, George W. Bush, who became the nation's 43rd President in 2001. Wife, mother, and future First Lady Barbara Bush looks on. During the son's Presidency, the similar names of the men were distinguished by the use of the son's middle initial, W., a letter which had become his nickname, as well. Some people referred to them by the number of their administrations, too, that is as #41 and #43.

HISTORIANS AND COMMENTATORS drew parallels between the Presidencies of George Walker Bush and his predecessors even before his administration ended. Bush, like Lyndon B. Johnson, drew criticism over an increasingly unpopular war. He faced unprecedented financial challenges, too, as did Herbert Hoover. During the contentious election of 2000 Bush became the first President in more than a century to reach the White House without carrying the nation's popular vote. Only John Quincy Adams, Rutherford B. Hayes, and Benjamin Harrison did likewise. Unlike them, Bush was reelected four years later. He and his father, the nation's 41st President, are the second father-son pair of chief executives.

A family tradition of elected public service began while George W. Bush was growing up in Texas. He was six years old when his grandfather became a U.S. senator. Twelve years later his father made his first bid for elected office. As a child George W. Bush played baseball and dreamed of becoming a star athlete. However, he shadowed his father's rise to political life by attending the same private high school as his father and the same college, Yale University. He graduated in 1968 with a major in history. Bush served in the Air Force National Guard during the Vietnam War and learned how to fly an F-102 fighter jet. Later he earned a degree from Harvard Business School.

In 1975 Bush returned to Texas and, like his father, found work in the oil industry. He married Laura Welch in 1977, just three months after they had met. The next year Bush made an unsuccessful bid for election to the U.S. House of Representatives. Later he became an owner and manager of the Texas Rangers baseball team. He was elected governor of Texas in 1994 and was reelected four years later.

During the Vietnam War, George W. Bush joined the Air Force National Guard (above). Questions over unfinished service requirements became a campaign issue during his presidential bids.

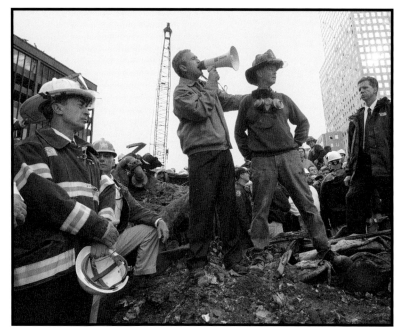

"America was targeted for attack because we're the brightest beacon for freedom and opportunity in the world. And no one will keep that light from shining."

George W. Bush,
September 11, 2001

The terrorist attacks of September 11, 2001 became a rallying point for the administration of George W. Bush. His leadership drew praise at first, particularly after his dramatic visit to Ground Zero at the site of the collapsed Twin Towers from New York's World Trade Center. Public opinion grew more divided later on.

Bush campaigned for the Presidency in 2000 against the sitting Vice President, Al Gore. Their contest ended with a hotly disputed debate over how to count election returns in Florida, a state governed by Bush's brother. Intervention by the U.S. Supreme Court some five weeks after Election Day secured the Presidency for Bush even though he trailed Gore nationally by more than 500,000 popular votes. Bush took office with only a narrow margin of Republican control in the House of Representatives and the first-ever equally divided U.S. Senate.

The Bush Presidency was barely underway before the catastrophic series of terrorist attacks of September 11, 2001, altered its focus from domestic to international concerns. The President's popularity soared as the United States invaded Afghanistan in an effort to capture those responsible for the attacks, including Al Qaeda terrorist leader Osama bin Laden. The decision to attack Iraq in 2003 as a protective necessity met with general support at first, but public opinion splintered as the war dragged on. Critics charged that Iraq had become a distraction from the so-called War on Terror, especially as bin Laden eluded capture.

Bush sought to strengthen national defense through the creation of a Department of Homeland Security. The lack of further attacks on the U.S. and a willingness among many Americans to "stay the

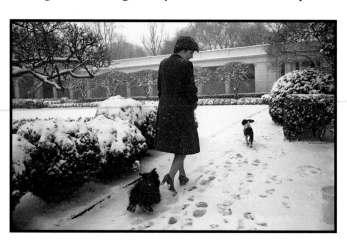

George W. Bush, the father of twin girls (left), brought a commitment to faith and family to the White House that was shared by his wife, Laura (center, during travels with the President). The First Lady (right, walking in a wintry White House Rose Garden) promoted literacy during her husband's administration.

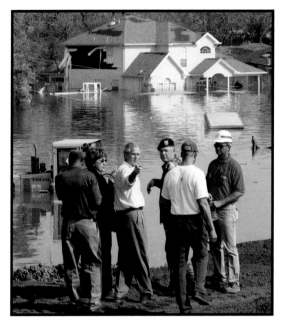

George W. Bush faced challenges both foreign and domestic during his two-term Presidency, most notably with international conflicts (left, meeting with advisors in advance of the Iraq War) and natural disasters (right, in 2005, visiting New Orleans in the wake of Hurricane Katrina). Six weeks after fighting commenced for the Iraq War, Bush helped pilot a fighter jet onto the deck of an aircraft carrier (below) and declared the war's "Mission Accomplished." His May, 2003 statement proved premature, and troops remained on duty in Iraq even after his Presidency ended almost six years later.

course" helped Bush secure reelection in 2004 against Democratic Party challenger, Senator John Kerry.

During his second term, the death of the Supreme Court's Chief Justice and the resignation of another justice enabled Bush to place two judicial conservatives on the nation's highest court. These appointments allowed the President to satisfy the interests of the Republican Party's influential conservative base and secured him an enduring legacy of influence over American policy through the court.

As President, Bush succeeded at implementing some domestic policy initiatives, such as his No Child Left Behind program for education reform, but he failed to win Congressional support for others, including social security modification and the reform of immigration laws. Charges of improper influence over the government by political appointees, especially in the White House and Justice Department, led to a series of high-profile investigations.

Growing public dissatisfaction with the Bush administration helped fuel midterm election victories

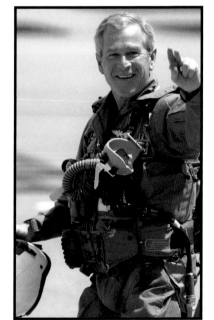

in 2006 that put Democrats in control of the House and Senate for the first time in 14 years. Bush's controversial 2007 initiative to bring stability to Iraq, the so-called troop surge, did help improve conditions there even as American forces remained on duty in Iraq and Afghanistan.

The administration's consistent support for tax cuts earned praise among conservatives, but were later seen as contributing to a dramatic rise in budget shortfalls. The wars became costly, too. The growing unbalance in the federal budget, sluggish economic growth, soaring oil prices, and Republican-led reductions in government regulation of financial industries helped contribute to a worldwide economic crisis near the end of Bush's Presidency.

The election of 2008 was widely seen as a referendum on the Bush administration. The outcome—with victories by Barack Obama and Democratic Congressional candidates—signaled the voters' readiness for change. President Bush retired with First Lady Laura Bush to their ranch near Crawford, Texas.

Election 2008

★ History in the Making ★

VOTERS ELECTED THE FIRST African American chief executive in U.S. history by choosing Barack Obama as the nation's 44th President on November 4, 2008. His victory for the Democratic Party capped a 21-month-long bid for the White House that many had dismissed as unlikely to succeed.

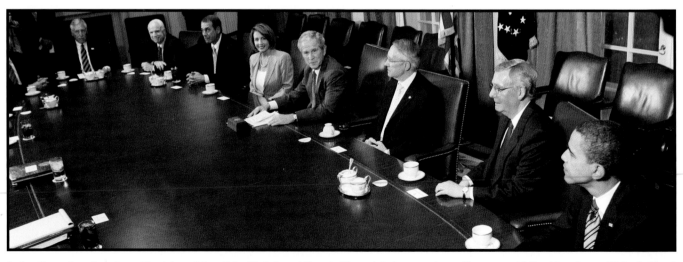

The two candidates face off in their first televised debate.

A relative newcomer to national politics, having only joined the U.S. Senate in 2004, Obama campaigned with promises for change in political leadership and tone. He secured his place in history with a decisive victory in the electoral college over Republican Senator John McCain. Obama won a majority of the popular vote, too, the first Democratic candidate to do so since 1976.

From the get-go, election 2008 promised excitement, drama, and the likelihood that history would be made. For the first time in more than 50 years, neither political party offered an incumbent candidate, someone already on the job as President or Vice President. Thus more politicians than usual vied to earn their party's nominations, as many as nine Democrats and 11 Republicans.

Among those competing were individuals offering the most serious candidacies yet mounted by an African American (Obama) and by a woman, former First Lady Hillary Rodham Clinton, both Democrats. The Republican field included the first bid for President by a member of the Mormon

In late September of 2008, presidential candidates John McCain and Barack Obama left the campaign trail to meet with President George W. Bush (fourth from right) and other national leaders to discuss the nation's deepening financial crisis. The economy became the dominant issue for the remainder of the presidential campaign, with Obama (far right) edging ahead of McCain (seated three chairs to Bush's right) in the public's perception of which candidate would better handle the crisis as President.

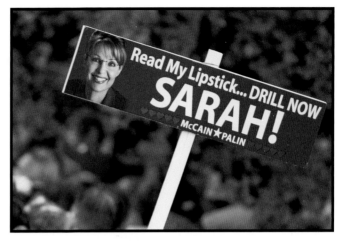

The 2008 presidential campaign featured two candidates who helped shatter the so-called glass ceiling that has kept women from holding national office. Democratic presidential hopeful Hillary Rodham Clinton (left) competed head-to-head with Barack Obama for months, before endorsing his candidacy in June. Republican candidate John McCain selected the first female candidate for Vice President in 24 years when he added Alaskan Governor Sarah Palin (right, pictured on a campaign sign) to his ticket in August.

faith, Mitt Romney, and an attempt by John McCain to become the oldest person ever elected President.

In early January of 2008—almost a year after starting his campaign—Obama gained national attention with his victory over party frontrunner Clinton during the opening of the primary and caucus season in Iowa. His campaign earned consistent praise for its organization and discipline as he and Clinton traded victories in the contests that followed. Obama set repeated fundraising records and drew campaign crowds of unprecedented size, attracting unusually large numbers of younger and first-time voters to the political process.

In June, after completing the full season of state-wide contests, Clinton threw her support behind Obama. Not since 1968 had it taken so long to identify a party's nominee. Obama and his running mate, U.S. Senator Joseph Biden, kicked off their fall campaign in August at the Democratic convention.

Republicans settled on their nominee well ahead of the Democrats, with John McCain securing his party's support in early March. His background as a decorated Vietnam War veteran and former prisoner of war resonated with voters concerned about the nation's continued military presence in Afghanistan and Iraq. His reputation as a so-called

maverick, or independent thinker, seemed to offer an avenue for extending Republican control of the White House despite President George W. Bush's poor standing in public opinion polls.

McCain's selection of Alaskan Governor Sarah Palin energized support among Republican conservatives as the party met for its convention in early September. But questions about Palin's performance as a governor and candidate became a concern among more moderate Republicans and independent voters.

Early campaign issues such as national security, health care, the environment, and immigration were overshadowed later on by the world's deepening financial crisis. Obama's steady, unflappable presence—and growing support for his commitment to change the tone of government—allowed him to pull ahead of McCain in the final weeks of the election. Voters turned out on Election Day and in earlier absentee balloting at higher-than-average numbers, drawn to the polls not just by issues but by the chance to cast a vote that would make history.

In addition to choosing the nation's first African American President, voters favored Democratic candidates for Congress, allowing that party to expand its control in the U.S. House and Senate.

Barack Obama

44TH PRESIDENT OF THE UNITED STATES ★ *2009 – present*

NICKNAME	Barry
BORN	August 4, 1961, in Honolulu, Hawaii
POLITICAL PARTY	Democrat
CHIEF OPPONENT	John McCain, Republican (1936-present)
TERM OF OFFICE	Jan. 20, 2009–present
AGE AT INAUGURATION	47 years old
VICE PRESIDENT	Joseph Biden (1942–present)
FIRST LADY	Michelle Robinson Obama (1964–present), wife (married October 3, 1992)
CHILDREN	Malia and Sasha
GEOGRAPHIC SCENE	50 states

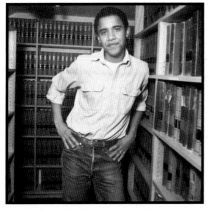

During his studies at Harvard Law School (above), Barack Obama became the first African American to head the prestigious Harvard Law Review. His father's enrollment at Harvard years earlier had separated him from his family when his son was only two. With the exception of a month-long visit when Obama was ten, the father and son never saw one another again. The future President spent five years of his childhood living in Asia when his mother, then divorced, married an Indonesian. Obama has a half-sister from that union.

IN 1901 THEODORE ROOSEVELT set off a storm of protest by inviting Booker T. Washington to be the first African American to dine at the White House. Some 100 years later, new generations of Americans were ready to elect an African American to live there. In addition to being the nation's first African American presidential couple, Barack Hussein Obama and his wife, Michelle, are the first since the Kennedys to bring young children to the White House.

Obama grew up during the Civil Rights era, the very period in U.S. history that would open the doors to his presidential candidacy four decades later. His biracial background, as the son of a white mother born in Kansas and a black father from Africa, gave him a window into two American experiences, one white and one black. Obama's mother and her parents raised him. After completing high school in Hawaii, Obama attended Occidental College and graduated from Columbia University. He spent three years working in Chicago as a community organizer before earning a law degree from Harvard. He went on to teach at the University of Chicago and practice law before embarking on his political career

by earning a seat in the Illinois State Senate in 1996. Eight years later Obama won election to the U.S. Senate.

Obama announced his candidacy for President on February 10, 2007, standing on the steps of Illinois's old state capitol building. At the time, he evoked the memory of another long-shot presidential candidate from Illinois, Abraham Lincoln. Obama's victory 21 months later secured his place in history even before he reached the White House. As was the case with Lincoln, Obama took office during a period of considerable national challenge with a commitment to heal divisions and secure the country's future.

In 2004 Barack Obama electrified the Democratic Party when he delivered a highly commended speech at its national convention. Four years later he was himself campaigning to become President (above).

Former Presidents

★ *Serving as Elder Statesmen* ★

FOR U.S. PRESIDENTS, it's only a matter of time before their jobs come to an end. No matter how popular they may be or how much they relish their work, four to eight years after taking office, they're out of work.

Presidents have completed their administrations when they were as young as 50 (Theodore Roosevelt) and as old as 77 (Ronald Reagan). Some have enjoyed lengthy retirements. Herbert Hoover's lasted 31 years. Others, as in the case of James K. Polk, are very brief. (He died fewer than four months into his retirement.)

Usually the nation has at least one living former President at any given time, but on five occasions there have been none. Richard Nixon was President during the last such period. There have never been more than five former Presidents alive at once.

Some former Presidents have continued in public service after leaving the White House. John Quincy Adams and Andrew Johnson joined the U.S. Congress. William Howard Taft was appointed Chief Justice of the U.S. Supreme Court. Others, like Herbert Hoover and Jimmy Carter, have played less formal roles but have assisted in government studies, peacemaking, or international humanitarian efforts. Carter earned a Nobel Peace Prize for his postpresidential work.

Other former Presidents have kept busy by writing and speaking about their lives, by teaching, with travel, or by just having fun. In recent decades former Presidents have spent considerable time helping to establish their presidential libraries, too.

In a show of respect, Chief Executives continue to be addressed as Mr. President even after they leave office. The earliest ones departed the White House with little more

Two years after his presidential retirement, John Quincy Adams won election to the U.S. House of Representatives. He served there for 17 years (above) until his death at age 80. William Howard Taft, who had always wanted to serve on the Supreme Court, earned that distinction (far left) eight years after leaving the White House. Bill Clinton, like many former Presidents, wrote his autobiography after leaving the White House (left, signing books). He campaigned actively when his wife, Hillary Rodham Clinton, ran for President in 2008.

than this title. Not until 1958 did Congress begin appropriating money for presidential retirement funds. Harry S. Truman received the first such pension; it totaled $25,000 a year. Presidential widows were granted pensions of $10,000; later this sum was increased to $20,000.

Today Presidents earn an annual retirement salary of about $200,000. In addition they receive office support, health care benefits, some paid travel expenses, access to free U.S. postage, and assistance with their presidential libraries. All former Presidents through Bill Clinton receive lifetime protection for themselves and their wives by members of the Secret Service. Subsequent retired Chief Executives are covered for ten years only.

Although Presidents have no formal role in the government after leaving the White House, they are usually viewed as important elder statesmen. Sitting Presidents may seek their advice. Former Presidents and First Ladies gather for important events, such as state funerals. Occasionally they may publicly

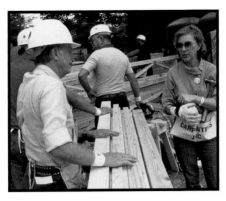

Former President Jimmy Carter and his wife, Rosalynn, volunteer each year as construction workers with Habitat for Humanity. "Now is the best time of all," Carter says about his retirement years. Writing, teaching, peacemaking, community service, fly-fishing—and being a grandparent—keep him challenged and fullfilled.

voice their opinions about government, especially in a show of support for the current President. Only rarely do they openly criticize a sitting President, and in such cases their views are treated seriously and with respect. They may offer their endorsement of new candidates for President, too.

Former Presidents often find that their popularity fluctuates with time. Even those who may not have been well regarded on leaving office can gain public support later on, as did Jimmy Carter, for example. Reputations continue to evolve and shift, even after the Presidents' deaths.

The death of a former President starts off a period of national mourning and recognition. U.S. flags fly at half mast for 30 days. Some Presidents may request simple burial services. Others prefer more elaborate events, such as state funerals at the U.S. Capitol. Whether simple or complex, funeral plans are prepared after each President leaves office then saved until the former leader's death.

Often the death of a former President brings together his surviving peers. Four former Presidents, George Bush, Jimmy Carter, Gerald R. Ford, and Bill Clinton, (clockwise from second row with their wives) joined President George W. Bush and his Vice President to mourn the passing in 2004 of Ronald Reagan.

Presidential Election Results

1789 – present

ELECTION YEAR	NUMBER OF PRESIDENCY	NAME OF PRESIDENT, YEARS OF OFFICE, AND CHIEF OPPONENTS	NAME OF POLITICAL PARTY	NAME OF VICE PRESIDENT	PERCENTAGE OF POPULAR VOTE	ELECTORAL VOTE
1789	I	George Washington, 1789–1797	Federalist	John Adams	Popular	69
		John Adams	Federalist		voting	34
		Others			began in	35
1792		George Washington, 1789–1797	Federalist	John Adams	1824.	132
		John Adams	Federalist			77
		George Clinton	Federalist			50
		Others				5
1796	2	John Adams, 1797–1801	Federalist	Thomas Jefferson		71
		Thomas Jefferson	Democratic-Republican			68
		Thomas Pinckney	Federalist			59
		Aaron Burr	Democratic-Republican			30
		Others				48
1800	3	Thomas Jefferson, 1801–1809	Democratic-Republican	Aaron Burr		73
		Aaron Burr	Democratic-Republican			73
		John Adams	Federalist			65
		Charles C. Pinckney	Federalist			64
		John Jay	Federalist			1
1804		Thomas Jefferson, 1801–1809	Democratic-Republican	George Clinton		162
		Charles C. Pinckney	Federalist			14
1808	4	James Madison, 1809–1817	Democratic-Republican	George Clinton		122
		Charles C. Pinckney	Federalist			47
		George Clinton	Democratic-Republican			6
1812		James Madison, 1809–1817	Democratic-Republican	Elbridge Gerry		128
		DeWitt Clinton	Federalist			89
1816	5	James Monroe, 1817–1825	Democratic-Republican	Daniel D. Tompkins		183
		Rufus King	Federalist			34
1820		James Monroe, 1817–1825	Democratic-Republican	Daniel D. Tompkins		231
		John Quincy Adams	Democratic-Republican			1
1824	6	John Quincy Adams, 1825–1829	Democratic-Republican	John C. Calhoun	30.5%	84
		Andrew Jackson	Democratic-Republican		43.1%	99
		William Crawford	Democratic-Republican		13.1%	41
		Henry Clay	Democratic-Republican		13.2%	37
1828	7	Andrew Jackson, 1829–1837	Democratic	John C. Calhoun	56.0%	178
		John Quincy Adams	National Republican		44.0%	83
1832		Andrew Jackson, 1829–1837	Democrat	Martin Van Buren	54.9%	219
		Henry Clay	National Republican		42.4%	49
		Others			2.6%	18

ELECTION YEAR	NUMBER OF PRESIDENCY	NAME OF PRESIDENT, YEARS OF OFFICE, AND CHIEF OPPONENTS	NAME OF POLITICAL PARTY	NAME OF VICE PRESIDENT	PERCENTAGE OF POPULAR VOTE	ELECTORAL VOTE
1836	8	Martin Van Buren, 1837–1841	Democrat	Richard M. Johnson	50.9%	170
		William Henry Harrison	Whig		36.6%	73
		Others			12.4%	51
1840	9	William Henry Harrison, 1841	Whig	John Tyler	52.8%	234
		Martin Van Buren	Democrat		46.8%	60
		James G. Birney	Liberty		0.3%	0
	10	John Tyler, 1841–1845	Whig	None		
1844	11	James K. Polk, 1845–1849	Democrat	George M. Dallas	49.6%	170
		Henry Clay	Whig		48.1%	105
		James G. Birney	Liberty		2.3%	0
1848	12	Zachary Taylor, 1849–1850	Whig	Millard Fillmore	47.4%	163
		Lewis Cass	Democrat		42.5%	127
		Martin Van Buren	Free-Soil		10.1%	0
	13	Millard Fillmore, 1850–1853	Whig	None		
1852	14	Franklin Pierce, 1853–1857	Democrat	William R. D. King	50.9%	254
		Winfield Scott	Whig		44.1%	42
		John P. Hale	Free-Soil		5.0%	0
1856	15	James Buchanan, 1857–1861	Democrat	John C. Breckinridge	45.3%	174
		John C. Frémont	Republican		33.1%	114
		Millard Fillmore	Know-Nothing		21.6%	8
1860	16	Abraham Lincoln, 1861–1865	Republican	Hannibal Hamlin	39.8%	180
		Stephen A. Douglas	Democrat		29.5%	12
		John C. Breckinridge	Democrat		18.1%	72
		John Bell	Constitutional Union		12.6%	39
1864		Abraham Lincoln, 1861–1865	Republican	Andrew Johnson	55.0%	212
		George B. McClellan	Democrat		45.0%	21
	17	Andrew Johnson, 1865–1869	Democrat	None		
1868	18	Ulysses S. Grant, 1869–1877	Republican	Schuyler Colfax	52.7%	214
		Horatio Seymour	Democrat		47.3%	80
1872		Ulysses S. Grant, 1869–1877	Republican	Henry Wilson	55.6%	286
		Horace Greeley	Democrat		43.9%	
1876	19	Rutherford B. Hayes, 1877–1881	Republican	William A. Wheeler	48.0%	185
		Samuel J. Tilden	Democrat		51.0%	184
1880	20	James A. Garfield, 1881	Republican	Chester A. Arthur	48.5%	214
		Winfield S. Hancock	Democrat		48.1%	155
		James B. Weaver	Greenback-Labor		3.4%	0
	21	Chester A. Arthur, 1881–1885	Republican	None		
1884	22	Grover Cleveland, 1885–1889	Democrat	Thomas A. Hendricks	48.5%	219
		James G. Blaine	Republican		48.2%	182
		Benjamin F. Butler	Greenback-Labor		1.8%	0
		John P. St. John	Prohibition		1.5%	0
1888	23	Benjamin Harrison, 1889–1893	Republican	Levi P. Morton	47.9%	233
		Grover Cleveland	Democrat		48.6%	168
		Clinton B. Fisk	Prohibition		2.2%	0
		Anson J. Streeter	Union Labor		1.3%	0

ELECTION YEAR	NUMBER OF PRESIDENCY	NAME OF PRESIDENT, YEARS OF OFFICE, AND CHIEF OPPONENTS	NAME OF POLITICAL PARTY	NAME OF VICE PRESIDENT	PERCENTAGE OF POPULAR VOTE	ELECTORAL VOTE
1892	24	Grover Cleveland, 1893–1897	Democrat	Adlai E. Stevenson	46.1%	277
		Benjamin Harrison	Republican		43.0%	145
		James Weaver	Populist		8.5%	22
		John Bidwell	Prohibition		2.2%	0
1896	25	William McKinley, 1897–1901	Republican	Garret A. Hobart	51.1%	271
		William J. Bryan	Democrat		47.7%	176
1900		William McKinley, 1897–1901	Republican	Theodore Roosevelt	51.7%	292
		William J. Bryan	Democrat/Populist		45.5%	155
		John C. Woolley	Prohibition		1.5%	0
	26	Theodore Roosevelt, 1901–1909	Republican	None		
1904		Theodore Roosevelt, 1901–1909	Republican	Charles W. Fairbanks	56.4%	336
		Alton B. Parker	Democrat		37.6%	140
		Eugene V. Debs	Socialist		3.0%	0
		Silas C. Swallow	Prohibition		1.9%	0
1908	27	William Howard Taft, 1909–1913	Republican	James S. Sherman	51.6%	321
		William J. Bryan	Democrat		43.1%	162
		Eugene V. Debs	Socialist		2.8%	0
		Eugene W. Chafin	Prohibition		1.7%	0
1912	28	Woodrow Wilson, 1913–1921	Democrat	Thomas R. Marshall	41.9%	435
		Theodore Roosevelt	Progressive		27.4%	88
		William H. Taft	Republican		23.2%	8
		Eugene V. Debs	Socialist		6.0%	0
		Eugene W. Chafin	Prohibition		1.5%	0
1916		Woodrow Wilson, 1913–1921	Democrat	Thomas R. Marshall	49.4%	277
		Charles E. Hughes	Republican		46.2%	254
		A.L. Benson	Socialist		3.2%	0
		J. Frank Hanly	Prohibition		1.2%	0
1920	29	Warren G. Harding, 1921–1923	Republican	Calvin Coolidge	60.4%	404
		James M. Cox	Democrat		34.2%	127
		Eugene V. Debs	Socialist		3.4%	0
		P. P. Christensen	Farmer–Labor		1.0%	0
	30	Calvin Coolidge, 1923–1929	Republican	None		
1924		Calvin Coolidge, 1923–1929	Republican	Charles G. Dawes	54.0%	382
		John W. Davis	Democrat		28.8%	136
		Robert M. La Follette	Progressive		16.6%	13
1928	31	Herbert Hoover, 1929–1933	Republican	Charles Curtis	58.2%	444
		Alfred E. Smith	Democrat		40.9%	87
1932	32	Franklin D. Roosevelt, 1933–1945	Democrat	John N. Garner	57.4%	472
		Herbert Hoover	Republican		39.7%	59
		Norman Thomas	Socialist		2.2%	0
1936		Franklin D. Roosevelt, 1933–1945	Democrat	John N. Garner	60.8%	523
		Alfred M. Landon	Republican		36.5%	8
		William Lemke	Union		1.9%	0
1940		Franklin D. Roosevelt, 1933–1945	Democrat	Henry A. Wallace	54.8%	449
		Wendell Willkie	Republican		44.8%	82

ELECTION YEAR	NUMBER OF PRESIDENCY	NAME OF PRESIDENT, YEARS OF OFFICE, AND CHIEF OPPONENTS	NAME OF POLITICAL PARTY	NAME OF VICE PRESIDENT	PERCENTAGE OF POPULAR VOTE	ELECTORAL VOTE
1944		Franklin D. Roosevelt, 1933–1945	Democrat	Harry S. Truman	53.5%	432
		Thomas E. Dewey	Republican		46.0%	99
	33	Harry S. Truman, 1945–1953	Democrat	None		
1948		Harry S. Truman, 1945–1953	Democrat	Alben W. Barkley	50%	303
		Thomas E. Dewey	Republican		49.9%	189
		J. Strom Thurmond	States' Rights		2.4%	39
		Henry A. Wallace	Progressive		2.4%	0
1952	34	Dwight D. Eisenhower, 1953–1961	Republican	Richard Nixon	55.1%	442
		Adlai E. Stevenson	Democrat		44.4%	89
1956		Dwight D. Eisenhower, 1953–1961	Republican	Richard Nixon	57.6%	457
		Adlai E. Stevenson	Democrat		42.1%	73
1960	35	John F. Kennedy, 1961–1963	Democrat	Lyndon B. Johnson	49.9%	303
		Richard Nixon	Republican		49.6%	219
	36	Lyndon B. Johnson, 1963–1969	Democrat	None		
1964		Lyndon B. Johnson, 1963–1969	Democrat	Hubert H. Humphrey	61.1%	486
		Barry M. Goldwater	Republican		38.5%	52
1968	37	Richard Nixon, 1969–1974	Republican	Spiro T. Agnew	43.4%	301
		Hubert H. Humphrey	Democrat		42.7%	191
		George C. Wallace	American Independent		13.5%	46
1972		Richard Nixon, 1969–1974	Republican	Spiro T. Agnew / Gerald R. Ford	60.6%	520
		George S. McGovern	Democrat		37.5%	17
	38	Gerald R. Ford, 1974–1977	Republican	Nelson A. Rockefeller		
1976	39	Jimmy Carter, 1977–1981	Democrat	Walter F. Mondale	50.1%	297
		Gerald R. Ford	Republican		47.9%	240
1980	40	Ronald Reagan, 1981–1989	Republican	George Bush	50.9%	489
		Jimmy Carter	Democrat		41.2%	49
		John B. Anderson	Independent		7.9%	0
1984		Ronald Reagan, 1981–1989	Republican	George Bush	59.0%	525
		Walter F. Mondale	Democratic		41.0%	13
1988	41	George Bush, 1989–1993	Republican	Dan Quayle	53.4%	426
		Michael S. Dukakis	Democrat		45.6%	111
1992	42	William Jefferson Clinton, 1993–2001	Democrat	Al Gore	43.0%	370
		George Bush	Republican		37.0%	168
		H. Ross Perot	Independent		19.0%	0
1996		William Jefferson Clinton, 1993–2001	Democrat	Al Gore	49.0%	379
		Robert J. Dole	Republican		41.0%	159
		H. Ross Perot	Reform		8.0%	0
2000	43	George W. Bush, 2001–2009	Republican	Richard B. Cheney	48.0%	271
		Al Gore	Democrat		48.5%	266
		Ralph Nader	Green		2.7%	0
		Others			0.8%	0
		Abstained				1
2004		George W. Bush, 2001–2009	Republican	Richard B. Cheney	51.0%	274
		John Kerry	Democrat		48.0%	252
		Ralph Nader	Independent		1%	0
2008	44	Barack Obama	Democrat	Joseph Biden	52.5%	364*
		John McCain	Republican		46.3%	163*

11 electoral votes undetermined at press time

OUR COUNTRY'S PRESIDENTS

CHART OF PRESIDENTIAL ELECTION RESULTS ★ 209

Index

Resource Guide

BOOKS

Allen, Thomas B. *George Washington, Spymaster: How the Americans Outspied the British and Won the Revolutionary War.* Washington, D.C.: National Geographic, 2004.

Bausum, Ann. *Our Country's First Ladies.* Washington, D.C.: National Geographic, 2007.

_____. *With Courage and Cloth: Winning the Fight for a Woman's Right to Vote.* Washington, D.C.: National Geographic, 2004.

Bunch, Lonnie G. et al. *The American Presidency: A Glorious Burden.* Washington, D.C.: Smithsonian Institution Press, 2000.

Ethier, Eric. *Wit and Wisdom of the Presidents.* Lincolnwood, Ill.: Publications International, 1998.

Friedel, Frank. *The Presidents of the United States.* Washington, D.C.: White House Historical Association with the cooperation of National Geographic, 1994.

Harness, Cheryl. *Abe Lincoln Goes to Washington, 1837–1865.* Washington, D.C.: National Geographic, 1997.

_____. *George Washington.* Washington, D.C.: National Geographic, 2000.

_____. *Thomas Jefferson.* Washington, D.C.: National Geographic, 2004.

_____. *The Revolutionary John Adams.* Washington, D.C.: National Geographic, 2003.

_____. *Young Abe Lincoln: The Frontier Days, 1809–1837.* Washington, D.C.: National Geographic, 1996.

_____. *Young Teddy Roosevelt.* Washington, D.C.: National Geographic, 1998.

Johnston, Robert D. *The Making of America: The History of the United States from 1492 to the Present.* Washington, D.C.: National Geographic, 2002.

Klapthor, Margaret Brown. *The First Ladies.* Washington, D.C.: White House Historical Association with the cooperation of National Geographic, 1995.

Kunhardt, Jr, Philip B., Philip B. Kunhardt III, and Peter W. Kunhardt. *The American President.* New York: Riverhead Books, Penguin Putnam Inc., 1999.

McPherson, James M., general editor. *"To the Best of My Ability": The American Presidents.* New York: Dorling Kindersley, 2001 (revised edition).

Provensen, Alice. *The Buck Stops Here.* New York: Browndeer Press, Harcourt Brace & Company, 1997.

Sandler, Martin W. *Presidents, A Library of Congress Book.* New York: HarperCollins Publishers, 1995.

Schanzer, Rosalyn. *George vs. George: The American Revolution as Seen from Both Sides.* Washington, D.C.: National Geographic, 2004.

St. George, Judith. *In the Line of Fire–Presidents' Lives at Stake.* New York: Holiday House, 1999.

_____. *So You Want to be President?* New York: Philomel, 2004 (revised edition).

Walker, Diana. *Public & Private: Twenty Years Photographing the Presidency.* Washington, D.C.: National Geographic, 2002.

VIDEOS AND TELEVISION PROGRAMS

1600 Pennsylvania Avenue: The White House. National Geographic Educational Film and Video, 1997.

Air Force One. National Geographic Television Special and Video, 1996.

The American President (listed as a book) is also a film series distributed by PBS.

Inside the U.S. Secret Service. National Geographic Channel, 2004.

Inside the White House. National Geographic Television Video, 2001.

The Presidents. The American Experience, Public Broadcasting Service. http://www.pbs.org/wgbh/amex/presidents/intro.html

PLACES TO VISIT

"The American Presidency," permanent exhibit, National Museum of American History, Smithsonian Institution, Washington, D.C.

The White House, Washington D.C.

See also pages 94-95 and each President's fact box.

WEB SITES

About Government, Dirksen Congressional Center http://www.aboutgovernment.org/index.htm

American Museum of the Moving Image http://www.livingroomcandidate.org/news

National Archives and Records Administration Electoral College http://www.archives.gov/federal_register/electoral_college/

Smithsonian National Museum of American History http://americanhistory.si.edu/

White House Historical Association http://www.whitehousehistory.org/

PRESIDENTIAL LIBRARIES
http://www.archives.gov/presidential_libraries/addresses/addresses.html

PRESIDENTIAL SPEECHES
http://millercenter.org/scripps/archive/speeches

Bibliography

Aikman, Lonnelle. *The Living White House.* Washington, D.C.: White House Historical Association and National Geographic Society, 1996 (tenth edition).

_____. *We, the People: The Story of the United States Capitol—Its Past and Its Promise.* Washington, D.C.: The United States Capitol Historical Society and National Geographic Society, 1991 (fourteenth edition).

Boller, Paul F., Jr. *Presidential Anecdotes.* New York: Oxford University Press, 1981.

_____. *Presidential Wives.* New York: Oxford University Press, 1988.

Brinkley, Alan and Davis Dyer; editors. *The Reader's Companion to the American Presidency.* Boston: Houghton Mifflin Company, 2004.

Caroli, Betty Boyd. *First Ladies.* New York: Oxford University Press, 1995 (expanded edition).

DeGregorio, William A. *The Complete Book of U.S. Presidents.* New York: Wings Books, Random House, 2005 (sixth edition, revised).

Freidel, Frank. *The Presidents of the United States of America.* Washington, D.C.: White House Historical Association and National Geographic Society, 1995 (fourteenth edition).

Graff, Henry F., editor. *The Presidents, A Reference History.* New York: Charles Scribner's Sons, 1996 (second edition).

Hamilton, Alexander. *James Madison and John Jay. The Federalist Papers.* New York: New American Library, 1961.

Kane, Joseph Nathan. *Facts about the Presidents: A Compilation of Biographical and Historical Information.* New York: The H.W. Wilson Company, 2001 (seventh edition), with new co-authors: Janet Podell and Steven Anzovin.

Keyssar, Alexander. *The Right to Vote: The Contested History of Democracy in the United States.* New York, New York: Basic Books, 2000.

Klapthor, Margaret Brown. *The First Ladies.* Washington, D.C.: White House Historical Association and National Geographic Society, 1999 (ninth edition).

Kruh, David and Louis Kruh; *Presidential Landmarks.* New York: Hippocrene Books, Inc., 1992.

Pearce, Lorraine. *The White House: An Historic Guide.* Washington, D.C.: White House Historical Association and National Geographic Society, 1999 (twentieth edition).

Purcell, L. Edward, editor. *Vice Presidents: A Biographical Dictionary.* New York: Checkmark Books, Facts On File, 2001.

Shaefer, Peggy. *The Ideals Guide to Presidential Homes and Libraries.* Nashville: Ideals Press, 2002.

The World Almanac and Book of Facts. New York: World Almanac Books, 2004.

Additional resources were consulted for individual essays, including presidential biographies, newspaper articles, and Internet sites.

★ ★ ★

Ann Bausum has written six other books for National Geographic: *Our Country's First Ladies; Denied, Detained, Deported: Stories from the Dark Side of American Immigration; Muckrakers: How Ida Tarbell, Upton Sinclair, and Lincoln Steffens Helped Expose Scandal, Inspire Reform, and Invent Investigative Journalism; Freedom Riders: John Lewis and Jim Zwerg on the Front Lines of the Civil Rights Movement; With Courage and Cloth: Winning the Fight for a Woman's Right to Vote;* and *Dragon Bones and Dinosaur Eggs: A Photobiography of Explorer Roy Chapman Andrews.* The daughter of a history professor, she grew up with a love of research and American history. She tackled each presidency as its own assignment, immersing herself in reference volumes, historical documents, and period anecdotes. Finding the facts she knows kids will love is her favorite part of research. A graduate of Beloit College, she has two college-aged sons and makes her home in Wisconsin.

Consultant **William B. Bushong** is currently the White House Historical Association's Staff Historian specializing in history of the executive mansion. He is a frequent contributor to *White House History,* and his publications include *Uncle Sam's Architects: Builders of the Capitol,* and *The North Carolina Executive Mansion: The First One Hundred Years.* He also administers the Association's Web site: www.whha.org.

Consultant **Dr. Robert D. Johnston** is Associate Professor and Director of the Teaching of History Program at the University of Illinois at Chicago. He is also the author of National Geographic's *The Making of America: The History of the United States from 1492 to the Present,* which was named a *School Library Journal* Best Book of the Year. Dr. Johnston Lives in Chicago with his wife, Anne, and two sons Sandy and Isaac.

Credits

Abbreviations:
LC – Library of Congress
WHHA – White House Historical Association
t–top, b–bottom, c–center, l–left, and r–right

Cover – Portraits courtesy WHHA with the exception of Barack Obama, Kwaku Alston/Corbis Outline; Flag Marilyn Mofford Gibbons

Page 1 Joe Sohm/Visions of America; 2-3 Paul Damian/stone; 6 WHHA; 7 The White House; 8 Stock Montage Inc

THE PRESIDENCY AND HOW IT GREW

10 (t) Portraits courtesy WHHA10 (l-r) National Archives; Chase Manhattan Bank, Money Museum; Chicago Historical Society; Doris S. Clymer; 11 (l-r) U.S. Supreme Court; New York Public Library, Stokes Collection; The Granger Collection, NY; Courtesy Alamo Museum; 12 WHHA; 13 (both) LC; 14 (l) LC; (tr) Frances Tavern Museum; (b) The White House; 15 (t) VA. Museum of Fine Arts, Richmond. Gift of Edgar & Bernice Chrysler Garbisch. Photo: Ron Jennings; 16 (tl) Courtesy Acacia Mutual Life Ins. Co.; (tr) Continental Insurance Companies; (b) Metropolitan Museum of Art, bequest of William Nelson, 1903; 17 LC; 18 WHHA; 19 (l) Adams National Historic Site/Bob Allnut; (r) Newsweek, 20 (t) Joe Bailey/Larry Kinney,NGS (b) Lisa Biganzoli, NGS; 21(l) New York Public Library; (r) Collection of New York Historical Society; 22 (t) The White House; (b) Smithsonian Institution; 23 (t) WHHA; (b) From the collection of Mac G. and Janelle Morris; 24 WHHA; 25 (l) William E. Ryder; (r) Vlad Kharitnov, 26 (tl) Collection of New York Historical Society; (tr) Courtesy Rhode Island Historical Society; (b) Painting by Thure DeThulestrup/Louisiana Historical Society; 27 (t) Marie-Louise Brimberg; (b) Painting by W. Goodacre, Betts Collection, Special Collections Dept., Univ. of VA Library; 28 (t) Arthur Liddov; (b) NGS Image Collection; 29 (top,both) Linda Bartlett; (b) Louis Glanzman; 30 WHHA; 31 (l) WHHA; (r) Eastern National Park & Monument; 32 (tl) New York Historical Society; (tr) Culver Pictures; (b) New Haven Colony Historical Society; 33 (tl) Painting by Thomas Brick/Jack Fletcher; (tr) James A. Sugar; (b) Newman Galleries Inc; 34 (t) The White House,Michael Evans; (bl) The Granger Collection, NY; (br) The White House; 35 (background) Vlad Kharitnov; (bl) Collection of New York Historical Society; (bc) Culver Pictures; (br) Bettmann/Corbis; 36 WHHA; 37 (l) Emory Kristof; NGS; (r) Pierre Mion, NGS; 38 (t) New York Public Library; (ctr) LC; (b) Taylor & Dull; 39 (t) James Russel; (b) WHHA; 40 WHHA; 41 LC; 42 WHHA; 43 (l) Joe Bailey,NGS; (r) Chicago Historical Society; 44 Chip Somodevilla/ Getty Images; 45 (t) Karen Kasmauski / NG Image Collection; 45 (b, l-r) Pool Photo/ Getty Images; Associated Press; 46 WHHA (WHC); 47 (l) Joseph H. Bialey, NG Image Collection; (r) Chicago Historical Society; 48 (tl) Collection New York Historical Society; (tr) LC; (b) Chicago Historical Society; 49 (t) Yale University Art Gallery/Ken Heinen; (bl) David S. Boyer; (br) Culver Pictures

FROM SEA TO SHINING SEA

50 (t) Portraits courtesy WHHA; 50 (l-r) Bettmann/Corbis; Werner Wolff/Black Star; LC; Bettmann/Corbis; 51 (l-r) Association of American Railroads, DC; Painting by William Heine from Mrs. Mary C. Owens/George Mobley, NG Historical Picture Services; Culver Pictures; Thomas Gilcrease Institute; 52 WHHA; 53 (l) LC; (r) Stock Montage Inc; 54 (t) Bettmann/Corbis; (b) Culver Pictures; 55 (t) Woolaroc Museum; (b) Colombia County Historical Society; 56 WHHA; 57 (l) Culver Pictures; (r) LC; 58 WHHA; 59 (l) Pierre Mion, NGS; (r) Benjamin Perley Poore; 60 (t) The White House; 60 (b, l-r) North Wind Picture Archives; Bettmann/ Corbis; Getty Images News Service; The White House; 61 Bettmann/ Corbis; 62 WHHA (WHC); 63 (l-r)

Bettmann/ Corbis; Bettmann/ Corbis; 64 (tl) Bettmann/Corbis; (tr) Culver Pictures; (b) LC; 65 (both) Culver Pictures; 66 WHHA; 67 (l) LC; (r) Culver Pictures; 68 WHHA; 69 (both) Culver Pictures; 70 (t) Corbis; (b, l-r) Flip Schulke/ Corbis; Corbis; Reuters/ Corbis; 71 Matthew Cavanaugh/epa/Corbis; 72 WHHA; 73 (l) Pierce Brigade, Conquered New Hampshire; (r) Culver Pictures; 74 WHHA; 75 (l) Bettmann/Corbis; (r) Missouri Historical Society, St. Louis

A NEW BIRTH OF FREEDOM

76 (t) Portraits courtesy WHHA; 76 (l-r) Lowdermilk Print Shop; Joe Bailey, NGS; Leslie Carlson; Bettmann/Corbis; 77 (l-r) LC; Western Historical Collection/University of Oklahoma Library; Corcoran Gallery of Art; The American Automobile Manufacturers Association; 78 WHHA; 79 (l) Lloyd Ostendorf; (r) F & G Unlimited; 80 (t) Chicago Historical Society; (b) LC; 81 (t) Bettmann/Corbis; (b) LC; 82 (top,both) LC; (b) Collection of New York Historical Society; 83 (tl) LC; (tr) Victor Boswell, NGS; (bl) Drawing by Beighaus, courtesy National Park Service; (br) Museum of the City of New York; 84 WHHA; 85 (both) LC; 86 (t) FDR Library; (b, both) Vlad Kharitnov; 87 (tl) Ripon Commonwealth Press; (tr) Bettmann/ Corbis; (bl) UPI; (bc &br) Brown Brothers; 88 WHHA; 89 (l) Chicago Historical Society; (b, both) LC; 90 (top,both) LC; (b) Bettmann/Corbis; 91 (tl) Bettmann/Corbis; (tr) LC; (b) Bettmann/Corbis; 92 WHHA; 93 Rutherford B. Hayes Presidential Center; 94 (t) Johnny Thompson; 94 (b, l-r) LC; Corbis; Abraham Lincoln Presidential Library & Museum; 96 WHHA; 97 Kiplinger Washington Collection; 98 WHHA; 99 (l) LC; (r) US National Park Service; 100 WHHA; 101 Bettmann/Corbis; 102 (tl) LC; (tr) Bettmann/Corbis; (bl) LC; (br) Bettmann/Corbis; 103 (t) Culver Pictures; (b) Bettmann/Corbis; 104 (tl) Smithsonian Institution; (tr) National Photo; (bl) Gerald R. Ford Library; (br) Bettmann/ Corbis; 105 Gerald R. Ford Library; 106 WHHA; 107 (l) LC; (r) Bettmann/Corbis

AMERICA TAKES CENTER STAGE

108 (t) Portraits courtesy WHHA; 108 (l-r) LC; LC; The LeBaron Collection; Ken Marschall; 109 (l-r) Bettmann/Corbis; LC; Archive Photos; NG Image Collection; 110 WHHA; 111 (l) LC; (r) Culver Pictures; 112 (t) Chicago Historical Society; (b) LC; 113 (t) LC; (b) Bettmann/Corbis; 114 WHHA; 115 (t) Bob Oakes, NGS; (r) LC; 116 (t) Culver Pictures; (bl) Culver Pictures; (br) FPG Int'l; 117 (tl) Brown Brothers; (tr) LC; (b) Theodore Roosevelt Collection, Harvard College Library; 118 LC; 111 (clockwise from up le) Alex Ross; LC; LC; The White House; The White House; Liaison; Corbis; 120 WHHA; 121 (l) LC; (r) Emory Kristof, NGS; 122 (tl) LC; (tr) Culver Pictures; (b) Culver Pictures; 123 (tl, tr, bl) LC; (br) George Mobley, NGS; 124 (t) John Kuo/ iStockPhoto.com; 124 (b) Corbis; 125 (t, l-r) Bettmann/ Corbis; JIM WATSON/AFP/Getty Images; 125 (b) Joyce Naltchayan/AFP/Getty Images; 126 WHHA; 127 (l) Punch; (r) LC; 128 (tl) UPI; (tc) Culver Pictures; (tr) UPI; (b) LC; 129 (t) Brown Brothers; (b) LC; 130 Mort Kuntsler; (b, both) Getty Images News Service; 131 (t) Corbis; 131 (b, l-r) Gustav LeGray, The J. Paul Getty Museum; Wally McNamee/ Corbis; Charles Ommanney/Getty Images; 132 WHHA; 133 LC; 134 WHHA; 135 (l) Bettmann/Corbis; (r) Stock Montage Inc; 136 WHHA; 137 (l) National Archives; (r) LC

SEEKING STABILITY IN THE ATOMIC AGE

138 (t) Portraits courtesy WHHA; 138 (l-r) Bettmann/Corbis; National Archives; IBM; UPI; 139 (l-r) Bettmann Corbis; NASA; Scott Shapiro/Index Stock; Black Star; 140 WHHA; 141 (l) Hartford University; (r both) FDR Library; 142 (t) Bettmann/Corbis; (ctr) Social Security Administration; (b) AP/Wide World Photos; 143 (tl) FPG Int'l; (tr) Hartford University; (b) AP/Wide World Photos; 144 (l) Bettmann/Corbis; (r)

FPG Int'l; 145 (tl) Bettmann/Corbis; (tr) Sandra Baker/Index Stock; (b) Time-Life Pictures; 146 (l) WHHA; (ctr) Bettmann/Corbis; (r) Louis S. Glanzman, NGS; 147 (tl) Joe Bailey, NGS; (tr) Liaison; (ctr) Steve Adams; (bl) UPI; (bc) LC; (br) Eric Thayer/Reuters/Corbis; 148 WHHA; 149 (l) UPI; (r) Harry S. Truman Library; 150 (l) US Army; (r) FPG Int'l; (b) UPI; 151 (t) Time-Life Pictures; (bl) Arthur Shilstone; (br) AP/Wide World Photos; 152 (t) Keystone/Getty Images; 152-153 Amy Sancetta/ Associated Press; 153 (t) Bettmann Corbis; 154 WHHA; 155 (l) Courtesy Dwight D. Eisenhower Library; (r) Bettmann/Corbis; 156 (all) Courtesy Dwight D. Eisenhower Library; 157 (tl) AP/Wide World Photos; (tr) UPI; (bl) AP/Wide World Photos; (br) Courtesy Dwight D. Eisenhower Library; 158 WHHA; 159 (t) Courtesy JFK Library; (bl) Fred Ward/Black Star; (br) Courtesy JFK Library; 160 (tl) AP/Wide World Photos; (tr) LC; (bl) Hulton Getty/Liaison; (br) Cecil W. Stoughton; 161 (tl) Hank Wolfe, Time-Life Pictures.; (tr) Archive Photos; (b) Hulton Getty/Liaison; 162 (t & bl)) James P. Blair, NGS; (br) LC; 163 (tl) LC; (tc) Bettmann/Corbis; (tr) FDR Library; (bl) Archive Photos; (br) Arlon Wiker; 164 WHHA; 165 (l) LBJ Library; (r) AP/Wide World Photos; 166 (t) George Mobley, NGS; (b) LBJ Library; 167 (tl) LC; (tc) LBJ Library; (tr) Dennis Brack/Black Star; (bl) Al Chang; (br) LBJ Library; 168 WHHA; 169 (both) National Archives/Nixon Archives; 170 (tl) Ken Garrett; (tr) James L. Stanfield, NGS; (b) The White House; 171 (t) National Archives/Nixon Archives; (bl) Joe Bailey, NGS; (bc) Black Star; (br) Stephen St. John; 172 WHHA; 173 (both) Gerald R. Ford Library; 175 Corbis; 176 WHHA; 177 (l) Jimmy Carter Library; (r) Grace-Sygma/Corbis; 178 (t) Wilbur E. Garrett, NGS; (b) Liaison; 179 (tl) D.B. Owen/Black Star; (tr) Alain Mingam/Liaison; (b) Getty Images;

FOOTPRINTS ON THE GLOBAL FRONTIER

180 (tl, tc) Portraits courtesy WHHA; (tr) Courtesy George W. Bush Press Office; (far r) Kwaku Alston/Corbis Outline; 180 (l-r) Anthony Suau/Black Star; Mike Persson/Liaison; Steve McCurry/Magnum; Reuters/Gary Hershon/Archive; 181 (r) Reuters/Rich Wilking/Archive Photo; Sonia Moskowitz/Archive Photo; Alexander Nemenov/AFP/Getty Images; Photo by Spencer Platt/Getty Images; 182 WHHA; 183 (both) The White House; 184 (t, l-r) David Alan Harvey, NGS; Consolidated News Pictures/ Getty Images; 184(b, l-r) Black Star; Archive Photos/ Getty Images; 185 (t, l-r) Larry Downing/ Woodfin Camp & Associates; Liason/ Getty Images; (b) Getty Images News Service; 186 WHHA (WHC); 187 (l-r) courtesy George Bush Presidential Library; 188 (t) Archive/ Getty Images; (c) Natalie Fobes; (b) Mike Theiler/ Archive Photos/ Getty Images; 189 (t, l-r) Newmakers/ Liason/ Getty Images; Brad Markel/ Liason/ Getty Images; (b) Adees A. Latiff/ Archive Photos/ Corbis; 190 (t) courtesy Clinton Presidential Library; (b, l-r) Bettmann/ Corbis; Getty Images News Services; 191 (t, l-r) Getty Images; The White House; (b) The White House; 192 WHHA; 193 (l) Archive Photos/ Getty Images; (r) Sygma/ Corbis; 194 (t, l-r) Sygma/Corbis; Mark Reinstein/Index Stock; (bl) Joe Sohm/ Visions of America; (br) Arnie Sachs/Archive Photo; 195 (tl) Jeff Swensen/Getty Images; (tr) George Widman-Pool/Getty Images; (b) Sygma/Corbis; 196 The White House; 197 (l-r) Newsmakers/ Liason/ Getty Images; Texas National Guard/ Corbis; 198 (t) The White House; (b, l-r) Getty Images; the White House; The White House; 199 (t, l-r) The White House; Larry Downing/Reuters/Corbis; 199 (b) Reuters/ Corbis; 200 (t) Jim Bourg/AFP/Getty Images; (b) Pablo Martinez Monsivais/ Associated Press; 201 (l-r) Robyn Beck/ AFP/ Getty Images; J.D. Pooley/ Getty Images; 202 Kwaku Alston/Corbis Outline; 203 (l-r) Harvard University/Corbis; Ethan Miller/Getty Images; 204 (t) North Wind Picture Archives; (b, l-r) Bettmann/ Corbis; Chip East/ Corbis; 205 (t) Black Star; (r) Getty Images.

National Geographic Society

John M. Fahey, Jr.
PRESIDENT AND CHIEF EXECUTIVE OFFICER

Gilbert M. Grosvenor
CHAIRMAN OF THE BOARD

Tim T. Kelly
PRESIDENT, GLOBAL MEDIA GROUP

John Q. Griffin
PRESIDENT, PUBLISHING

Nina D. Hoffman
EXECUTIVE VICE PRESIDENT, PRESIDENT OF BOOK
PUBLISHING GROUP

Prepared by the Book Division

Nancy Laties Feresten
VICE PRESIDENT, EDITOR-IN-CHIEF OF CHILDREN'S BOOKS

Bea Jackson
DIRECTOR OF DESIGN AND ILLUSTRATION

Jennifer Emmett
EXECUTIVE EDITOR, REFERENCE AND SOLO, CHILDREN'S
BOOKS

Amy Shields
EXECUTIVE EDITOR, SERIES, CHILDREN'S BOOKS

Carl Meheler
DIRECTOR OF MAPS

Staff for this Book

Priyanka Lamichhane
PROJECT EDITOR

David M. Seager, Ruth Thompson
ART DIRECTORS

Lori Epstein
ILLUSTRATIONS EDITOR

Judy Klein, Margo Browning
COPY EDITORS

Matt Chwastyk
MAP RESEARCHER

Connie D. Binder
INDEXER

Jennifer Thornton
MANAGING EDITOR

Grace Hill
ASSOCIATE MANAGING EDITOR

Heidi Vincent
DIRECTOR OF DIRECT RESPONSE SALES AND MARKETING

Jeff Reynolds
MARKETING DIRECTOR, CHILDREN'S BOOKS

R. Gary Colbert
PRODUCTION DIRECTOR

Lewis R. Bassford
PRODUCTION MANAGER

Susan Borke
LEGAL AND BUSINESS AFFAIRS

Manufacturing and Quality Management

Christopher A. Liedel
CHIEF FINANCIAL OFFICER

Philip L. Schlosser
VICE PRESIDENT

Chris Brown
TECHNICAL DIRECTOR

Nicole Elliott
MANUFACTURING MANAGER

For Jake and Sam
— AB

★ ★ ★

Acknowledgments: The publisher gratefully acknowledges the kind assistance of Michael Beschloss, Presidential Historian, who reviewed the first edition in page proof form; Bill Bushong and the White House Historical Association for their generous support of the project; Lynden Steele from the White House; Anne Heiligenstein from the Texas Governor's office; Jeanette Larson, Texas librarian; Beloit College Library; Beloit Public Library; Lyle Rosbotham; and Betty Behnke and Vlad Kharitonov of the National Geographic Image Collection. Special thanks go to Robert D. Johnston, Ph.D. of the University of Illinois at Chicago for reviewing and commenting on the updated and new material in the second and third editions.

The type for this book is set in Hoefler Text.
Design by Bea Jackson

Printed in the United States of America

Library of Congress Cataloging-in-Publication Data
Bausum, Ann
Our country's presidents: all you need to know about the presidents, from george
washington to barack obama / by Ann Bausum
p. cm.
First Edition ISBN 0–7922–7226–9
2nd Trade Edition ISBN 0–7922–9329–0
3rd Trade Edition ISBN 978-1-4263-0375-3
Library Edition ISBN 0–7922–9330–4
3rd Library Edition ISBN 978-1-4263-0376-0
1. Presidents—United States—Biography—Juvenile Literature. [1. Presidents.] I. Title.
E176.1.B28 2000
973'.09'—dc21
[B]   00-042164

Front cover: (from left to right) Presidents George Washington, Thomas Jefferson, Abraham Lincoln, Franklin Delano Roosevelt, and John F. Kennedy. The United States flag in the background is a Shutterstock image.
Back cover: The seal of the President of the United States. This seal was redesigned by President Truman in 1945.
Half title page: A detail from the original seal of the President of the United States, where the eagle's head faced the arrows clenched in its talons. The eagle now faces the olive branch.
Title page: The faces of Presidents George Washington, Thomas Jefferson, Theodore Roosevelt, and Abraham Lincoln are carved in stone at Mount Rushmore, in South Dakota.
Foreword page: The Oval Office in 2004.

Founded in 1888, the National Geographic Society is one of the largest nonprofit scientific and educational organizations in the world. It reaches more than 285 million people worldwide each month through its official journal, National Geographic, and its four other magazines; the National Geographic Channel; television documentaries; radio programs; films; books; videos and DVDs; maps; and interactive media. National Geographic has funded more than 8,000 scientific research projects and supports an education program combating geographic illiteracy.

For more information, please call 1-800-NGS LINE (647-5463) or write to the following address:

National Geographic Society
1145 17th Street N.W.
Washington, D.C. 20036-4688
U.S.A.

Visit us online at www.nationalgeographic.com/books

For information about special discounts for bulk purchases, please contact
National Geographic Books Special Sales: ngspecsales@ngs.org